THE WORST OF TIMES

'Those who cannot remember the past
are condemned to fulfil it' –
George Santayana (1863-1952)

The Worst of Times

An oral history of the Great Depression in Britain

NIGEL GRAY

Preface by Richard Hoggart

Wildwood House
London

For Letty, who also knew hardship

First published in Great Britain in 1985 by
Wildwood House Limited
Gower House, Croft Road
Aldershot, Hampshire GU11 3HR

Copyright © 1985 Nigel Gray
Preface copyright © 1985 Richard Hoggart

The worst of times
1. Labour and labouring classes—Great Britain
—History-20th century 2. Great Britain
—Social conditions— History-20th century
I. Gray, Nigel
305.5′62′0941   HD8391
ISBN   0 7045 0513 4

Typeset in 10 on 12 point Times by
Tellgate Limited, Swinton Street, London WC2
Printed in Great Britain by
Billing & Sons Ltd, Worcester

Contents

Acknowledgements

As well as those people who were good enough to write to me and to talk to me, I would like to thank John Gorman for the use of photographs from his private collection; Richard Hoggart for his Preface; David Craig, who taped the interview with Marion Watt on a visit to his home town of Aberdeen, for his help; and Martin Bailey and Jeremy Seabrook for their assistance and encouragement.

Preface

It is unusually difficult to find the right epithets to describe the over-all impact of this book. Engrossing and vivid—sometimes very funny—it certainly is. More: it is at one and the same time shocking and heartening.

Even to someone who, like myself, was brought up in a poor working-class district in the Twenties and Thirties, and who has tried to remain aware of that background, the record as it is filled out in these first-hand accounts is startling. Inevitably, the full impact of what the terms of daily life then were for so many people becomes blurred over the years. Detail after detail in these accounts calls it all up and sets off a flood of feeling: the abomination of the Means Test, the shame of living on 'tick', the horrors of petty provincial snobbery at the tradesman or small industrialist level, the indignities and injustices suffered at the hands of those dreadful in-between people, the bosses' men, the sheer meanness of endless petty and large exploitation, the continuous thread of generosities and decencies, the recurrence of the gas–oven or emigration as the two extreme solutions; above all, an endless fight to preserve self-respect. That is why this book is, in the end, heartening; all in all, the victims come out of it with immense dignity—but far too much patience.

All this, as I say, seems startling at this date, even to one who lived through it. To others, it should come as a revelation. I do not believe that these things are by now sufficiently well-known. Indeed, a great many instruments of modern society are devoted to making sure that we do not know or conveniently forget this part of our immediate past. To judge by recent political choices, or failures to choose, that process is well-advanced.

It is shocking that so recently—less than forty years ago—the largest empire on earth and one of the richest nations should have treated the bulk of its citizens in these inhuman ways. The lack of adequately-evolved public provision in so many sectors (housing and hospitals above all), the grossly inadequate educational system which threw so much talent on the waste-heap, the consistent pressure at all levels to prevent the unions from working effectively for a more just system; all this and much more are a shame to our history. Some of these ills could, in the two pre–war decades, be explained by the world–wide recession; but not by any means all. There was a deep and gross divisiveness at the very heart of British society which radically separated the consciousness of a Lancashire millworker— underschooled, underhoused, underpaid, undercared for in almost all respects and with no reasonable hope of betterment, from an Old Etonian—sure of a good job in the City, sure of a world which embraced the best clubs, Ascot, Lords, an attractive house and a wife to match it all. In less evident ways that divisiveness remains and is being strengthened even now.

In 1939 the two went to the War together, with the Etonian as the officer of course. Six or seven years later they came out to the beginnings of a different world. The first post–war Labour government did not overturn the system, but within its own modes and hence relatively quietly it set off a profound social revolution which was still going on until four or five years ago. Whatever remains to be done—and some of the more difficult moves towards a juster society have still to be faced, but the present government has set them back—this book can help us, first of all, to recognise how far we *have* come since the great watershed of the War.

It is an exceptionally timely book. Unemployment is once again a major problem, a misery for millions. Just now the Trade Union movement is receiving from the bulk of the mass media and from government even more than its usual share of prejudiced attention. No reasonable person—beginning with most Trade Union leaders—will try to justify either a blind restrictionist rejection of any new methods or an equally blind wish to exploit collectively a commanding position in the economy. But the great bulk of people are immensely more responsible than that. If they are slow in welcoming 'progress' which is likely to put them out of work, when they can see no other provision being made for them, that is because they have justifiably long memories of the horrors of the Thirties, and because they see the new unemployed all around them. It is easy to be brain–washed these days by all the special articles on the 'attacks on liberty by the big Unions'. This book puts the picture in a better perspective. It reminds us, among much else, that until quite recently in some of our major industries if you became known as an 'agitator' for better conditions you were giving yourself a ticket for the dole queue. The Unions had good grounds for building up foot– thick defensive attitudes and they will let them go only slowly, as they see a decent future more firmly secured.

It is a pity, but such is the nature of our communications system, that most people who read this book will be already sympathetic towards it. It *should* be read by the more avid subscribers to the right–wing popular and not–so–popular press and above all by the members of the present government. But I guess these organs and people will ignore it, or perhaps will dismiss it as an out–of–date attempt to 'stir up class hatred by harping on ills which have long been swept away'. It should also be read in most schools (beginning with Eton). It does indeed show that we have come quite a distance—but from a starting–point which was decades and decades behind where it should have been.

The book also sets off a stocktaking. How far have we *really* come? What are the next frontiers? Are we making the correct interpretations of needs so that we get the direction and shape of our plans right for the day when under another administration we move again into overdue reforms? At this point we are brought up short. Consider only one issue: housing. In the last thirty years we have cleared away throughout Britain the bulk of that squalid working-class housing which is described in this book. But it is now evident that in far too many instances we have replaced that housing unimaginatively, that we have destroyed not only the rotten old terraces but the chance of retaining the better forms of community life which had grown up within them. The interiors certainly have more comforts and conveniences than would have been dreamt of in the Thirties. But all too often the new districts as a whole give the people who live in them hardly any foothold for creating a proper community life. Instead they make them feel anonymous, fragmented, of no account, 'the hinds of industry' for the late twentieth century. The rebuilding of much of Hunslet, Leeds, where I was brought up, the redevelopment of parts of Deptford, in South East London, where I now live, are in many parts so brutally mechanistic, so un-human in a strict sense of those words, that you wonder what sense of the people who were to live there the planners had in their minds. As I write, the 'new' Hunslet is being torn down— sometimes we move forward.

There is still a very long way to go, a long way towards a more adequate understanding of our nature and our history and so of the lives we want to make for ourselves and to help one another make. This book could greatly help that process of rethinking.

Richard Hoggart

Introduction

This book came about as a result of the anger I felt when I first encountered the arguments of a school of economic historians who claim that there was no Great Depression in Britain between the wars. Broadly, they suggest that while some traditional industries were badly affected, new ones like man-made fibres and electricity supply rose to prosperity. The gross national product increased over the period, and many people became steadily more affluent. Radio sets, seaside holidays, even family cars, became commonplace.

This seems to me so glib that it is an insult to millions whose experience of living at that time ran quite counter to this rosy analysis. For people involved in the older industries like mining, steel, cotton, ship-building, agriculture, the 1920s and '30s were years not of increasing wealth but of uncertainty, long-term unemployment, continual humiliation and deep poverty. I felt that representatives of those people should be given the chance to speak up and answer back. Most often, history has been the history of the privileged minority. Occasionally we had a history of the common people written by a sympathetic scholar, and we were grateful for that. This book is intended to be an evocation of life during the Depression in the words of the people themselves. (It should be said that, since I gathered this material, much work has been done by the History Workshop at Ruskin and others, so that now, the testimonies of ordinary people are more properly valued.)

Neither historian nor sociologist, I did not approach the project with academic rigour. I merely wrote a letter, inviting people to write to me about their memories of the Depression, and sent copies to sixty national or regional newspapers, periodicals and magazines, twenty-eight of which published it. I received over four hundred replies, entered into further correspondence with over fifty of these contacts and taped interviews with thirty-nine of them. In several other cases I launched into lengthy correspondence.

Because of the rather haphazard and random nature of this method there are numerous gaps—whole industries and areas which are not touched upon. There is no voice from Northern Ireland for example, my own part of the world (which many might feel exists under a cloud of permanent Depression—where, in fact, continuous high unemployment was a not insignificant contributory factor in the re–emergence of the 'troubles'). This was simply because no one from Northern Ireland wrote to me.

It may well be wondered why I followed up certain letters and not others. Again, there was no scientific basis for this. My attention would be caught by a striking phrase in perhaps the briefest of notes. Often it was no more than a hunch. In the end I selected the dozen edited contributions and a final section made up of extracts from correspondence and interviews not used in full, which collectively seemed to me to create the fullest representation of the times.

Perhaps because I did not myself approach any of the contributors—my published letter allowed them to approach me—I was never made to feel, during the interviews, that I was *intruding* into people's private lives. They told me only what they wanted to tell, although, of course, I asked questions, and when we seemed to have touched upon a rich vein I dug deeper.

Not having carried out any interviews before, compiling this book was a voyage of discovery for me. Despite being forearmed with the knowledge that ordinary people are as capable of being interesting and eloquent as the privileged, I was continually surprised by my interviewees' skill as story-tellers, and often by the good-humour and decency they had maintained despite the violence that had been done to their lives. It was one more reminder of that absurd and unforgiveable waste, that worst of all waste, the waste of human potential engendered by unjust societies.

I met the interviewees in their own homes, and the atmosphere was always that of a neighbour popping in for a cup of tea and a chat. I made it clear that my visit could be as brief or as extended as my host wished, and I merely repeated my invitation for them to tell me about their memories of the Depression without suggesting when or what I thought the Depression was. We would settle down together in facing armchairs, and very soon my companion would forget about the existence of the microphone and begin to talk directly to me. The longer the interview lasted, the more tea we consumed, and, if so inclined, I could have carried out a survey of toilets in working-class homes in tandem with collecting material for the book. In all cases, I think it is true to say, I was accepted as a friend, as an ordinary person like themselves, who was interested in their lives, and to whom their experiences were of significance.

One thing I discovered was that people, in general, given time and encouragement, talk in circles. Initially, they will give the 'news headlines' so to speak—a brief summary of what seems to them the most noteworthy items. It is as though they have found that people as a rule are in too much of a hurry to listen to them, and that the headlines is all that there is time for. At this point I would prompt them by saying, 'You mentioned such and such a thing—tell me more about that.' The second time around the stories would be more detailed and the details themselves would jog the memory of the story-teller and would lead on to summaries of other stories. At the end of this round I would prompt again, and round we would go again with further additions, more details, new anecdotes. It would be like a journey on a circle line train, pausing briefly, initially, at only the main ports of call, but on each orbit making longer stops at an increasing number of stations.

Clearly then, editing the transcripts (and editing the correspondence, which followed a similar pattern) was a major undertaking. There was a complicated process of fitting the pieces of the jigsaw together, as well as the obvious re–ordering and pruning away of repetitions, irrelevancies, sidetracks and so on. Sadly, when you represent speech in print you lose a great deal of individual and regional richness and colour, but in the interests of clarity and ease of reading I have not attempted the impossible task of trying to reproduce that here. Much material, obviously, has been cut away from the interviews (which lasted up to five hours) and the protracted exchanges of letters, but I have added nothing.

For some, the Depression lasted from 1931–1933; for others, it stretched from 1921–1938, a period of pain enclosed by the ending of one world war and re–arming for the next. These years brought malnutrition, shabbiness, dirt, industrial strife, the indignities of the Means Test and the threat of the workhouse. They also brought out the strengths of traditional working–class life: solidarity, resourcefulness, good neighbourliness, political determination, and moments of intense and long-remembered delight. Lest I be accused of romanticism, it has to be said, too, that the brutality of living conditions played its part in provoking meanness, deceit, violence and injustice within the stricken communities and families. The harshness of the times inspired both the best and the worst of human behaviour.

There are other books in which can be found the facts and figures of the period; almost certainly, memory will have distorted them here. But despite gaps and errors, I believe this book gets near to the truth about the Depression as it was experienced by very many ordinary British people. It is intended to put some human flesh on the academic bones.

I embarked upon this project way back in 1974. As well as being a memorial to those working-class people who suffered so badly between the wars, it was intended to be a warning that we were heading towards a new Depression. That was clear then, even to someone as ignorant and ill–informed as myself—'the man in the street' if you like. Why then was it not clear to the politicians? Or, if it was clear, how would Prime Minister Thatcher excuse the decisions of her government that have exacerbated that situation instead of alleviating it?

I don't wish to suggest that the present Depression is as cruel as the Depression remembered in this book. Three and a half million unemployed then was a greater proportion of the workforce than it is now. (And if so many young men had not been slaughtered in the First World War the numbers of unemployed would have been far greater.) More pertinently, we are cushioned now by the rag-ends of the Welfare State which was so proudly and laudably delivered by the 1945 Labour Government. But it is also clear that the present Tory regime is as intent on destroying that Welfare State as it is on destroying the Trade Union movement.

'Conservative', then, is a misnomer. Given that Britain's imperial past—a history of lies, deceit, bullying, cheating, greed, exploitation and murder—is a matter of the greatest shame, it was only those decencies of greatly extended free educational opportunities, a free National Health Service and so on, that gave us some right to regard ourselves as civilised. And yet it is these very assets that are under constant and vicious attack from our present government—a government which has no interest in conserving anything other than its own power and privilege. It would be more honest to rename the Tories 'The Reactionary Party'. They are, after all, reactionary in the literal sense of the word: a backward tendency from progress. Thatcher has publicly stated that she wants the country to return to the values of the Victorian era. Enough, surely, has been written about that infamous period for us to know what that implies: inhumanity and hypocrisy; vast wealth and appalling poverty; the philosophies of Gradgrind and Bounderby[1]; the excesses of Veneering and Podsnapery. The poor, from infancy, worked as much as fourteen hours a day for a pittance in the mines and mills dragging

---

[1] The Penguin edition of *Hard Times* comes with the bonus of a lucid, sane and informative introduction by David Craig which contains concrete examples of Gradgrindery in practice.

coal tubs on their hands and knees or turning the handle of the bar loom till their brains were irreparably damaged, or were in servitude at the constant beck and call of their masters, or prostituted themselves as their only means of survival, or were free (in that great age of 'free enterprise') to die (separated from their spouses) in the workhouses (Bastilles, the people called them) or starve of hunger and cold on the streets. And Thatcher's route back to those glorious times cannot but pass through the valley of the Great Depression.

As a footnote to all this, readers may wonder why it has taken so long for this book to appear in print. Ironically, this was partly due to the financial crisis recently experienced by the publishing industry in this country—a crisis which was to a large extent the result of the high interest rates created by Thatcher's policies during the first four years of her reign. Many publishers saw and thought highly of the manuscript, but felt it was not 'commercial' enough to satisfy their business needs in that difficult financial climate. Clearly, the manuscript would need to find its way onto the desk of a committed and far-sighted publisher. The search took ten years, and the Depression it wanted to warn against is a long-accepted fact of life.

One of the tragedies of this time-lag is that the majority of the contributors to this book are now dead and so have been denied the personal satisfaction of seeing their words in print.

Although too late now to caution us against the present Depression, there are still important ways in which these testimonies stand as a warning which we will ignore at our peril. Readers, I am sure, will be struck by numerous echoes and correspondences between the 30s and the 80s—examples of what Jeremy Seabrook has called, 'the epic circularity of the capitalist project'.[2] The book reminds us of that great error of the labour movement—the assumption that progress is a once–and–for–all irreversible advance. The endless and thankless struggle against tyranny is more like the continual shoring up of a sea wall against the relentless and destructive forces of wind and ocean.

Particularly remarkable are the parallels between the story of the South Wales miner and the latest coal dispute which is in its tenth month as I write. It is astounding to me that MacGregor and Thatcher can be talking publicly about the future privatisation of the pits when the memory of the evils of private ownership is so painfully alive in the coal–mining communities.

[2] Jeremy Seabrook. *The Landscape of Poverty* (1985)

(Only yesterday, by chance, I was in a many–roomed 18th century mansion which had marble doorways and frescoed ceilings and even a high, unobtrusive balcony from where servants could peep down to admire the great ladies and gentlemen making their elaborate entrances to grand occasions in the famous Long Gallery. The house stands imposingly in thirty-eight acres of historic grounds and gardens containing many follies including one of the earliest and most extensive in Britain. This was a coal-owner's house.)

I said earlier that the present Depression is less cruel than the one remembered in this book. I think, too, that it is more cruel than many people believe it to be. Often, we measure 'progress' against the known horrors and familiar abuses, and thereby fail to recognise new symptoms of the old disease. People are quick to throw up their hands in shock at the 'contemporary' problems (so beloved by the popular press) of drug and alcohol abuse, glue-sniffing, soccer hooliganism, muggings, rape and other violent crime, but rather slower to see the connections between these 'private tragedies' and the basic philosophy of our way of life. To quote Jeremy Seabrook's new book again, 'It has been the greatest triumph of capitalism to make socially and economically created evils appear as though they were the problems of disordered individuals'.

We must be aware, too, that however much worse Thatcherism is than the Macmillan or Heath brands of Toryism, they are all servants of an old and evil ideology. They are the heirs of those who introduced the Poor Law Amendment Act of 1834, the heirs of those who left market forces to 'cure' the Great Hunger in 19th century Ireland, the heirs of those who foresaw national ruin in any abridgement of the hours of child labour. The mask of humanity they wear is one that was forced on them by us, and they will claw it off if they can.

Despite all this, in comparison with many countries, Britain in the 1980s is for many people a pleasant place to live. But our way of life has always been blighted by great inequalities. And after the brief interlude of the 1950s and 60s, the gap between affluent and poor is again increasing. I hope that the insights and perspectives given here, placed in their historical context, will make a real contribution to an understanding of that dark time of the Great Depression which is so near to us in years, yet in many ways so extraordinarily remote. It is only by remembering the past that we can interpret the present and plan for the future.

Nigel Gray, December 1984

Manchester

Joseph Farrington

In 1928 my father was working at Metro Vickers, Trafford Park. He worked as an iron moulder. He was a shop steward. They called him the sailor. They didn't call him his name. They called him the sailor because he'd always been a sailor. If you were ever in trouble in the foundry you went to the sailor. He was on the pricing committee. One week, the foreman gave him a job. It was an angle iron what you put in a thing for holding coke. They wanted thousands of it, at fivepence-halfpenny a box. He went and got the card out to look at the price. Well he rolled his sleeves up and set off and worked hard all week. And that week his wages were £16. The manager said, 'He's earned more than me.' He come to my father and said, 'I want to shake hands with you. I'm very proud of you.' My father said, 'Yes, but listen to what I'm trying to tell you. I've been day work for two years on £2.5s a week. Now I've got piece-work I can make £16. I still worked as hard on day work. As a matter of fact I've not worked as hard on this because it's not a skilled job. And that's your trouble in this shop. You put one man against another. And that's why you're ruling.'

He led the men on strike for eighteen weeks. It was through this strike he got barred by the Masters' Federation. When he got sacked he come home, black with being a moulder, and said to my mother, 'I've lost my job'. Any road he went to Labour Exchange. So they asked him what he got sacked for. He said, 'I don't know. What *have* I been sacked for? What have they put on?' The manager said, 'It's strictly confidential. What have you been doing?' My father said, 'It's strictly confidential'.

He was out of work about six months and then he got a job at the Linotype in Altrincham where they make printing presses. He worked there one week. On the Friday night the foreman came to him and said, 'I'm very very sorry, I've got to sack you'. My father said, 'Why?' He said, 'I don't know why, but I've been told to give you your cards'. My father said, 'There must be some reason for them sacking me. I've not made a bad casting or anything'. 'No,' he said. 'You're one of my best workers. I know you are. But I've had orders to sack you. And I'm very very sorry to lose you.' Well with that my dad walked home. He sat down and put two and two together. He said, 'I've been sacked through taking the moulders on strike. Through being a shop steward'.

After he came out of work things was grim. There was Betty, she was the eldest, there was me, Emma, Carrie, Edie, and a baby in between, John. He was about eighteen months when he died. He was just walking. My dad used to send him for a meat and potato pie. They were only tuppence. He used to go round this shop. My dad used to watch him. This particular night he was a long while. He come back with the pie. My dad said, 'Where've you been?' He couldn't talk but my dad could understand him. He puts the pie on the plate for my dad. My dad washed his hands and rolled his sleeves up. Big muscles. He were only a small man but he were fit. He gets a knife and fork, the salt and pepper and a few rounds of bread, and he takes the top of the pie up. When he looked in the pie, there's no meat and potato in. So he looks at John. 'Where's the potatoes and meat?' John points to his mouth telling him that he's eat them. So my dad says, 'Here's another twopence. Go and get me another'.

He was heartbroken, my father, when John died. He thought the world of him. He was just starting to talk. Only my mother and father went to the funeral because we couldn't afford to all go. And a couple of aunties went. But us kiddies didn't go. We was minded by Aunty Ada. It broke his heart.

Anyway he was out of work. It was Christmas time, and my mum was expecting. He had to go to the dole. £2.5s on the dole. He got as much out of work as he did on day work. But he'd been a piece–worker. He'd worked at lots of foundries. He was a good moulder. But he chased money because he had to do. If there was no work, or better money somewhere else, he used to be off. On piece work you could earn money. This particular winter my mother was in hospital expecting Billy (he was born on December 28th) so Dad didn't know what to do. He'd never been on the dole in his life. Christmas time and no toys.

My father goes to the Public Assistance and sees a fellow called Mr Coalcart who give him a two pound food ticket. He said, 'You'll have to go to a shop in town. There's only certain shops that'll take a food ticket'. My dad says, 'All the way to town? How am I going to get to town if I've no money?'

We lived in West Gorton. Into town was into Manchester. Any-way we had this food ticket so he said, 'Well, we're all right for a feed. We'll go down and see what we can get'. He put two of us in the pram, I walked with Betty, and my other two sisters were on the other side. He had a patch that he'd sewed on his knee, but he was smart. He'd put a collar and tie on. And we walked through Piccadilly. As we were going past the Queen Victoria statue a man got hold of my arm. He said, 'Is that your father?' I said, 'Yes'. He said, 'Are all them his children?' I said, 'Yes.' He said, 'Here'. And he put half a crown in my hand. He said, 'God bless him'.

We went a bit further. One pulled my sister to one side. Give her five shillings. We got across the road and a feller came up, loaded up with parcels, and he had a toy aeroplane on top. He looks at my dad and he scratched his head. He said, 'Are all them yours, Pal?' My dad said, 'Yes'. And he gave me the aeroplane. Well we got down Market Street to the shop. My dad got what we needed. Some syrup, butter, sugar, I remember him tying it up in a big brown parcel. He puts it on top of pram and off we goes. Then a women came up to me. She said, 'Where d'you live?' I said, 'West Gorton'. She said, 'Have you got to walk all that way home?' I said, 'Yes'. 'Here's some tickets', she says. 'Come to my Sunday School party.' I've never seen my father look so happy as he did that day. Everyone seemed to like us. So we had a good Christmas. He made dolls for the girls out of packing and paper and put faces on with indelible pencil. He was clever at making things with newspaper. He'd make a tablecloth with a pattern—just by tearing.

He took us to see Mum who was having a baby in Withington Hospital. We walked all the way there, and we had police clogs on. Police used to give free clogs to poor children and Wood Street Mission used to give you a jersey and cap. When we got to the hospital the matron said, 'You can't fetch all those children in here'. My dad replied, 'Where I go, these go', and marched us to the ward and the clogs didn't half make a row. The nurses and sisters stared in amazement and a nurse near me said, 'What a man!' All the nurses knew my mother because she read teacup fortunes for them.

So then my dad joined the Labour Party. Because he was unemployed it was a penny a week. He used to fight people's cases. He was on the committee. He started getting men interested outside the Labour Exchange. He used to stand on a soapbox and hold a meeting. There'd be thousands round one Labour Exchange (like at a football match at Maine Road today) waiting for the dole. From 8 o'clock while nearly 4 o'clock before they could get their money. He used to take us with him. If we were off school he had to because my mother was more times than not in the hospital having a child. That's how I come to know my father more than anybody else. I was called after my father. I loved my father. He was a good man.

He was friends with all the Labour Party men. Like George Hall (he was the one who got arrested for playing bowls on a Sunday). My father used to say, 'We want free milk for the children. We want wash-houses where we can go and wash us clothes'. All the washing them days was hung in the streets. Fellers like the communist Jock Patterson used to speak on my father's platform. They wanted to speak on his platform because he had the crowd with him. They were all out of work. They were all on the same level. They held meetings in Blackfields Park, where Manchester City play, Sunday afternoons at 3 o'clock. There used to be thousands there.

My dad was a very popular man in the Labour Party. He wasn't popular like Harold Wilson. He was a back room boy. If anybody wanted to know anything they went to my dad. He said to Leslie Lever, 'I'll get you in as a councillor in West Gorton,' and he got Leslie Lever in. He got George Hall in. George Hall had been knocked out thirteen times in another part of Manchester. My father said to him, 'George, come to my place. I'll get you in in West Gorton'. It was a Conservative ward then. 'I'll get you in if it's the last thing I ever do.' So my father got a big handbell and ringed it in the street. A lot of kids come. And he made up a song!

Vote vote vote for Georgie Hall
He is sure to win the day
And by voting very fast
We'll have him in at last
And we'll throw the old Conservatives away

He had them all singing down the street. He phoned the newspaper. He said, 'I've got a big stunt coming off and I want you to watch it'. And there must have been 6,000 children marching behind him and all singing.

We all had voting balls in them days. We used to get a newspaper and roll it up, tie a piece of string round it, and we used to hit one another with it. If there was a Conservative you used to go up and bonk him on the head. And of course we used to gang up and fight one another. All us lads in Dawson Street used to fight the lads in Grantham Street. It was just the next road, but they were like foreigners.

My father was related to H. & J. Quick. Quick's of Trafford Park, chief agents for Fords. They were my dad's cousins. He went down for a job at my Uncle Harry's. I went with him that morning. It was about 9 o'clock. We walked all the way to Chester Road, and stood at the gate. A commissionaire come and said, 'What do you want?' 'I want to see Mr Harry Quick'. 'Have you got an appointment?' 'No'. 'Then you can't see him, Pal. He owns the place'. He came with a chauffeur driving him. He got out of the car, he had a trilby on, and my father shouted him from the railings. 'Hello, Mr Harry'. Mr Quick came. And they looked like brothers. He said, 'I don't know you, but you're one of the family'. 'Aye, I'm Leslie's lad'. 'Oh, come in.' We went in the Board room. My dad asked Uncle Harry for a job. He said, 'I cannot give you a job because you'll get more money out of work than what you'd get working for me. I could only give you 38 shillings. I'll tell you what I'll do. When they're all grown up, come and see me and I'll give you a good job.' We went to his house in Mere. He was chairman of the Mere Golf Club. He give my dad £10, and he took us to see his mother, my dad's aunty, and she give him £10.

In our house we had steel fire irons. We used to polish them with spit and emery paper every morning. They'd shine lovely when the fire was lit. All blackleaded grate. We had horses what my dad had made in the fireplace. We had an oven and a fireplace and a pot. We used tin plates for our dinner and jam jars for cups. We used overcoats on the beds. We only had a few old blankets. All the best things went to the pawn shops. I've seen hundreds of women standing outside a pawnshop Monday morning at 7.30 waiting to pawn their husband's suit, blankets, rings, anything they had to get a bob or two to see them over the week. We had flag floors. No carpets. No oilcloth. We used to whitestone round the edge of the house and then put newspapers down and make a rug of us own. My dad used to get two canvas bags and sew them together. He'd cut up different coloured coats and make a pattern. It was as though he'd bought it in a shop when he'd finished it. He was clever with being a sailor. He could knit, he could splice a rope, he could do anything. He even used to cook the meals because my mother couldn't cook. We got a big goose one Christmas. The British Legion at Belle Vue gave us a ticket to get one free. There were thousands going. Nobody had any money. My dad cooked it and made the stuffing himself.

I was delivering and selling papers one time. I wasn't supposed to sell. I didn't have a permit. I was too young. There'd been a law passed. But I used to go round with papers to help my dad out. I used to get fourpence a dozen for the penny papers and sixpence halfpenny a dozen for the *Sunday Chrons* and *Empires* on a Saturday night. I used to sell programmes at the football matches at Maine Road and Belle Vue. Every time Maine Road was away Broughton Rangers were at home. I used to get nearly as much as my dad sometimes. Of course it was supposed to be unknown to the authorities.

This particular time I was selling papers and I was coming alongside Gorton Park. I used to collect my papers from Ashby Station and run all the way through the streets. I used to deliver some and occasionally people bought one. By the time I got to Gorton Baths on Hyde Road I'd nearly got rid of them. Anyway I'm along with my papers under my arm and I sees this rabbit in the park. I chased it. I was a good runner. It couldn't get through these railings and I shoved my paper bag over it. It was a big one. I took it home. We had a cupboard with a gas meter in and there was a little bit of space. So I got some straw, and some cabbage leaves. Shops used to have cabbage leaves what they put the food on outside. I went on for two or three days feeding this rabbit and I come home on the Saturday and I'm looking for it. I said, 'Hey, Dad, where's the rabbit?' He said, 'It's all right. Not to worry, Son. I've got a customer for it.' Then at dinner time we were all sat round table. We had rabbit stew.

Another time I'd just started work. I was 14. A turner, a lad called Johnny, got sacked for being a five-thousandth part of an inch under on this brass casting. He were nearly crying. He was just coming out of his time. I used to go for cigarettes for the manager. I go down to the cigarette shop on Hyde Road and there's a chap passing with a flat cap on. He said, 'Do they want any men in there, Son?' I said, 'Well, they just sacked one.' And he run. When I got back he was coming out. He said, 'I got that job.' He worked there a week and on the Friday night he says to me, 'I've got a present for you.' I went to his house and he give me a big white angora rabbit. And we didn't have that a week. That went in the pot. My eldest sister sat down and started crying. She said, 'I'm not eating any of that.' We'd called it Betty after her.

They set my dad on Means Test. They sent him to Nell Lane. He walked all the way there. Walked all the way back. It's about three miles. He was digging dead bodies up, transferring coffins and that. They had to do it to get their relieving money. He came home and sat down. He said, 'I don't know why I should have to go and do that. Just for three shilling a day.' So next morning he put his old shoes on, put cardboard in them. They had big holes in. He put an old pair of trousers on that were all ripped under the crutch. He only had an old coat. He put that on. And he goes to Nell Lane. They said, 'You'll have to clean the windows in the hospital today.' He climbed up a ladder and the matron looked up and seen him. 'Come down, Mr Farrington. You're showing all your privates.' So he came down. She said, 'You cannot go like that.' He said, 'This is the only pair of trousers I've got.' She said, 'Well you'd better go and tell them at the Public Assistance.' So off he goes and sees Mr Coal-cart. 'The matron says I can't work like this.' And he got a note to get trousers, stockings, shirt, coat, all the lot. Well the next morning he were all dressed up. He went to the first man and says, 'You'll have to do what I did. Come in your oldest clothes. They'll give you a brand new strip.' Well he didn't tell one man. He told them all. Next day they're all at the Public Assistance. Mr Coalcart give two or three but when he seen the queue outside he thought, 'There's summat going on here.' So he goes and sees his boss, Mr Hyam. Then Mr Hyam come out. He said, 'That's one of Farrington's tricks. Send Mr Farrington here.' He said, 'What did you go and tell all them men for?' And they wouldn't let him go on the Means Test no more.

If there was a march he'd go out at night with a bucket of whitewash and he's gone and written on the road, not on a wall, on the road, BIG MEETING, BLACKFIELDS, SUNDAY. He worked hard. He'd come home. He'd get some sheets and some poles and put on FEED THY LAMBS; DOWN WITH THE BABY–STARVERS; SUFFER THE LITTLE ONES TO COME UNTO ME, making banners for people to carry in the demonstrations. Because people were pretty hungry like. Everybody was out of work. Out of five houses there'd only be one with anyone working in. Some streets had none working. I've seen the landlord come down the street in his car and he's got nothing. Nobody had any money.

My dad led 35,000 up London Road on a hunger march. The Labour Party band was in front. There's one lot coming down Fairfields Street, another lot coming up Hyde Road, and another lot coming from Hume. The police lined up across the London Road, and the fire brigade with hose pipes. The Labour Party brass band was playing *It's a long way to Tipperary*. And they all met together. There was one or two rowdy ones in, ready to fight the police. They had pokers down their trousers. I was with my dad. He had money boxes strapped to his wrists. I was holding on his coat. We were right at the front. We came to the police and we all stopped. The chief of police, Mr Maxwell, came across and spoke to my father. All the Labour Party leaders were there. He said, 'You can't go through. You must turn back.' The Sheriff of Lancashire read a scroll out. He had a black uniform on with a red sash. So we all sat down in the road. Nothing could pass. A big cart came along full of bricks—a big shire horse pulling it. Some fellers jumped in and started throwing bricks down to their mates. The band was playing *Goodbye, Dolly, I must leave you.* Everybody was singing. The police were lined up. Then as the band stopped playing, a big feller called Johnny jumped up. He said, 'Come on lads. Up and at 'em. Let's give them a taste of the 1914 stuff.' Well they went for the police. They was throwing bricks. The police went in with their batons. They were knocking people down. They turned on the hose pipes. There was fifty troops marching at the back. I could see the soldiers with fixed bayonets. I don't think we'd have got in town because they'd have put the guns on us. There were women screaming and men fighting. There was skin and hair flying. My dad said to me, 'Make your best way home, Son. Get off home.' As I was going I see this big policeman go to grab him, and Dad hit him with money box. Cracked him and knocked him down.

There was another occasion at Belle Vue. There was about 45,000 there, up Mount Road, Hyde Road, all stood outside docks. They had a feller played the trumpet. Someone said, 'Sound the call! We're gonna march!' There must have been 600 police lined up across Hyde Road. They read the scroll again. *If you're not dispersed in so many minutes . . .* I forget the whole rigmarole. They give so many minutes and if you're not dispersed they come at you. This man blew the trumpet—and only five men fell in. All the rest walked away. There was five men stood there: Jock Patterson; my father; a big feller that played in the jazz band; a deaf and dumb man; and Mr Griffin. Maxwell, the chief of police, says, 'You're five brave men.' And they were arrested on the spot. They went to court. They let Mr Griffin off. They let the deaf and dumb man off—he'd been through the 14/18 war. They let my father off—he had a lot of children. And they let big Tommy off. But they got Jock Patterson—because he was a Communist. He went to America and the Americans put the guns on him. So he had to go to Canada. He was an orator. He could rouse people up.

The Blackshirts used to get together. They'd be marching down Hyde Road, the Communists would be marching up, and the police were in the middle, and they'd knock the stuffings out of one another. I've seen Mosley march to Belle Vue with 600 men all in uniform. Black shirts, belts, truncheons, jackboots. Mosley at the head of them.

Times were grim. One day we had no coal. He said, 'I'll go and see the church and see if I can get a bucket of coal.' He went to the minister, Mr Binch. He said, 'Can I have some coal to keep my family warm?' The minister said, 'No you can't. I'm not giving you any.' My father came back. He slung the bucket on the floor. He said, 'None of you lot are going to church no more.' Before that we all went to Sunday school. We had little cards with Jesus on. I had a book full of them. And he goes in the kitchen and there was such a blinking crash. He hit the door. He was a strong man. He knocked it right off its hinges. He gets a big hammer and breaks it all up and puts it in the fire. Then he started with the chairs. My mother says, 'Hey, we'll have nothing left.' 'Never mind that,' he says. 'If I've got no fire I'll burn everything in this house. Them babies have to be kept warm.'

One time he went to see Mr Hyam. Mr Hyam only had one eye. My father said, 'I want a food ticket.' Hyam wouldn't give him one. My father took four of us kids. He said, 'I want a food ticket or you'll have to keep these children. I've got no food for them.' Hyam said, 'I'm not giving you anything.' So my father went to the police station. He said, 'I'll prosecute him. If I steal a loaf you'll give me six months.' They give us a cup of cocoa in the police station and a big cheese butty. The next day he went to a Poor Lawyer and he got three shillings for a summons to summon the Relieving Officer. It'd never been known before. Then Leslie Lever, George Hall, the Labour Party city councillors and that lot said, 'Please don't take him to court.' Why? Because their position was in danger. Because they worked hand in hand with them. 'Alright,' he says. 'But if he refuses me once more, I'll have him. And I'm a man of my word.'

Things got worse and worse. My mother paid sixpence a week to the doctor for years. Then three of us, me, Emma, Carrie, went in hospital with diphtheria. Emma was bad a long while. About 12 months. And Carrie was bad a long while. I came out after about a fortnight. My mother was very anaemic. She had fourteen children in twelve years. Six of them died. Some died in childbirth. We give her up three times. She was told not to have any more children. Hyam once told my father not to have any more children. Dad said, 'I'll have as many children as I want. I got married to have children.

If it wasn't for you they'd all be alive.' He had no family left of his own. He'd been a Petty Officer stoker but he deserted the navy to get to France to see his brothers. He joined the 156th Nova Scotia Highlanders and became a sergeant. But he never saw them. They were all killed in the war. Emma and Carrie came back home. Then my mother had twins—Violet and Mary. Mary died when she was about 7 days old. Violet was right poorly but she was alive. Things were getting on top of my dad. He was going to get a boat for Canada, get a job there and then send for us. He went to Liverpool and signed on this boat and at the last minute he said, 'No, I can't do it.' He come back home. He stood at the door crying. Tears were running down his face. He never cried. He said, 'I'm never going to get a job. But I'll stick at home.'

It was a cold winter in 1932. I had no shoes to go to school. My soles had come off the uppers. There was six inches of snow on the ground. My mum said, 'Come on, we'll go and get you some shoes. We'll get you something.' She only had 1/3d. Her last 1/3d. She bought me a pair of canvas pumps with rubber soles. I came out of the shop with her and stood on the doorstep and we looked at the snow. And my mum looks at me. She was a nice woman. She'd welcome anybody. And she looked at me and I could see the tears in her eyes. She said, 'Never mind, Son, it'll not always be snowing.'

I went to school in these pumps. The teacher used to give me a meat and potato pie for dinner every day. After I'd been home for dinner he used to say, 'Are you hungry?' I'd say, 'Yeah.' 'Eat that.' And I used to have to eat that meat and potato pie in front of the class. He gave me a pair of football boots. He had a lad as old as me. He used to call me Lordy Farrington. It was comical—I always tried to look smart. If I had old clogs they were always polished. I always had a tie on—even if it was only my dad's tie. My hair was always cut short. My dad didn't believe in long hair. He had two pair of clippers he got off the Flat Iron—the market in Salford. No messing. All off. He used to smack me on the neck and say, 'Smack my neck, I'm a Manchester lad.'

We had a board where we put our shoes. He could tell if there was one missing because the shoes wasn't there and he'd be off after them like a shot. He's come to the park many a time about ten past eight. 'What have I told you? 8 o'clock you come home.' I used to look at clock at library and I'd say, 'I'm going, lads. I've got three minutes to be home.' Summer time he used to let us stop out till about 9, but winter time we'd all be in bed early. We'd be washed, hair parted, one of Dad's shirts or something on for a dressing gown. Up to the age of 21 I was always in bed by 10 o'clock, unless I told him where I was going. Then he allowed me half an hour to an hour. I went to the Hippodrome one night to see the famous Houdini. It were only a penny. I used to go in the gods. He said, 'All right. But be in for 10 o'clock.' Well I couldn't get in the first house, so clever me, I thought I'll stop for the second. I was with the lads— lads bigger than me, 16 and 17—so I thought, I'll be all right. It finished at 10 o'clock and I run all the way home from Ashton Road, and I could run. They used to say, 'Look at that lad, he can fly.' I could catch pigeons then. I got home in ten minutes but he'd locked me outside. He said, 'You're not coming in.' I said, 'Let us in Dad.' He said, 'Stop there, and don't make a noise.' So I stood there. Well all lads came down the street. Big John Llewellyn knocks on our door. 'Are you there?' he said. 'Let him in off road.' My dad come out and looked at him. He said, 'Go home to your father. Go on. Sling your hook. I'm in charge of him, not you.' 'You don't want to be like that,' John said. 'If I told him to be in here at ten o'clock I mean ten o'clock. Not five past ten or ten past ten. Ten o'clock.' So one thing led to another. All lads started shouting and bawling and he chased them down the street. Then he said to me, 'Go on, get your clothes off, have a wash, and get in bed. And don't dare do that no more.'

We used to have a special place to put us clothes. All our shoes, stockings, together in a row. When we got up in the morning we used to go out to the cold water tap, washed, dressed. My dad got up at six in the morning. He washed in the yard. He wasn't lazy. He was a very active man. If he had some money he'd buy a bit of wallpaper. Make the house look decent. We used to get a lot off the rag bone man. Second-hand things. There was gypsies at the back of us that lived in houses. Joe Barlow's father was a gypsy. He had a black moustache. He used to go all the way up Knutsford and them nice posh places. He used to get furniture give him, and different things. Coats. They were off people who had money. If we seen a pair of trousers we used to give him a penny for them. My dad used to get hold of him. 'That gramophone, I'll give you a shilling for it.' 'It's broke.' 'I'll mend it.' He took the motor out of one and the spring flew right across the house. It was broke at the end where it fastened on. He made a hole in it and screwed it in the opposite way round. Plenty of vaseline and he got it going. Same as a clock. If it was broke, he'd mend it. He didn't sell them. He did it for nothing.

People would come and say, 'Would you have a look at it, Joe?' and he'd mend it.

He had a mate called Purdie, a weight lifter. He used to paint on his wall, lions and that. It were like a jungle on his wall. 'Joe, I've got a good record. I've been up Flat Iron. Give me a penny, you can have it.' 'What is it?' 'Caruso.' He loved Caruso, my dad. He had all Caruso's songs. We had some little records from Woolworths. They was threepence a piece. Sandy Powell was on one of them. It was about school. 'Hello little girl. What's your name?' She said, 'It starts with M.' He said, 'Mary?' 'No.' 'Martha?' 'No.' 'What is it then?' She said, 'Emma.' Dad had got a big sea chest off a captain, all made of oak, and he had it full of records. He was record mad. There was no wireless. If you had a wireless you was a millionaire.

He did things for us. One day he bought a penny worth of dolly mixtures. But he wouldn't give one more than the other. He'd tear up a piece of paper and make little cone-shaped bags, twisted round underneath. 'One for you, one for you, one for you, one for you.' There was three sweets over. He put them all in his mouth and said, 'Now you've all got the same.'

He said to my sister one day, 'Betty go and get me a loaf.' She said, 'Let him go.' He never said anything to her. He just put the threepence back on the mantelpiece. I said, 'I'll go, Dad.' He said, 'It's all right. Don't bother.' He sat down in the armchair and got the one o'clock out to have a look at the horses. He used to have three-pences on the horses. Never spoke. Then our Betty says, 'Dad, I'll go for a loaf.' 'No, don't bother. But the next time I want a loaf you'll take the money and run.' He was like that. He wouldn't hit you. But if you didn't do it he'd have another way to beat you. He sat there for three hours and nobody had owt to eat. Dinner time come. We were all sat their waiting for summat. He said, 'Betty.' 'Yes, Dad.' 'Fetch the threepence and go and get me a loaf.' 'Yes Dad.' And she run. He had discipline. You couldn't answer him back. If he said, 'Go and do the lavatory out', it meant you'd got to go and do the lavatory out because if you didn't he'd have you doing the yard out an' all. He used to get us all together, even the smallest one. He'd say, 'I want this house cleaning. You wash the pots. You clean the fire irons. You do this. You do that. Don't do any more, only do that.' And you got the brush and shovel or whatever and you done the job. We'd get it all washed while he was making the dinner or something.

If any of the lads called for me, 'Is your Joe in?' my dad looks at them. 'Beg your pardon? I've got no lad called Joe.' 'You know, your Joe. Your Joey.' He said, 'His name's Joseph, not Joey.' He was strict like that. If you didn't say anything right he'd correct you about it. He learnt us the 24 manners. Knock at the door. Wipe your feet when you walk in. Say thank you when you receive anything. He knew all the 24 manners. He was a good writer. He could read Shakespeare a lot. He sat in many a time telling us stories about the war—stories what he'd done himself. How he'd joined the navy and all about it.

He was a musical man. He had an old rosewood concertina. And he could clog dance. He used to put his silk scarf on and clog dance all the way down street. He could make them rapple. He could stand on his hands. Do cartwheels. When he'd had a pint or two down the pub he'd say to my mum, 'Are they all in?' Then he'd get his concertina out. He'd say, 'In this box are three dices. Two are white and one is black. And the man that draws the fatal dice shall do the dirty work.' Then he'd say, 'Oh hello, good sailor.' And in a different voice, 'And who the heck are you?' 'Jolly Jack the sailor,' and start to play the Sailor's Hornpipe. He'd get us singing. He'd say, 'I'll give you a penny if you can sing a song for me.' He was a good singer.

My mother used to get groceries from the corner shop on tick. My dad sent me with the book one day. He said, 'Go and get me two Oxo cubes off Harold Fairfield.' He kept a shop on Gorton Lane. His mother was a great friend of my mum's, and her Harold ran the shop. So I went round to Harold. I said, 'Two Oxo cubes,' and he puts 'Goods 2d.' That was Tuesday. And my dad put it on a list pinned up on the wall. We got something else next day, 2 oz of cheese or whatever we could afford. He was very strict with money. He used to calculate how much he had to draw and how much he had to pay out. On the Friday he got his dole. He was looking at the book, reckoning up. So he gets his list off the wall. And where the tuppence was, there's a shilling added. 1/2d. He went round. 'What's that 1/2d please?' Harold said, 'It's goods, what you've had.' 'That's what I've had off you this week, and that's what you're getting paid for. You've been robbing my wife you have. No wonder you've got a good job. You'd rob a man with 8 kiddies? I'd give you 6 months. Don't you ever come near my house no more.' Harold went white. He said, 'I'm sorry, Mr Farrington.' My dad says, 'You've been doing it through the book for years. No wonder the girl's had no money. You want flogging.' He'd speak his mind but he didn't believe in violence. He walks out and he come home and sat down. He said, 'How can one of your own kind do that?' About half an hour after, a knock came at the door. Harold Fairfield had got a big box of food. 'Is your dad in?' I said, 'Dad, it's Harold Fairfield.' He went white at the gills. He said, 'I told you I don't want to see you no more, and I meant it.' Harold said, 'Please Mr Farrington, accept this.' But my dad wouldn't take it. Then Harold's mother come. She said, 'Give him another chance, Mr Farrington.' 'I'll forgive him,' he says, 'but I'll never forget. I'll give him another chance but let him accept it with two hands. He's not to be trusted.' She said, 'I've had a word with him and told him never to do it again. It's a wonder he's not had his head chopped off. Many a man would have belted him up and down the road.'

Another time we had us gas meter robbed. That was when my dad took us to see *Ben Hur* at the pictures. The old silent picture. He took us all on a Saturday afternoon. They had to have three shows that day at the Savoy picture house, there was that many there. The Corona was the posh place and the Savoy was the small one for the rough 'uns. We used to sing songs. *Who's afraid of the big bad wolf?* Then there was Amy Johnson the famous airwoman. We all used to sing:

Amy, wonderful Amy
I'm proud of the way you flew
And believe me, Amy
You cannot blame me, Amy
For falling in love with you.

And while they were showing the advertisements there was a man playing away on a piano, and if he was playing a rotten tune and nobody was singing we'd get a piece of orange peel or something like that and throw it at him, have a bit of fun. They used to have a big feller who was the chucker–out. 'Hey, move up there.' They only had forms, and he'd push them and push them until he'd pushed somebody off the other end and he'd have to run round and get on again. Half way up was posh red seats. We used to crawl on the floor and get in a seat. We used to make us own fun.

We used to play marbles—flirting. We used to make a ring of tin milk tops. If you hit one with the marble you took it out. We used to play with money, when we had money. We used to play on the corner where everyone stood and where my dad used to get up on his soapbox. These lads of 17 and 18 used to kid my dad on. My dad used to stand up and say, 'I want wash houses for people to do their washing. I want school milk for the kids. I want free dinners for the kiddies.' He was thinking of a plan of knocking down the houses and rebuilding them where they were. His idea was to knock four rows down, put the families in houses somewhere else and then rebuild and put them same people back in again. Because the people all knew one another. They had their friends, and their enemies, but they all knew one another. I could reel the names off now of the people who lived in our street.

The house we lived in was full of bugs and vermin. No matter what you did in summer, whitewash, paint, disinfectant, fumigation, you could not shift them. Bugs used to walk on the walls with whitewash camouflage. It was terrible. I was full of bug bites. *We* tried, the Corporation Public Health tried, but we could not get rid of them. People in our street used to sit on the doorsteps till about 10.30 because of the bugs. In our house we had a special bug. It became one of the family. We never slept in the back room. All ten of us slept in the front room in a row, and this bug used to wake us up in the morning regular as clockwork. First it used to drop off the ceiling onto my dad. Then my dad used to knock it off his forehead onto my mum and so on and the last one, Jimmy, used to knock it onto the floor. Then it proceeded to walk up the wall onto the ceiling and do the same thing all over again. We always knew when it was morning. My father once set fire to the house trying to shift the vermin with a blow lamp.

We weren't getting the food that we should be getting. We were all losing weight. So my dad went to the Public Health. Dr Fitzclerk come to see us. He went to the chemist's shop just around the corner and fetched their scales in. He weighed and examined us. 'Can I go upstairs?' My father said, 'Yes, but I'd better warn you. You'll have to disinfect your clothes when you leave.' He said, 'Is it that bad?' He got a knife out of his pocket and he lifted the plaster off the wall. He said, 'We're going to fumigate your house.' My dad said, 'It's been fumigated.' He said, 'Well I'm going to fumigate it again. Can you go somewhere for a day?' He sat down and wrote a note out. He said, 'I'm going to give you 14lb of oatmeal a week, 7lb of butter, 7lb of meat, and 5 pints of milk a day.' My dad said, 'Aye, but they'll take if off me at the P.A.C.' He said, 'No they won't. I'm giving you that. And your children have got to have school dinners.' Well I'd never seen a man like that in my life. We got this stuff and it did help us a lot. We used to have porridge in the morning with a bit of syrup on. We were getting better off.

When I was about 14 I went to town and there was seven of us waiting for this job. The first one went in and came out smiling. I said, 'Have you got the job, Pal?' He said, 'No, I don't want it.' So I thought, 'I've got a chance here.' Well, every one that come out was smiling. I was last. 'Come in. Are you strong?' I said, 'Yes.' 'Well I want you to walk down Piccadilly every day from 9 o'clock while 4 o'clock in the afternoon. All you do is walk down Piccadilly with a sandwich board with a little window in so you can see where you're going.' CHERRY BLOSSOM BOOT POLISH, ONE PENNY. It was a big board. I'd have needed a pair of high-heeled shoes to get it off the ground. It was really heavy. I said, 'How much will you pay me?' He said, 'Ten bob a week.' I said, 'No thank you.'

My father got a job as a boilerman—because he'd been a stoker—after being out of work about seven years. He was told he'd get fifty shillings a week. We give him a clap when he come down the street in his brown overalls. He was a fit feller. He'd been a boxer. He fought Bert Lynch in America. He was a Royal Marines champion. He fought Seaman Hayes, Billy Merchant. He was a featherweight. Anyhow, when he got his wages he got 45/-. So he packed it in. Hyam said, 'We've got him now.' So they took him to court for malingering. They had a King's Counsellor. He babbled on and babbled on, saying how long my dad had been out of work, how he'd got this off the Public Assistance, how he'd got that off the Public Health. My father let him carry on. Then he got up. Fair hair. Nice looking feller. Cap under his arm. Swore to tell the truth, the whole truth, and nothing but the truth. Then he started. He said, 'I was told fifty shillings a week. The man that was doing the same job on the other shift, he was on fifty shillings. They gave me forty–five shillings. I said, "If you give me another five shillings I'll stop. But if you don't, I'm going." Five shillings is a lot of money to me with my family. And you,' he said to the KC, 'don't you call me lazy. Look at my family. You couldn't look after them, you. I haven't been to Oxford, Eton, Harrow, or Cambridge, but I don't want you telling me what I should do. I brought my family up. They're not dragged up. And if they'd offered me forty-five shillings I should have been there for forty-five shillings. But they offered me fifty shilling and I want fifty shilling.' The Judge said, '*Sine die*—dismiss the case.' The lawyer looks at my dad. He said, 'What a clever man. Where have you been educated at?' My dad could speak better than me. He could put words there that I couldn't. I'm not clever enough. I only wished I could have took notice of him years ago. The lawyer said, 'Well how have you learnt?' He said, 'I've taught myself. By sitting in the library and reading. I learnt the law. I learnt what you can do. I learnt what I can do. You don't need all these big words.' The KC must have thought, 'I'll get this feller.' He offered my father half a crown. My father was out of work then mind. So my father said, 'I cannot accept that.' The lawyer said, 'I beg your pardon?' He said, 'If you give me half a crown I've got to declare it to the Public Assistance. But I'll tell you what you can do. You can buy me a drink. There's no law against that.'

My father was my friend. He was my best friend. He always helped me. I hit a policeman when I was 17. When I went into work I had to show a pass to a policeman. Well one day I took the wrong thing and I never tumbled to it. I opened it and walked past and he said, 'Ay, come here.' He got hold of me by the scruff of the neck. 'Get in there.' I had a big mark on my neck. 'What's this?' 'Oh,' I said, 'I made a mistake.' 'Don't come that game with me.' Next minute he hit me one. Well I left fly at him. Bang! On chin. I was boxing then. I knocked him on floor. Broke his teeth. So police came and took details but didn't arrest me. He let me go in work. I was working for a firm inside English Steel doing asphalting on the road. My case didn't come up for a bit. Then I went before a judge. He'd just given a woman three years for telling lies. The police sergeant gave evidence. Then the judge said, 'Have you got anybody to speak for you?' I said, 'There's only my father.' He stood in the centre of the court with his flat cap under his arm. He said, 'Did you strike Inspector Lawrence first?' I said, 'No. He pulled me in the office first by the scruff of the neck, then he slapped me behind the earhole. So I let him have a left hook.' The judge said, 'What's a left hook?' I said, 'Well I hit him with my left hand.' 'And where did you learn that at?' I said, 'Well I fight for the Mill Street Lads Club. That's the police club.' And all the policemen in the court started laughing. He said, 'Order in court!' My dad explained what a good lad I was. The judge said to me, 'Joseph Farrington, can you hear me? I'm going to give you a chance. I'll let you off this time. Now I don't want to see you no more because if I do I will give you three years.' I said, 'Thank you very much. You won't see me no more.' I wouldn't of got off only for my father. He had that character. He could speak in a court. He wasn't frightened of anybody. He was a man. He was somebody you would look at. He walked straight–backed. I walked round–shouldered, and when I did he used to put his fist in the middle of my back. 'Straighten your back up. Even if you've got no money in your pocket, walk as though you own the place. It belongs to you.'

Caerphilly

Kenneth Maher
I am a native of Caerphilly, South Wales, the son of a miner and a
miner myself until ill health stopped me. All I remember of the 1921
strike, I was six years old then, was going with my mother to a house
at the end of a row of houses, and a man stood inside on the garden
with a big boiler full of soup kept hot with a big coal fire. He took my
mother's pint jug and scooped up this soup. That was fed to me and
a younger brother. My mother got nothing. When I look back we
were really starving. But there was worse to come.

When trade started to decline from about 1922 on, the pits were
owned by lots of companies. These companies started to go under.
It was the weakest to the wall. Some of these companies had been
good to work for. Others had been bad. Now, in their place, was rising the big combines. And the combine that will live in my mind as
long as I live was the Powell Duffryn Steam Coal Co. They caused
more men to leave South Wales than any other firm. (About
400,000 left between 1921 and 1937). They bought up pit after pit
and shut them down, keeping open only the most productive, also
creating a surplus of men.

A man only had to raise his voice in protest and he was a marked
man, sacked at the first opportunity. Then came the 1926 strike.
The miners in South Wales, being the most militant men in the
country, were in the forefront of everything. As soon as the strike
started, the Education Committees and the South Wales Miners'
Federation got soup kitchens going right away for children five to
fourteen years.

These soup kitchens were always sited in the vestries of chapels—
the chapel being the biggest building in any village. The yard outside the vestry would look like an army camp. As many as a dozen
boilers going at the same time. Steam and coal smoke everywhere.
Always attended by men and our food always given to us by men. I
never remember a woman serving us.

Discipline was strictly enforced by the men who cooked and
served our meals and by a very formidable schoolmaster, name of
Edmund Griffiths. Each class lined up like soldiers, all with a letter

and a number. Mine was B2. And if any boy got out of hand he could get a belt across the ear from one of the men. Plus six of the best, compliments of Mr Edmund Griffiths, with a length of the very best Welsh oak.

Looking back now, it was a farcical situation. Children of the working class didn't get enough to eat before the 1926 strike, and thousands certainly didn't after—what with local strikes, shut downs, short-time working, unemployment, and low wages. I would think that during that eight months strike we children of miners, between five and fourteen years, were better fed than normal.

The cups we used for the soup kitchens were made from milk tins with a little bit of tin soldered on for a handle and our plates were always tin plates. The food was plain but good. For breakfast it was always porridge, bread and marge and jam, and cocoa. For dinner it was always potatoes, greens and rice pudding after. For teatime it would be, without fail, bread and jam and banana and two cups of tea. We got no more until next morning. It was no good asking your mother for anything. There was very little in the house. Although many mothers went without to give to their kids. Our parents were starving. The wives did get a few shillings from the Parish Relief (which all had to be paid back when the strike ended). The men got nothing. I remember that once or twice the men got a shilling each, sent by the miners of the U.S.S.R.

I also remember an allocation of cheese coming from somewhere. It was about two ounces each. A lot of the men were up on the mountainside picking coal out of the colliery tips, or, due to where I lived, some of the coal seams outcropped to the surface of the mountain, so they would dig down ten or more feet to the coal seam. A lot of men made quite a few shilling out of this digging for coal but a few lost their lives by it where their little pits caved in. There had been a lot of narrow shaves, especially in tips that had been put down in the latter part of the last century. These tips were rich in coal due to the fact that grading of coal wasn't very important then. It was only lump coal wanted. Small coal (duff coal it was called in Wales) was not used at all. So these tips were like rabbit warrens and the men dug into them to very dangerous depths. But to come back to the cheese. Us lads went like the wind up the mountain to tell our fathers and others. I didn't find my father so he didn't get his cheese. There were plenty of tears in our house that night.

Another thing I remember was, due to no coal being mined, the G.W.R. were using coal sent from America. Now Welsh coal gave off very little smoke. But this American coal, we had never seen such smoke. A train would be puffing up the valley and the valley would be full of smoke. American Western films remind me very much of those trains.

As the days of the strike lengthened into weeks, the mass meetings of men increased and it was then that the militant Communists of South Wales were born. Men like Arthur Horner, A. J. Cook, S. Davies and Jas. Mainwairing, not forgetting Aneurin Bevan. These men were brave men. The named and a lot of unnamed, because once branded as a Communist you would never work again.

Due to the idleness, the younger men started to form what was called jazz bands. They made uniforms out of crepe paper and bought things called gazoots which they blew through. They would have a big drum and two or four kettle drums. Then they did hours of practice until they were as smart as anything the army turned out. Then they started to compete with each other. Perhaps the whole valley would compete with another valley, and believe me, the competing was life and death to some of them. The prize would be perhaps 50/-, and that was a fortune. One of the favourite tunes was *Moonlight and Roses*.

When the strike was total, which I think lasted nine days, the only news anybody could get was through the B.B.C. That was if somebody had a wireless, which very few people did have.

The South Wales Echo tried to put out a leaflet printed by scabs. It only came out once—it was just two pages of a brownish or yellowish colour. They were soon put out of action by strikers in Cardiff. The only movement on the roads were food lorries, the word FOOD in big letters on the windscreens. A lot of these lorries were the famous Ford T model 'tin lizzies'. The country was at a complete standstill. The country was beginning to realise that the miners were not animals after all. But the South Wales coal owners still did think it. They would not give one inch.

Working hours were eight hours a day, six days a week. The wages were about £2.5s a week. The coal owners were tyrants of the first order. Their spokesman was a man named Iestyn Williams. I'll never forget that name as long as I live. The strike dragged on and on. Then the railwaymen's leader, J. H. Thomas, turned tail, backed down. The railways and all other industries went back to work, all except the miners. The miners never forgave J. H. Thomas for what he did. He was a close friend of King George V.

The miners still stuck it out. Towards the end of the strike things were awful. No coal, no clothes. We were in rags and a lot of us had no shoes. I remember going with my mother and my brother to a colliery tip about four miles away. The weather was getting very cold. It took us all day to pick two buckets of tiny bits of coal. The tip had been picked clean. Then after eight months the strike collapsed in Nottinghamshire. There was a drift back to work. But in South Wales it wasn't going to be as easy as that.

The miners went back to work completely crushed—worse off than before. The Powell Duffryn Company came into its own, buying pits up for a few thousand pounds, shutting them down, throwing hundreds out of work. Thought for the community never entered into it. In the pits they didn't shut down they put their own breed of managers, under–managers and deputies. In some places they put up semi–detached houses with indoor toilets and bathrooms, which was out of this world. Into these they put these bosses. In other new houses they built they put their screened and selected workmen, who would be uprooted from a village maybe fourteen miles away. These bosses never mixed with the rest of the community, nor did their wives. They were a law unto theirselves. They didn't drink a pint of beer in the same bar as the workmen—unless he was one of the selected ones. They would all get together in the 'best room' with the manager and talk nothing but work. (The manager and under–manager never paid for a round of drinks). If any of the miners was seen talking to them he was mistrusted by the rest. I even remember lads delivering newspapers refusing to take papers to the hated P.D. houses. In school the village children wouldn't play with children from the P.D. houses.

Managers and under-managers came and went like football managers today. The slightest drop in output, and *bang*! they'd had it. The P.D.s were wicked taskmasters. They not only took their pound of flesh, but took a man's soul, his dignity and all. If a colliery had a tyrant of a manager, these junior bosses had a worse life of it than the workmen. I have known cases where deputies and overmen have had to have a day off to get away from the pressures and stresses of the job. But he wouldn't dare go out. They all lived near one another and it would be known at the pit within the hour. He would be sent for and told that if he could go out he could go to work. I knew one deputy who worked nights regular, who I never remember having a night off in years, and that included Saturday and Sunday nights. He died a few years ago of pneumoconiosis.

The village of Aber Cridwr was one of two villages in the Aber

Valley. The valley is only about five miles long. But what went on there was going on all over South Wales. The other village in the valley is called Senghenydd. Two villages—two collieries. In 1927 P.D. bought Senghenydd colliery and shut it down, putting two thousand men out of work. Some of them got work at the other pit. The rest were left to rot. No hope, no prospects, absolute despair. The younger men started to look for work at other collieries in other valleys, where they wasn't known. It meant they had to walk over the mountains, which could be six or seven miles. A lot got jobs. They knew what it meant. But they were desperate men. They were getting up in the morning at three, walking all that way in the dark to be at the pit for six, doing a hard shift for eight hours and then walking back, getting back about four or five. Just imagine what it was like on a cold wet winter morning. And there were no pithead baths in those days.

I remember another evil which degraded men lower than the floor and which the management had to a fine art. All the coalgetters were on piece work, either yards of coal cut and filled, or tonnage filled. If a collier was in a bad working place, i.e. bad roof, very hard coal, a lot of water, etc., and couldn't earn much, he would have to report it at the offices on Wednesday so he could be made up to the legal minimum wages. He would get his pay docket on a Thursday and find he had not been made up. Perhaps there would be as little as 25/- on his docket but he couldn't see anybody until the end of Friday's shift, say three o'clock. The man he would see would be the under–manager. This man would have come up the pit at say one o'clock, gone home, had a bath, a cooked meal, put on clean warm clothes and come back to a warm office at the pit. There would be perhaps fifty men waiting to see him outside the office window. The only way they could see him would be through a hole in the window where a pane of glass would have been taken out. If it was a very cold day, these men would be stood there frozen, still in their pit clothes, sweaty and dirty (and wet through if they worked in wet conditions). Then it would start. Him inside in the warm. Them outside in the cold and wet. He would be doing nothing but calling them filthy names, calling them liars, sneering and abusive. Some men would get maybe a note for ten shillings, some fifteen, some nothing. All this would be going on till five or six o'clock. Then they would set off and walk over the mountain to their homes with perhaps a pay of thirty shillings after a hard week's work of forty-eight hours.

One man who got in such a state because of the insults said, 'I have a woman in the house who thinks of me as a husband and a man, three children who look up to me and think they see a man, their father. But I can't be a man to put up with this.' He put his arm through the hole and grabbed this under–manager by his necktie, pulled him forward against the window breaking his nose with the force, and was slowly strangling him. It took four men to get him to let go. He was sacked there and then but he could hold his head up. He didn't grovel to them. He moved to the Midlands.

In 1929 South Wales hit rock bottom. The giant steelworks at Dowlais near Merthyr Tydfil shut down. There were at least half a dozen pits belonging to G. K. Nettlefolds supplying coal to the steelworks. They all went under. Twelve thousand men out, miners and steelworkers, all in one day. There was utter despair. Family businesses disappeared overnight. The main shopping streets of Merthyr were boarded up within weeks. The only shops left open were some food shops who soon were to issue food on foodnotes issued by the Board of Guardians. The miners in that valley were now going as far as the Swansea valley pits twenty-five miles away looking for work. There were more buses coming on the road by then, so them men who did get work were travelling up to fifty miles a day. They also came down to the area where I lived looking for work, but the pits there were full. At 9 o'clock every night before the Dowlais steelworks closed, the furnaces went into blast for the night shift. The glare from them lit the countryside.up as far down as where I lived twenty miles away. Now that had gone. An old man I knew said, 'The light is gone out in South Wales.' It had. There was despair and poverty everywhere. A year or two later King Edward VIII visited Merthyr Tydfil. His words when he saw the state of things were, 'My God, something must be done for these people.' But nothing was done.

We kids used to be in bed when my parents quarrelled. But we could hear them going at it hammer and tongs. My father was a gormless selfish sort of a man who only thought of himself. He also drank, and would get drunk every Saturday night—like many more. He was six foot four and 16 stone. We hated and detested him. We adored my mother. She was only five foot tall but she was a match for my father. And to his credit—he never struck her. There were of course a lot of happier couples in the street. Men that didn't spend their money on drink and earned better money than my father.

He always worked on the night shift. His week would go like this:

Stay in bed all day Sunday (except for meals) getting over Saturday night. No Sunday night work unless he was asked to go. Monday, shaved and dressed for eleven a.m. A lot of looking in the mirror. He was a very vain man. Then pestering my mother for 'a few bob, Bid.' (My mother's name was Bridget.) If he didn't get any he would go stomping out. Although he would pester my mother, he always had money in his pocket. Back about three p.m. three parts cut and quarrelsome. We kids dreaded him like that. Nothing but drunken talk, talk, talk. Then go to bed about five p.m. Call him at nine o'clock for work. He would get up evil and looking for a row. His pit clothes would be laid out around the fire and if they were not warm to his liking, look out. Then out to work, without as much as saying 'Good night.' Next morning in bed for nine o'clock. Stay there until five p.m., then up, eat his dinner, read the evening paper, then back to bed until nine o'clock. Tuesday, Wednesday, Thursday. Then on Fridays he would get up at twelve o'clock to go for his pay. Before he got home the pub would get the first pull of his pay. The quarrelsome drunken talk all over again, just like Monday. Then Saturdays, up for twelve, out for one o'clock. Back home to bed, then up and out again for six-thirty. This was the night we really dreaded. We were terrified of him. The biggest dread we kids had was that he would hit our mother and kill her. Another fear we had was that he would fall against the kitchen table, knock the oil lamp off, and set fire to the house. This was very real to us.

My father was no different to a lot more men. It must have been the times they lived in. Endless struggling to live. My father was not a collier but a 'company man', so was never on piece work which meant his wages were never as much as the colliers'. His work was repairing the roadways to the coal faces. In those days all colliers worked on the day shift (six a.m. till two p.m.). I remember colliers who never worked on any other shift. These men would have as many as three sons working with them. So there would be good money going in the house. Most of these men belonged to working men's clubs and they would be at the club without fail every night of the week to drink four or five pints of ale and talk nothing but work, politics or rugby football. Never family life, and never sex, except for maybe a dirty joke or two.

It was a man's world. The lot of most wives was pure drudgery. There was no recreation for women. Especially young women with kids. Only the cinema. And that only if one child was old enough to look after the others. No such thing as baby-sitters. Men did not and would not look after the children. And a young married woman would never be seen going out on her own. The older women of sixty or sixty–five would go to a pub. But only to the 'Jug and Bottle', a small room with two benches to sit on. The room might hold ten people. There would be some scandal thought up there. Women never went in any other room. If one did go in, she would more than likely be on the game. But they were few and far between.

As for the clubs, they were strictly taboo to women. Right up to the war. I remember men who never took their wives out in twenty or thirty years. When the women were allowed in the clubs it was one night a week. To most men, their wives was only somebody to go to bed with, cook their food, have and look after kids.

Our house was two rooms down, three up. They were built of concrete blocks and were very damp. There was no scullery so the sink was in the kitchen between the chimney breast and the window. There was a little pantry in the corner. The fireplace in the kitchen was a five bar grate standing about 12″ high. One hob was brick, the other the cooking oven. The grate in the front room was more posh. It was five bars and had a cast iron hob each side and down the front. In the kitchen was a table, a wooden armchair, three wooden kitchen chairs and a horsehair sofa. Two home-made mats on the floor made out of bits of rags. The floor was flagged. Our lighting was a two-wick oil lamp set on the table. Over the fireplace was a shelf with a thin brass border. On that would always be kept the tea caddy and other odds and ends. Then above that was a picture of some buildings in Dublin and a string of faces underneath with the words 'Brave sons of Ireland'. My parents were Irish. Other households would have pictures of 'Monarch of the Glen' or Lloyd George, or a son who had joined the army. The army got plenty of human fodder through that period. There was a steel fender around the fireplace. The fireplace was cleaned with blacklead, which for some reason did a better job of shining if some cold tea was added.

In our front room we had another kitchen table covered with a cloth which had tassels round the edge. On the table was a brass candleholder in the shape of a snake rearing up. The candle would be stuck in its mouth. (This candleholder was very useful for going to the pawnshop. It would fetch 1/6d). There was a Welsh dresser, a what-not, a sofa, four chairs with cloth seats, and over the fireplace what was called an overmantel with a mirror in it. One Saturday night my father came in drunk and fell on the what-not and that was the end of that.

The stairs had cheap oilcloth held with thin brass rods. My mother's bedroom held an iron bedstead with brass knobs—one on each corner—a straw mattress covered by a flock mattress, a little dresser, a wardrobe, a mat or two on the boards, and the inevitable chamberpot under the bed. Our bedroom had just the iron bed in it. The lavatory was outside, about twenty yards down the back. All the houses in our village had flush toilets but some villages had earth lavatories which could be up to seventy yards away from the house.

My mother would go to the ends of the earth for her kids. She was quite a character. She kept chickens on the coalhouse, and had a chicken pen on the small garden. Then she got herself an allotment. She dug it, with my help. Then she went and got a pig, and built a pigsty. Again with my brother and myself helping. She even took this pig to the boar and got a litter of piglets. My father took no part whatever. The only thing she asked him to do was to bring home from the pit two pieces of pit prop, about twelve inches in diameter, six inches long. She burnt a hole in each with a red hot poker and put the axle off an old pram through. She nailed on some boards and a pole to pull it with. This was to carry bracken on—bedding for her pigs.

The easiest place to get bracken was on the side of Caerphilly Mountain. But to get there we had to go along the main Cardiff Road, where all the shops were. My brother and I went one Saturday morning. It was twelve o'clock by the time we had got enough bracken in three huge sacks. Then we had to come through Caerphilly Main Street. The pit prop wheels were not very round—they were the nearest you could get to square wheels. The bundles of bracken kept falling off. The people out shopping were roaring with laughter.

I was lucky. I started work at fourteen in January 1930. One morning I'm still going to school, the next morning I'm getting up at four-thirty to be down the pit at six. No training. A lad was chucked in at the deep end. A little boy one day, nearly a man the next. My wage for six eight-hour shifts was 12/4d a week. The pit I started in is still working. It's called the Bedwas Navigation Colliery, about ten miles from Newport, Mon. This colliery employed two thousand men. It was not owned by the evil P.D. but by a firm called S. Instone and Co. Sir Samuel Instone was at that time also Chairman of Imperial Airways. It was a good and fair company to work for. Even the boys had their own dockets so they could draw their own pay. No other pit in South Wales did that. It worked full time because it had some of the best coking coal in Wales. Also a contract to supply the G.W.R. with coal.

By this time, nearly all the pits in Wales were on short time. Even then the coal owners and the government of the day kept bashing the miners. The favourite trick was to work on Monday and Tuesday, off Wednesday, work Thursday, off Friday, work Saturday, or off Monday, work Tuesday, off Wednesday, work Thursday, off Friday, work Saturday. In this way the men could not claim any dole. They were taking home maybe three days' pay—about £1 or 25/-. That was bad enough but those on the dole were in an awful plight—18/- for a man, 6/- for a wife. Then came the Means Test. If somebody had a decent home, the man from the Means Test came and made a list of what you had. Then you were told to sell a wardrobe this week, some chairs next week, some pictures the week after, until you perhaps only had your bed, two chairs and a table left. Only then would you be able to claim something off the Public Assistance.

This Act drove many more young men and women away from home than anything else, because if you had a son working, and the father was out of work, the son was made to keep him. It was one of the reasons why so many left for the Midlands and the London area. I remember seeing whole rows of houses empty and stripped of window frames, floorboards, doors, even the slates taken off the roofs and the rafters taken for firewood.

The shops that did the most trade through these years were the pawnshops. Every biggish village had one. All the pawnshops were owned by a man named Abraham Shibko who lived in Cardiff. He must have made a fortune. I have taken my father's suit and even his working boots (when he didn't need them) to the pawnshop many times. I would then go to the butcher's shop and get six pennyworth of scrag ends for Sunday dinner.

The P.D. bought a hooter off one of the Cunard liners. It was the method used to let the men in our area know there would be no work the next day. It gave off a terrific blast. It would blow at six for one pit, six-thirty for another, seven for another and so on. The Union would let the men know by flashing it on cinema screens.

On my fifteenth birthday, after working one year, Bedwas colliery closed down, bankrupt. I was out of work four months. You couldn't claim dole till you were eighteen. My father had worked at Bedwas so he was also out of work. There were about twelve lads my age all in the same boat. Someone must have told the Salvation

Army about the plight we were in. We were starving. So they organised a dinner for us every day for three months. The dinners were plain but good. Potatoes, sausages, peas, a bowl of rice, two slices of bread and jam, and a mug of tea. The same every day.

The only place to look for work was at a P.D. pit. My younger brother who had just left school and I walked to a colliery named Penalta eight miles away to try to get work. Sixteen miles there and back. It was a P.D. pit employing three thousand. There were men from as far as the Rhondda Valley twenty miles by road, and Cardiff sixteen miles away, working there. Due to the pressures and treatment by the little Hitlers (under–managers, overmen, deputies), it was a death pit. I worked there six months. In that time five men and a 16–year–old boy were killed.

I was put to work with a man named of Jim Beard, and he was a bastard. He was also a bosses–man. He was working what was called a main heading. As the heading advanced forward, work places called stalls were set out each side of the road. The stalls were allowed one tub at a time to fill. The heading was allowed two. The two tubs we got were always full of stone (called muck). One end of every tub was a door that was opened, and the muck shovelled out into the waste where the coal seam had been taken out. Then the door was shut and the tubs filled with coal but not with a shovel. There was very little market for small coal at that time. So when the collier pulled down a pile of coal with a pick we lads got down on hands and knees and scraped the lump coal with our bare hands into a curling box. This was a piece of steel plate about thirty–six by twenty–four inches, with the sides turned up. If you fell across it it would cut you in two. We carried these to the tubs. They were so high we had a block of wood twelve to eighteen inches high to step on to get the coal into the tub. It was murder. There would be about forty pounds in the box but it was a hell of a lot of boxes to fill that tub. Our hands were raw with scraping and our bellies raw with carrying the box. The small coal that was left would be thrown in the waste with a shovel.

When the coal was level with the top of the tub you still wasn't done with it. The collier would now start racking the tub. That meant he would build up lumps of coal like a dry wall at least two foot six high. The middle was filled in with little bits of coal. If this job wasn't done with skill the coal would be off the tub on the way to pit bottom. It meant that each tub would hold 2 ton 10 cwt. It required three of these tubs each day to pay a man the minimum

wage. This man Beard drove us merciless. Eight tubs to fill, plus the
muck to empty first. He was paid sixpence each for these.

The dust and heat was awful. All lads carried an oil lamp for light.
The collier had an electric lamp of 4 volts. Our lamps would be hung
on a prop about two feet off the ground. Within half an hour they
would be too hot to touch. By food time, the flame would be so
weak due to the lamp being chocker block with dust you couldn't
see anything. A crust of coal dust would have formed on the wick.
While we were eating our food the collier, and only the collier,
would take the lamp and lower the wick till the crust cracked. Then
he would raise it again. Then gently slap the side of the lamp until
the broken crust fell away, and hang it up again. This colliery was
working full time at this time, six days a week. But our friend Mr
Beard couldn't be in on a Saturday. According to the Coal Mines
Act no boy under 21 must work on his own. But the other lad and
myself were there. There must have been a backhand somewhere.
The nearest collier was told to watch out for us.

Our stint for a Saturday was to fill two tubs. These had to be filled
and up the pit for eleven a.m. They wouldn't go into that week's pay
if they wasn't. Then we had to fit up a hand-operated boring
machine. We would bore four holes five feet long. These would be
charged and fired on the following Sunday night. We cleared the
stone and set the timber.

Boys did not collect their own wages at the offices. If a collier lost
a week his boy could have worked with five or six different colliers.
That boy could spend two hours on a Friday afternoon looking for
those men. I've known boys run about all the following week after
their money. Mr Beard wouldn't pay us lads on pit top. He made us
come to his house. What his reasons were I never knew. He lived in
the village nearest the pit. I lived eight miles away. The other boy
lived five miles away. It meant I had to find sixpence bus fare which
was a lot to me. But that didn't bother our Mr Beard. My pay at that
time was 18/3d a week. He would give me the eighteen shillings but
never the threepence. He's been dead now many years but I hope
the bastard rotted in hell.

In September of 1931 Bedwas Colliery was opened up again, not
by Instone & Co. but by Barclays Bank who were owed a million
pound by Instones. That was another nightmare. My brother and I
got work the first week. The first move by the bank was to sack the
agent, manager, under–manager, overmen and some of the
deputies. They then brought in an agent from the Durham coalfield

and a manager named Ashurst from Wigan. The under–managers and overmen they enticed away from P.D. This was because a lot of the men and all of the Union committee were Communists. These men would call a strike at the drop of a hat. This pit was called the umbrella pit because it was always opening and shutting. The Instone Co. wouldn't stand up to them. The new management did. The P.D. were angels compared to them. It didn't take long before there was trouble. Six men on the screens was supposed to have let some lumps of stone pass them into the coal trucks. The G.W.R. complained because it was loco coal. The six men were sacked on the spot. That did it. STRIKE. It lasted eight weeks. The management brought in the scum of South Wales supposedly to work the pit. Men from Merthyr and Dowlais who hadn't worked for years. There were too weak and undernourished to work. The scum and down and outs from Cardiff and Newport docks area. They were the worst type of scab. Every day the buses brought the men from Cardiff and Newport. Every day all the windows were smashed in the buses. The men from Merthyr came by train. The train was run into the pit sidings. It dare not stop at Bedwas station. And every day all the windows were smashed. It was even derailed twice. There were at least fifty policemen billeted in the colliery offices.

One day in the last weeks of the strike I was upstairs looking out of a billiards room window. There was a large crowd of people on the road. I think they were going to attack one of the buses. There were also old people standing on their doorsteps. There were dozens of policemen there. Half a dozen mounted. Then one of them pulled a paper out of his tunic and read something. I was too far away to know what he said, but the next thing the police drew their truncheons and charged. Straight into the crowd. Men, women, children, even the old people standing on their doorsteps were struck. I saw one chap run into a school yard, pick up half a brick and throw it high into the air. Down it came and struck a policeman on the head. With that I backed into the room very frightened. The outcome of it all was that six men and two women got six months' jail at Monmouthshire assizes. I think it was 1932. I remember one woman was Mrs Ludlow. She's dead now. One of the men's name was William Saunders. He did get work again—but not until the coming of the N.C.B. The last I heard he was still alive and still has the paper binding him over for the rest of his life.

Barclays Bank had won. The Union said every man for himself, but the management had something to say about that. They went through everybody with a fine tooth comb. All the reds and the militants were out. They didn't get work again until the war in 1939. I went back without any trouble. I was only a lad. My father was also taken on. He'd never caused any trouble. Now the management brought in their own union. It was called the South Wales Industrial Union and was an offshoot of the bosses' union in Nottinghamshire, the Spencer Union. There were four men running this union. Nobody really ever got to know who they were. They were from outside South Wales, and had never been down a pit in their lives. No man could get a job unless he joined this union. His union dues which were fourpence a week were stopped on his docket. This had never happened before in the history of mining. The easiest way to get the sack was to go to the time clerk before you went down the pit and tell him you wasn't going to pay any more union. Your cards were waiting for you when you came off shift. I knew a few men who were sacked when they told the time keeper to cancel their union dues.

For the next four years it was hell on earth. I remember one deputy hit a man across the face with a spanner and cut his eyebrow open just because the man stood up for himself. Nothing was said to the deputy. I can only describe the conditions as tyrannical, brutal, callous. It was nearly parallel to the conditions set up by the Nazi SS in Germany at that time except they didn't shoot you.

Nearly all Welsh pits are very gaseous and dusty. Bedwas was no exception. The system of work, due to the gradient and know-how of that time, didn't make it a paradise on earth. And of course, because of the most important item to all colliery managers before the coming of nationalisation, cost, the Coal Mines Act was flagrantly broken day in day out, year in year out. Safety more or less went by the board for years. There was no money spent on safety. The system we worked was called longwall. Stall work was not possible due to the grade of 1 in 3, so we had conveyors on the full grade about 150 yards long. The weight of the coal pushed the steel troughs down the grade. The coal tipped into tubs on the roadway below. Where the coal tipped into the tubs the dust was awful. That dust would blow back along the roadway and settle. It was rarely cleaned up. Then coal dust would leak out of the tubs all the way to pit bottom until it was ankle deep. The law required that it was cleaned up and stone dust spread. This was rarely done. Fine warm coal dust will burn like petrol. Looking back we were working in petrol tanks.

Due to poor ventilation we were troubled with methane gas. We were often sent home because of gas trouble. We then lost a day's pay. When the wind was from the south-west the air would be saturated with moisture and become heavy and sluggish. Then the gas would creep out of the coal seam, the roof and the waste. When there was 3½% all work stopped. It was then just right for ignition.

The airways carrying the return air were always badly neglected. Low, narrow timber supports broken down, falls of roof levelled out and left. How they got past the inspectors I'll never know. Tubs in bad repair with coal dust pouring out, roadways neglected until tubs were catching in the roofs and sides. Where there were falls on the haulage roads only enough dirt would be cleared to see the rails. Dirt would be left from the rails to the roadside. The roof would be left unsupported and left to arch. Things were that bad that the leading tub of each set would have a locker in each front wheel to push the dirt out of the way. Haulage ropes were neglected. Some broke with a resulting hell of a mess. It would take us days to get it right again. Where the rails spread we couldn't get sleepers to repair it. To get dog nails to fasten rails down, we had to take old nails to the blacksmiths and get them straightened. The fishplates that held the rails together had four holes in them. There should have been four bolts to a joint. They were cut in two so there were two bolts to a joint. A lot of threads on the fishplate bolts got damaged, but we couldn't get new ones unless we took the old ones to the stores. It was economy till it hurt. It was getting to be a death trap. It was the time of the owners' union.

Another bright economy was to stop the big Parsons compressor at 1 o'clock on Sundays. All the pumps stopped. There were two districts which made a lot of water. When the Sunday night deputies got to these districts there would be water everywhere. The pumps had to pump Sunday afternoon's water as well as Sunday night's and if a pump broke down that poor deputy could look out on Monday morning if coal filling was held up by water, and yet it wasn't his fault. The sump below the pit bottom where I worked would fill up with water and spread out over the pit bottom for about 150 yards. The first men would be the night overman and the deputies. The cage would be slowed until it was inching down. Then slap! into the water, men and all. By the time it came to rest they would be standing in about three feet of water. They would walk to the edge of the water and change into spare trousers. But that little caper only lasted six months. Not because of the men but because the tubs could not be slowed down on a Monday morning on the wet rails, and would go crashing into the sump or the cage.

The most important man at that pit was the splicer. His name was Sid Newcombe. He was the only man there who could splice a rope. He was always at the pit. His shift was two till ten but it was mostly two till six the following morning, five nights a week. Then about twelve hours on Sunday. Once the main haulage rope broke about a hundred yards from the tubs. We couldn't get hold of Sid. So the overman, a bright young thing, somehow managed to tie a knot of sorts. When the weight of the twenty tubs was taken the knot was still as large as a football with two broken rope ends sticking out. The tubs were sent off to pit bottom one–and–a–half miles away. Well, you never seen such a mess. The knot and rope ends caught in everything. It ripped up every sleeper for a mile. Ripped out supports where the rope ran in the side of the roadway, so the roof collapsed. It took about fifteen men three days and nights to put it right. Needless to say that overman was sacked as soon as he stepped off the cage.

Another time a full set of twenty tubs was being pulled out of a conveyor road which was nearly flat, on to the main haulage road which was 1 in 3. The points were turned and the twenty tubs started for pit bottom when BANG! the coupling between the nineteenth and twentieth tubs broke. Away went the tubs at sixty miles an hour. They crashed about two hundred yards away. The man in charge of the set got a bill for damages from S. S. Cowley, the colliery agent. The bill was for £250. Sam's wages were £2.5s a week. Even the owners' union couldn't wear that. Nothing came of it.

The coal face I started work on was about 150 yards long and all roof supports at that time were wooden props. There was no roadway to bring props in at the top end of the face—cost again. So all the props had to be carried up the face. The seam was six feet thick, so all props were 6 ft. 6 ins. The timber used was French fir. It had very thick bark. The man who carried those props was Hayden Williams. He was about twenty–five and as strong as a bull. He had to be. There were eight colliers and each would want about six to eight props. Say fifty to sixty props. Some of these props were twelve inches thick and wet. Hayden carried them one at a time up that grade of 1 in 3, on a floor like glass, sometimes having to cross over the conveyor. It was slavery. His wages were £2 per week for six days.

Another time, I was working on a panel of coal that had been left to the side of the roadway so it was like stall work. It was sheer hell. After we were down about six yards we were out of the main ventilation. It was as hot as hell, and the dust was wicked. We also had a pneumatic pick which made the dust worse. There was twelve inches of soft roof to be got down to get to a very hard roof, so that dirt had to be cast uphill behind us before we could get more coal. It was so steep we couldn't throw coal with the shovel to the far end of the tub, so we carried lumps of coal to fill that end. When the tub was full, I had to walk up that grade, then a hundred and fifty yards back along the roadway to the haulage engine, pull the full tub out, take an empty tub in. The further we got down, the longer the walk up that grade. When we had filled eight tubs we took them five hundred yards to the parting on the main road. I would wait there until the main set went by and let the rider know we wanted more tubs. It was always cold on the main haulage so I would be chilled to the marrow after the heat of the working place.

I got me a bad back working in that place which is with me to this day. The conditions were terrible. But nobody dare raise his voice or he was victimised and sacked. The management at that time should have gone to jail for what they got away with. The man I worked with is still alive. He didn't have a watch. The deputy would come around once. (He should've come twice according to the law.) He let us know the time. After that we would guess it. The nearest men to us was about a thousand yards away through old workings. Sometimes I would have to go and find the time off them. I used to be terrified. It was an awful walk and in some places I had to crawl. But I would never let it be known I was frightened. It wasn't done to be frightened down a pit.

Another job that I had to do on overtime after my shift was finished was to move the pans from the conveyor. They were 11 feet long and weighed 2 cwt. Where there was a bad roof and the props were close together we wouldn't be able to get them through and had to drag them a long way round. Sometimes we couldn't get a bolt out due to a damaged thread, so we had to drag two pans which would be 22 ft long up a grade of 1 in 3 on a floor like glass. When I was on two till ten shift I might have to work three extra shifts a week up till six next morning. Then home to bed until twelve–thirty and back again.

All faces used the same air. The first face to get the air was the newest one furthest in. It would travel back through six or seven faces. The temperature would be anything up to a hundred degrees.

You couldn't see your hand in front of you during coaling, for dust. Then you'd walk out to pit bottom with that heat on your back and go up the pit to a temperature of perhaps freezing point. Before the air reached the last face it was as rich as petrol. One spark, and oblivion one and all. The deputies had a hell of a job trying to keep the workings clear of gas.

It wasn't till 1926 that a doctor realised that the deaths from t.b. and bronchitis were being caused by the dust. The outcome was the Silicosis Act. This only covered men working in stone. The silica was only supposed to be in certain types of stone so not many men could claim. And the man would be gasping and choking to death before he was certified. The lungs would be solid with stone dust. I knew a lot of men who died of it. There was one family, name of Armitage. There were two brothers who had two sons each. They all died of it. And many, many more. The coal dust was deemed harmless. We were supposed to be getting rid of it every morning in our motions. I bored many a six foot hole for the borer in payment for about two inches of chewing tobacco. After the hole was bored you blew the dust out with a copper pipe. You ended up like a baker. Covered in white dust. It wasn't till 1939 or 1940 that a German scientist discovered that certain coals also contain silica. But it never seemed to bother us. The coal-cutting machines cut out the bottom of the seam, raising clouds of dust. When the compressed air exhaust caught it, when the colliers shovelled on to the conveyors, when it tipped into the tubs, it was like a black fog travelling in the ventilation. A miner in South Wales who is free of dust is called a wet lung. There is a difference between silicosis and pneumoconiosis. The stone dust sets like cement but coal dust doesn't. Particles of silica cut into the lung and kill the tissue. I remember taking my wife to my brother's home. We saw a man leaning over a low wall. My wife said, 'Whatever is the matter with that man?' 'That,' I said, 'is what dust does to a man.' He was gasping and coughing his lungs up. He was dying on his feet. He was 45 years old. He was dead a few months later.

Bedwas colliery went on strike again in January 1933. I was sixteen at the time. This strike was in its sixth week when a few lines appeared in *The South Wales Echo* which said 'The Powell Duffryn Co. are reopening the Bute district at Cilfynydd colliery if they can get sixty boys'. (It was nearly impossible to work a pit at that time without boys.) This colliery was about seven miles over the mountain from our village. But with my father and brother also out of

work because of the strike we were desperate, so with the impetuos-
ity of youth I set off to get a job. First I walked up the Little Aber
valley about five miles to Sengenhydd, then struck off two miles
over the mountain into the next valley, the lower Taf valley. On that
side of the mountain it was down a gradient of 2 in 3 on the tram
road that brought the pit dirt from the pit I hoped I was going to get
a job at. It was very cold with about twelve inches of frozen snow. I
got to the colliery about one o'clock. It had taken me about three
hours. I was signed on within minutes but the timekeeper said the
job was nights, regular, and could I start that night. Well nothing
daunted I said I would. I set off home again up the 2 in 3 mountain
through the frozen snow, and it was getting colder. Over the top and
down to Sengenhydd and through Abertridwr to Caerphilly. I got
home about five. I well remember my mother storming at me, and
crying that I was doing such a foolish thing. But there was no stopping me. I had a job. I went to bed but couldn't sleep. I went out at
quarter to nine and got a lift from Ivor Jones to Sengenhydd. He
tried to put me off by saying it was too cold to go over the mountain.
I had no top coat and my pit clothes were threadbare. But go I did.
The cold was intense. I got to the pit at ten-fifteen. The shift started
at ten-thirty. The working place was about a mile in, and I had a set-
back straight away. The coal seam was only 36 inches thick and I had
never worked in a thin seam. So it was down on your knees—and no
such thing as knee pads. It was also very hot but I didn't mind that so
much. But it was murder on my knees. By four-thirty in the morning
I was going cross–eyed for want of sleep. I had walked eighteen
miles the day before, and then worked this shift in the terrific heat.
My body was crying out for rest. Anyhow we filled about five tubs of
coal which was about eight tons. The shift ended at six a.m. We left
the workplace about five–thirty. The walk to pit bottom was a nightmare. The roadway was a return airway which meant the air was hot
and coming from behind you. The pit shaft was the upcast shaft,
which meant the air was hot all the way to the top. Then the cold. I
was wet through with sweat and the cold was breathtaking. Stun-
ning at that time in the morning. I put my lamp in the lamproom.
Left the pit yard and crossed the road to the track that took tubs of
dirt up to the tip. I had been told the first set of tubs left the pit yard
at six-twenty. I could get on and ride up to the top (although it was
against the law). When I got there the set of tubs was about two
hundred yards up, so that was that. The ground was pit dirt frozen
solid and smooth. Two steps up, one back. I got hold of the track

rails, which were so cold they felt red hot. By the time I got to the top I had lost track of time. I was too late now to get a lift from Sengenhydd with Ivor Jones. I kept walking. I dare not stop. When I was about half a mile from home I was light-headed and sleepwalking. I kept going by rubbing my hands against walls and hedgerows. So as well as raw knees, raw hands, made worse by frost getting into them. I got home about ten o'clock. Drank a cup of tea then laid down in front of the fire in my pit dirt and slept all day. While I lay sleeping, a mate called to say that the strike at Bedwas had been settled and the pit would start on the following Monday. I never went back for that shift's pay. It would have been about 3/-. It would have cost me half that to get there by train.

Men who were hurt were taken to the miners' hospital. They could claim compensation, but there would be a lot of disputing it. They were always trying to do the men by saying it was their own fault. The company doctor for Bedwas was Dr Wallace, the doctor for Cardiff prison. He was a bastard. His sole aim was to get men off the comp. and back to work before they were fit enough. My right foot was crushed between a girder and a coal tub. He certified me fit to go back. I wasn't. I've suffered with a bad ankle to this day.

I was eighteen at the time. Pit safety boots had just come on the market. They had steel toecaps and steep plate in the heel. They could only be bought at the colliery stores, so much a week deducted out of your pay. I had some on. If I hadn't I would have had my foot off. As it was, I fractured both fibula and tibia bones where they joined my ankle bones. I also had a cut about three inches long.

I was in charge of a set of coal tubs pulled by a rope from a compressed air drum haulage engine. One of the tubs had come off the rails, and I was working it back on (scheming it we called it) with a round piece of wood to one side and a short piece of rail turned on its side on the other. I then signalled the engine man to pull very slow. I didn't see this girder because of the coal dust lying about. The tub missed going on and fell towards me, trapping my foot. I grabbed for the signal wires and the tub stopped. I fell down. The deputy in-bye came back to see why I was stopped so long. I was sitting there with my leg quite numb. He went back in-bye to get his first aid tin, and brought three men back with him. One man took the set of tubs forward to be filled at the face conveyor—production dare not stop. The tubs were filled in minutes and coming back, so I was put in the side until they passed.

The deputy cut my stocking off and bandaged my ankle up. Then he said, 'Patsy,' (I was known by my second name) 'you've lost me £5 by this accident.' He only had two men to spare. They were not colliers. He dare not take a collier off the coal face, so these two had to manage. The pit bottom was two miles away and, except for a short length, was down a gradient of 1 in 3. It was murder. It took two hours to get to pit bottom. For some reason the deputy decided I only had a bruised ankle, so I hobbled with my arms around the men's shoulders. It was the main haulage road for tubs to pit bottom. They ran in sets of twenty one-ton tubs. No unauthorised person was allowed to travel this road. The walking road for men was the return airway. That road didn't have tubs running on it. The used air from the coal faces travelled that road, and it was in a bad state of repair. I couldn't have managed it. It was too low and narrow and hot.

Anyway we set off down old 1 in 3. The first thing to watch for was that either man didn't put his foot on the rails. Second, every thirty yards was a frame with a roller in between the rails. These were to carry the haulage rope which ran along the floor. The empty train of twenty tubs was in-bye of us when we started out, but it wasn't long before they were changed for twenty full ones ready for the run to pit bottom. The man in charge of them, the rider, came running down to warn us to get out of the way. The Coal Mines Act requires that refuge holes must be provided twenty yards apart. At that time they were very much neglected. So we tucked ourselves in the side of the road. The set of tubs would be travelling up to thirty miles an hour. The rider stopped them just above us, then signalled to the engine driver to lower them slowly past us. Then, 'ding, ding, ding', the bell in the engine house, off came the brakes and the train was gone like a bullet. Now the third hazard. The rope holding the tubs was one–and–a–quarter inches in diameter, and while the set of tubs was travelling it was swinging about like a deadly bar. As soon as the tubs landed at pit bottom it stopped and dropped on the floor. Then it was hitched to another empty set, and up comes the rope again. If it caught a man it would cut him in two. Nowhere between us and those tubs was safe from that rope, so we had to wait until the set of empty tubs went roaring by.

We finally arrived at pit bottom, then up the pit (which is a thousand feet deep) into the lamproom to report the accident, then into the ambulance and home. I had the ambulance stop out of sight of the house so as not to frighten my mother. My doctor came later and put four stitches in the cut. Three days later the cut turned septic and my leg was twice its normal size, so I ended up in hospital where I should have been taken in the first place. But it wasn't for me to reason why. The deputy wasn't a bad sort. He came to see me in hospital and give me a packet of fags.

There were two wards of 24 beds for men, and one for women. All the staff, except the matron, came from mining families. I was in there three months, in 1933. While I was in, there was a very bad explosion at Gresford Colliery in North Wales; 250 men were killed.

We were awakened at five a.m. for a cup of tea with bromide in. Then a wash in a bowl. I'll never forget the soap. It must have been made of pumice stone, and smelt vile. I had about two ounces, and it lasted the three months, it was that hard. Breakfast was at seven. One rasher of bacon and one slice of fried bread and a fried egg if you could provide your own, and a small bowl of porridge. Eight, bedmaking and temps. Eight–thirty, the girl cleaners with blocks of wood on handles about nine foot long. There was squares of velvet nailed to the blocks. They used to swing those blocks back and fore like nobody's business, and all of us whistling and beating time.

The wound on my ankle was septic and some cuts on my hands were also septic. I was taken to a small room where they had four or five cylinders like tea urns, all boiling hot, sterilising bandages and sundry utensils. It was about a hundred degrees in there. There was a bowl of boiling hot water put on the floor and I was told to get my foot into it. I was left on my own, thank goodness, and my foot didn't go in till it was cooler. The sweat used to pour out of me when I eventually got my foot in. The steam would be pouring out of these cylinders all the time. I would be in there nine–thirty till eleven–thirty, with the nurse nipping in odd times. Then back into bed to have my hands done. That was another carry on. The nurse would come with a bowl of scalding water and some cloths about six inches square, put one in a bigger cloth and soak them in the water. Then wring them out. The small cloth would be slapped on my cuts. I would rise a yard off the bed. All that went on for a month. The septic then disappeared.

Twelve o'clock was dinner time. We didn't put any weight on with the amount of food on the plate. Then it was always rice pudding. The afternoons were spent reading and sleeping. Teatime was four o'clock. Two cups of tea, and bread and butter. We had to find jam or cheese if we wanted it. Then we had a cup of cocoa at seven and that was it.

While I was there a lad named Victor Rees was brought in with his right leg off halfway between his knee and groin. He was in terrible pain and he let the nurses and sisters know it. His language was wicked to them. Now everybody was getting fruit brought in by families and friends. One night, out of downright cussedness, Vic Rees started to throw grapes at a lad across the ward. The lad started to throw grapes back. Some hit me so I started to throw. By now everybody was roaring with laughter. Then one man name of Wilmot shouted he'd shit the bed with laughing. Well what a to–do. There was one man name of Archer who was recovering from an operation for ulcers. He burst his stitches. The next morning the reckoning. The matron, the hospital secretary, everybody was there in the ward. The walls were in a dreadful state, stained from top to bottom. Without any hesitation, Vic Rees was put outside the main door on a trolley and his parents sent for and told to get him away as best they could. No ambulance laid on. The rest of us were severely reprimanded.

In my last week, I was walking about the ward helping the nurses. Just after five a.m. the phone started to ring in the nurses' room. We knew when it rang that time in the morning it was a pit accident coming in. Later we got to know the accident was coming from Bedwas. At six forty-five the accident arrived on a trolley at the door of the ward. Five men with it. One of them was my father. I went towards him, pushing past the trolley. I glanced at the accident victim and asked my father who it was. It was my brother. The stone side of a roadway had fell out on him, cutting him to the bone over the right eye, cutting the bridge of his nose open, splitting open knuckles on both hands, and cutting him badly above the right knee. He was also badly shocked. He recovered in about two months and was back in work ten weeks later.

Every pit lad's ambition was to be a member of the working men's club, in my case the Caerphilly Social Club. It was a very proud and conservative club, and had upward of two thousand members. To try to get in there if you wasn't a member was like trying to get into jail if you hadn't committed a crime. My introduction was on the first Friday night after my eighteenth birthday, but with a tried and trusted member, Ivor Jones. Everybody's eyes were on me. They were holding an inquest on me with their eyes. My legs were like jelly. My mouth dried up with nerves. The first pint didn't touch the sides. When it came to my turn to call, I gave the money to Ivor and he got the drinks. A non–member was not allowed up to the bar. Then the older men want to know who I was. Ivor Jones speaks up:

'You know Martin Maher working nights in Bedwas? Well this is Martin's oldest boy, Patsy.' 'Oh aye. How's things, Patsy?' 'Working in Bedwas is it?' 'On the coal is it?' 'Rough working in Bedwas so I'm told.' 'Wouldn't work in Bedwas for a pension.' 'Diw diw boy, working in Llanbradach, us.' 'Better there, look you.' Then an inquest all round on the merits of different collieries and men. There was more work done there, and more dust produced, than down any pit. Then a bit later someone would put a beer mat on top of his pint glass. That was the signal enough had been said about pits. The dust was getting in his beer. All this time I was seen but not heard. About eight weeks later, January 1st, the books were opened to new members and six were taken on. But only because six had passed on. If these six stalwarts had not gone six feet down into the land of their fathers, there would be no new members till the next year.

The pit was a man's world. The club was also a man's world. No woman dare enter over that doorstep. I'd really got hair on my chest now. Working with men, drinking with men. The beer was cheaper and better than pub beer. Concerts would be booked from all over, and some of these singers had it all. Besides these there would be impromptu singers. The chairman would call 'Can I have a volunteer?' Without fail, up would jump Evan Davies, known far and wide as Ianto Undertaker because he drove the two–horse hearse. He was always dressed in a black coat and pinstripe trousers with a Gladstone collar cutting his throat. His song without fail would be 'Donald is waiting for you tonight'. 'Thank you Mr Davies, and here is a ticket to get a free pint.' Another to get up was Ben James. He stood there like a ramrod with an expression like Buster Keaton. His song would be 'The Umbrella Man', as flat as a fart. A shout from the back: 'Mr Chairman, give him a ticket to put him out of his suffering.' 'Thank you, Ben. Give him a clap boys. And here's a ticket for a pint.' Another would always come on with 'There's a little green-eyed goddess to the north of Katmandu'. Will Perry would stand there like a rod of steel and roar out 'And six stalwart sergeants to carry him.' But for all that there would be some lovely voices get up there. As good as any opera singer.

There was one room called No. 10 because there was more holding forth on how the country should be run than there ever was at No. 10 Downing Street. There were about twelve or fifteen of them. All potential prime ministers. They would sort out everybody's problems from Alaska to Cape Horn, from Spain across to China.

Three or four were dyed–in–the–wool reds. They would weigh in with the Utopia we were missing by not having Joe Stalin for our guiding light. Another, a North Welshman, would be on about how this country would never be the same because Lloyd George was not prime minister. The main theme of one of the reds was that somewhere in Russia there was a little village by the side of the Trans-Siberian railway: it was reported to Moscow by the village soviet that there was a very gifted child in maths. So without any more ado the mighty Trans-Siberian express was stopped to pick the child up. He was taken to the best school in Moscow, and then the express was stopped again in the evening to put him down. Could you imagine the capitalists of this country doing that for a working man's child? Then it was 'Drink up boys and have another.'

There was times when it would get a bit boring at the club; a few of us would gang together and nip off to Cardiff, to the docks pubs in Tiger Bay. That was a different world altogether to the valleys. One word out of place there and you were flat on your back with your two eyes filled in. It was said that there was more prostitution in Tiger Bay than in any other port in the world. On summer evenings we would walk to the little pubs dotted about the mountains. Some of them little thatch and whitewash places. One of them, the Travellers' Rest on Caerphilly mountain, had a marvellous view. Stand outside the door and look south. The city of Cardiff, the Bristol Channel and the coast of Somerset in the distance. Walk a hundred yards north. Caerphilly, the Aber valley, the Rhymney valley stretching for twenty miles. To the left the smoke haze over the Rhondda valley. To the right Newport and the western valley of Monmouthshire.

The event of the year was the club outing. It would take at least four trains and two paddle steamers from Cardiff docks. The pub and shopkeepers of Weston–Super–Mare would be rubbing their hands together, I can tell you. Another favourite place, but for men only, was Bristol. There could be parties from other valleys there at the same time, so it was 'lock up your daughters, Bristol'. But at Hotwells Road Pier that night, the Bristolians would come out in their hundreds. There'd be more than two thousand voices, and all Welsh, singing 'Abide with Me', 'Jerusalem', 'Myfanwy', 'Jesu lover of my Soul', and the famous 'Cwm Rhondda'. More than one Bristolian would get out his handkerchief and blow his nose.

I had an aunt who was head cook at a big house near Clifton suspension bridge. One Saturday when I was sixteen I went to see her.

I went in at the servants' door. My aunt told 'Upstairs' I was there so she was told to take me up to meet them. They were both in their seventies—retired Indian Army. They had never seen a miner before. I've never had so much fuss made of me before or since. The old girl was crying because I looked so pale and wan. They couldn't believe I went a thousand yards underground every day. The old man wanted to keep giving me beer to get some colour in my cheeks. And I've never eaten so well in my life. It was a day to remember. The boat left Bristol at nine o'clock. It was a rough crossing and we didn't get to Cardiff till after the last train had left. I walked home ten miles from Cardiff docks to our house, up one side of Caerphilly mountain and down the other. I got home at five in the morning dead on my feet.

I thought more of Ivor Jones than I did of my own father. I was a school chum of his son. He had been a miner, but had to get out of the pit because of nystagmus (eye trouble miners got because of bad light in the pit). He got a lump sum of £150 and bought himself a lorry. He carried miners from Sengenhydd to Llanbradach colliery. He prospered, and then bought a six-wheeler bus with a Chevrolet engine. Chevrolets were all the rage then.

Another character I remember had the nickname of Coffee. I didn't know anybody who knew his proper name. Coming home from work one Friday afternoon he went, as usual, into his pub and got a skinful of ale. After leaving the pub he had to pass the railway goods yard. Seeing a goods van with the door open and some straw on the floor, Coffee got in to sleep the ale off. To quote him: 'I woke up and this van was going like hell. It was pitch dark. So I got my head down again. When I woke again and looked out I was in the biggest sidings I'd ever seen. Seeing a passing railwayman I asked him where I was. "Old Oak Common," said the railwayman, eyes popping.' Coffee was still in his pit clothes and pit dirt. As black as ink. Coffee now found he'd lost his wages. So the goods station master phoned through to the colliery manager in Wales to vouch for Coffee. The manager paid the fare and took it out of next week's wages.

By 1937 there was a slight wind of change. There was a movement started by a moderate group of men to get the S.W.M.F. back in (now the N.U.M.). Leaflets began to appear in all sorts of odd places like under a beer mat in a pub, hidden in the newspaper, or slipped in your pocket on a bus. These were given out by unemployed men who had nothing to fear from the colliery or this other union. These four men were running about in big cars by this time. One in a Rolls Royce. He also had a bodyguard. A punch-drunk boxer by the name of Billy Green. Eventually things came to a head. There was a strike. But this strike was something very different. It had never happened this way before. The strikers would not come up the pit at the end of the shift. It was the first sit-in ever in this country, and it was the miners of Bedwas Colliery who did it. They stayed down the pit four days and nights. It was across the country in every newspaper. The colliery management were at a complete loss to know what to do for a time. There was only one answer. They had to get rid of this fascist union which they promptly did. But it cost the N.U.M. £10,000 to get rid of these four men.

By this time Hitler was raving and ranting. All the old pithead gear at derelict pits, old coal tubs, any old iron, was being taken away for the coming war. The giant Dowlais steelworks which had stood idle so long was now being dismantled and cut up. When it was done, and it will last for ever, it left a mighty tip of solid iron slag which nothing will ever grow on. In the next valley to Merthyr Tydfil there is a little village called Pontlottyn. In the park there, planted in a block of concrete, are two huge pit wheels—the symbol of coal mining. They are 22 feet in diameter. They stand as a monument to an era of misery, poverty and despair, a monument to men and women who were born, bred and maimed, and who struggled all their lives.

Some things people would never forget. Like when Churchill said the dole ought to be cut, and it was. And when he said, which damned him for evermore, 'Two shillings a week is enough to keep a miner's child on.' In 1947 came nationalisation of the mines. The management of the N.C.B. was handed over to the men already running the old companies, and because Powell Duffryn were the biggest they took over.

At six o'clock on the morning of January 1st 1947 at the area A.G.M. a man named Corfield who had been dictator of the P.D. for years, came to speak to the day shift before they went down the pit. He said that now the pits were owned by the people we must all pull together. A voice in the crowd shouted out, 'Tell them about all the children you starved to death in Merthyr, Dowlais and the Rhymney Valley, you bastard.'

London

Gladys Gibson

I was employed by what was known as the U.A.B. as investigator, in the East End of London, untrained, as were all my colleagues. Most of the men had come over from Public Assistance after the 1934 Act, when powers and duties were passed to the U.A.B. With some exceptions investigators had a low opinion of the unemployed, and the general opinion was that they could find work if they tried a bit harder. My colleagues were badly paid and most had a family to support so they hated to see the unemployed 'getting money for nothing'.

Most of the unemployed were genuinely seeking work. A heavy snowfall was a blessing, when men with broken boots earned a little money by sweeping the streets. The Boroughs took on unemployed, in strict rotation, for thirteen weeks of unskilled work. It sometimes put a man back in benefit and took him off the hated dole. The situation began to change after Munich, when more men found work. Salvation came with the War, when the despised unemployed became valued workers or serving soldiers.

Quite by chance I came across Mary Hughes, daughter of Judge Hughes who wrote *Tom Brown's Schooldays*. She was then a tiny, frail woman of about seventy, still a J.P. and much given to talking about the devil's unemployment when on the bench. She was well known as a magistrate and a councillor but she once disguised herself as an old beggarwoman, spent the night in the workhouse and, in the morning, when the skilly came round, banged on the table with her spoon and shouted, 'We want a hot drink and some bread and butter.' All the women joined in. There was such din and disorder that the workhouse master was called in. Then she stood up, all five feet of her, and said, 'I am Mary Hughes and a justice of the peace. I demand that these women be given a proper breakfast'. So there was no more skilly.

She believed that all crime was the result of poverty. She was very tolerant of theft, even from herself. She often said, 'If my children needed bread I should not think it wrong to take it'. This did not endear her to her fellow magistrates but they had great respect for her. (Incidentally the trustees who had the disposal of her money gave her house to the newly formed Family Service Unit who have done great work ever since.)

Mary Hughes told me there was a room to let in the street round the corner. It was an L-shaped room, quite large but filthy. I had it cleaned and distempered but had a fearful struggle against bugs. The tenants of the house were an elderly couple of Russian Jews who made a bare living by selling bagels in Wentworth Street, the permanent street market that crosses Petticoat Lane. At six in the morning the boy from the baker brought a sackful of bagels—glossy rings of bread, boiled before they were baked—and these were on sale in a basket outside the door. They sold at a halfpenny apiece or five for twopence and were good but indigestable. People dropped their coppers into the basket.

The old couple were very friendly. It was a second marriage in each case. He was said to have lived a raffish life but she had always lived in extreme poverty. As she came from Odessa, a fine town favoured by the Czar and his family, she thought London a very backward dirty place. She never learnt to read and write. She could not even read the numbers on the trams but he was intelligent and had had some education.

I used to go down for a meal in Passover week, for gefilte fish and almond macaroons and we were on good terms but he was devoured with curiosity about my past. 'Education is not to be picked up off the ground' he said. He would try to get me to tell him my troubles and I used to turn his questions off with a joke. He longed to be rich. 'But what would you do with all that money?' I asked him. 'I should speckerlate. I'd wear a silk hat and smoke cigars all day long. Also diamond rings I should have on every finger.'

It was a poor house, three storeys high, with an air of respectability, in a terrace occupied by Jewish people, many very old, the women still wearing wigs. On warm evenings they brought their chairs out on the pavement, a practice not followed by non-Jewish people.

The old couple kept a kitchen and a small back bedroom for themselves. The ground floor front was occupied by a rather fierce woman, a tailoress living apart from her husband. He came to see her every evening and they quarrelled incessantly. The couple on the first floor had a fearful struggle to live. He had been a silversmith but was trading in anything he could afford to buy, from skipping ropes to fly papers. I remember helping them to dress little celluloid dolls in Cambridge colours before Boat Race day—a large blue ribbon and some sparklers gummed on the chest. We worked until after midnight but he was out at dawn the next day. He helped with furniture removals and with Jewish weddings and, as a street trader, went as far as Nottingham Goose Fair. He was small, stringy, rather monkey-like in appearance. He had come from Russia as a teenager and though he had never been to school he could read, write, and imitate any kind of accent. His wife, a plump cheerful young woman, made a tiny profit by selling candles, soap and such things to neighbours. At last they had a baby girl who brought them luck, they said, for he got back his old job as silversmith.

There were no amenities in that house except a lavatory on the first floor. I had to carry up water from a tap at the turn of the stairs and to carry dirty water down. I kept my coal in a shed in the yard. The house was lighted by gas. The pressure was low so that extra cooking in one room meant dim lights all round. On Friday a young woman who was not Jewish came to wash the passage and kitchen and on Saturday morning children came wanting to light fires for a copper or two. A man came down the street selling carbolic. Everybody bought some. The whole street reeked rather pleasantly of carbolic.

The street was always teeming with life. There were two schools, one a huge council school, the other a church school, an old grey stone building next to the church. There children could be heard all day chanting their lessons. There were some pollarded willows in the narrow churchyard, the only spot of greenery in the road. There were two synagogues, one tiny, and a Jewish Welfare Centre. A brewery at the far end sent an overpowering smell when the wind blew from that direction. It was not exactly a slum street for, though people were poor, they were 'respectable'. When the cats'-meat man came on his bicycle calling 'Meat! Meat!' hundreds of lean cats streaked out to follow him. There was a young nanny goat who lived in a yard full of crated hens, destined for ritual slaughter. She clattered up and down the street, pushing her nose into shopping bags in search of greenery. Some cows lived in a dark shed where one could buy milk in a jug. Or, after dark, one could put a penny in the slot machine on the gate.

People who lived in the street did not see it as picturesque, but though some had ambitions and would work to all hours, the atmosphere was friendly. People made easy contacts. One worried little woman stopped to ask me, a total stranger, 'Does rock salmon eat good?' There were several small shops where women lingered over their meagre shopping and were always ready for lively gossip. Kippers and smoked salmon came direct from the smoke sheds of Limehouse and one could buy minute quantities of salmon at rock–bottom price. Fruit and vegetables came from Spitalfields market on the barrows, or in the street markets. Food was cheap. I lived on about thirty shillings a week and managed very well. A friend came to live in two rooms above the church school tuck-shop that dealt in farthings and we both went to the Dewdrop Inn on Friday night for a bath and a talk with Mary Hughes. It was through her that I got to know a great many people, most of them left-wing.

I was gradually drawn into political movements such as demos. Once I went with a small crowd of Stepney people on a march in Herts, organised by a woman pacifist and socialist. I carried a pole with a French loaf and some rambler roses nailed to it and the words, *Bread and Roses for all God's children*. We had tea in a village institute and then sat in a field listening to cheery words from Ernie Bevin.

My first demo happened by accident. I had not been in Stepney more than a few weeks when I noticed a small crowd going to a Town Hall afternoon meeting. The great hall was crowded, mainly, I think, with unemployed men but there were a good many housewives. The speakers were all loud-voiced and excitable but I chiefly remember the last, a dynamic young man who told us about the situation in Germany where Trade Unionists like Thaelmann, as well as Jews, were rounded up into concentration camps. He then talked about Austria under Doctor Dolfuss (this was in 1934) and the machine-gunning of the workers' flats in Vienna, of which I had known nothing.

Then he organised a demo for us, illegally I suppose, as we kept to back streets and had no police escort. 'Come on, you lot!' he bellowed. 'Don't go slinking off. Join the demo. Show you've got red blood in you.' We followed him in a procession, two by two, with no banners. We marched with the right fist doubled and raised. We shouted 'Release Thaelmann! Release the Austrian workers!' The people we passed seemed interested and certainly not hostile. The stallholders in a Jewish market that was just closing shouted 'Bravo. Attaboy!' They knew far more about what was happening on the Continent than we did. We dispersed at a convenient spot near a main road and went off feeling rather pleased with ourselves.

Soon I became involved in big demos, for May Day, for Aid to

Spain and particularly in the great Anti-Fascist demos. Many contingents marched behind their banners—very fine works of art, marshalls marched beside us shouting slogans that we took up, and impassive policemen walked beside them. But demos became more and more exciting as the numbers of Blackshirts grew. Oswald Mosley was determined to get into the East End. The people were determined to keep him out, and the police were powerless. Wherever they tried to steer a way through for Mosley they found barricades and angry crowds. Mosley once got into Cable Street but never any farther.

Both Fascists and Anti-Fascists decided to hold meetings in Victoria Park, Bethnal Green, on the same Sunday afternoon. Mary Hughes wanted to go but was dissuaded. 'It's no use talking about Jesus where half the crowd will be Jewish,' somebody told her. I marched with the Anti-Fascists, passing many blocks of flats bristling with Union Jacks, with women at their windows screaming that we were traitors and Jewish scum. The police were there in force to keep the two crowds apart. After a wild meeting we reformed our ranks and were very glad of police protection as the Blackshirts ran alongside shouting 'The Yids. The Yids. We gotta get rid of the Yids' and trying to get at us. Many a citizen of Jewish appearance who had been an onlooker was glad to join us to escape the rage of the Fascists who, only a week before, had thrown a Jewish baby through a plate glass window.

After dark, people went out in small groups with a bucket of whitewash and a brush, to daub slogans on the pavements—when the police were not about. So in the morning we read as we passed by:

DOWN WITH THE MEANS TEST.
DOWN WITH MOSLEY AND HIS BRUISERS.
THEY SHALL NOT PASS.
WORKERS OF THE WORLD, UNITE.
LEARN THE TRUTH. READ THE DAILY WORKER.
DOWN WITH CHAMBERLAIN AND HITLER.

One young man spent a long time decorating the pavement round the Tower with slogans, not knowing he was being watched by soldiers. When he had finished they said 'Now you can clean up the mess. This is Crown property.' Many people in the East End rejoiced at the so-called peace settlement in Munich but next day the street slogans told them exactly what they could expect.

The political ferment of those days did mean intellectual ferment too. Communists, some with little education, grappled with Marx, Engels and dialectical materialism while Blackshirts were studying Carlyle. A young man I knew started a study group in a docker's flat. I don't know why I was invited to join. We read William Morris and talked about everything under the sun. The docker's wife had been annoyed by the visit of a Duchess, interested in poverty, who looked round the nice clean flat and exclaimed 'But your furniture is quite good'.

The docker in whose flat we met once a week was an outgoing, exuberant man in middle life who, though not a 'regular' man at the docks 'walked in' when there was work and did not have to attend the call-on. He was of Irish descent and a natural leader. He collected seven or eight men, all dockers or stevedores, with names such as Bill, Joe or Ted. It was a change for me to be among men who were not unemployed but were able to live fairly comfortably with a wife and children on earnings of about sixteen shillings a day—more with overtime.

Morris expected the triumph of socialism. He looked forward to an idyllic society with England once more a green and pleasant land, where men were craftsmen rather than factory workers. The dockers doubted whether it would be acceptable to the working classes. 'They'd chuck litter about. They'd smash things up. They wouldn't want to work. They'd never be educated up to it.' 'Youngsters want to get down to a job and have some money in their pockets. Young chaps on piece work, they kill themselves to earn a bit more than the next man.' 'But under socialism they'd forget about competing. They'd co-operate.' The docker's wife, the hostess, made tea and handed it round. She had taken no part in the discussion but she was not hostile. 'There's more tea in the pot,' she said, taking off her apron. 'I'm off with Emmy to the *Gunboat* for a split Guinness.' All the men agreed that Morris was right in saying that gangs of hooligans would do battle to break up the socialist society. Fascists. They could understand that.

This odd little study circle came to an abrupt end with the outbreak of war in Spain. The men formed an anti-fascist group of dockers and portworkers and threw themselves into the struggle to aid the Spanish government. They organised meetings, collected money and added their weight to the big organisations working for the same cause.

The office of the Unemployment Assistance Board was in Limehouse. It covered a wide area, part of Stepney, Bethnal

Green, Spitalfields, Shadwell and Wapping. The Unemployed Workers' Movement was very strong, Communist orientated and militant. It was perhaps because of their resistance that the second part of the 1934 Act was never put into operation. All over the area Communists and Blackshirts were at loggerheads. On the whole the Blackshirts produced more bruisers. In one house I would be confronted with a smiling picture of Stalin; in another of Mosley. It was very difficult for me not to show bias. The police favoured the Blackshirts whom they regarded as patriots because their rostrums were draped in Union Jacks. It was not unusual to hear a London Bobby softly whistling the fascist song, known locally as the Horse Whistle.

When I went to the U.A.B. my position was difficult. My colleagues, one woman and a number of men, all came in from the suburbs. They thought I was mad to live in Stepney. I was not happy in the atmosphere at the office, where there was not much sympathy for the unemployed. The constant cry was 'Don't forget it's public money these people are getting.' Some people we visited were resentful of our right of entry into their homes, but most took it as a matter of course. One man told me to fill up my bloody form in the street but it did him no good. He had to go to the office to be ticked off.

I suppose the investigators were the lowest in the hierarchy in our office. The area officer once said to me, 'You surely don't want to be a common investigator all your life?' The porter, an Irishman, had been an N.C.O. in the British Army and when he had nothing to do he whistled a martial air and went through his drill, an imaginary musket on his shoulder. It was his job to see to the men in the waiting room, some called up for interview, some to report a change in their circumstances. He was anti-semitic, believing, against all the evidence, that no Jew ever fought in a war. One day he came with blazing eyes to tell me that one of my men, Jewish of course, was trying to get out of having me call by pitching a yarn about a visit to hospital. 'A nasty type. Cheeky. Know the feller? He drags a leg.' As he limped across the room to show me, I looked at the yellow card without which an unemployed man would be lost. 'It's an honourable limp,' I said. 'He draws a disability pension for it.' 'What! That cock sparrer? Who's the girl he's after seeing?' 'His daughter, in a sanatorium. His wife died of T.B. Please return his card, say I'll make another appointment and give him my best wishes.' I doubt whether the man got my good wishes but he caught his bus.

The office was usually crowded with people reporting changed circumstances or simply asking for more money. Occasionally a man twirled a razor blade on a string or clung to the legs of a table or chair. Most of the cases of threatening behaviour took place in the registry, a large room where there were several desks and a table for interview. I don't think I actually saw any violence though I heard scuffling and shouting when an offender was being hustled out by the porter. I came back one afternoon to write up my reports and found a broken window and some ruffled tempers. I was told that the porter was not to be found at the time. 'Where were you when the affray took place?' the area officer asked him. 'Sure I was like the Bobby when there's a bit of trouble. I was just around the corner.'

The morning the men barricaded themselves into the waiting room was exciting. They came in a body when the office opened, handed their yellow cards to the porter, hustled out the few men not involved and barred the door. We in our room heard singing, mostly music hall songs such as *Lily of Laguna*. There was consternation among the officers because our book of rules gave no instructions that met the case. The porter could hardly be restrained from battering-in the door. The area office rang up a higher authority for instructions. The men inside wanted to send out a delegation of three to discuss their demands and the porter was delighted to bawl a refusal through the door. We had to go on our way but we heard later how the door had been lifted off its hinges and the contingent bundled out, laughing.

One of my colleagues was a plump, lugubrious little man whose parrot cry was 'Roll on Friday'. He said he was paid for only half the week. He had sailed the China seas selling whisky, but all good things come to an end. Most of the people were terrified of him. He said to me, speaking of a man I knew well, 'Why doesn't that young chap get himself a job?' 'He has a duodenal ulcer. Last time he was doing his stint on the Borough he collapsed.' 'They all say that,' he grumbled.

An older, well educated man who had been a geologist was very popular. The people liked him for his courtesy and his even temper. They referred to him as a nice old gent, a proper gentleman. He regarded himself as a cut above his colleagues and, when asked to go on an office outing, he replied, 'I wouldn't be seen dead among such people.' These words, often quoted, caused no resentment.

There was one who specialised on fraud cases. The whole business of prosecuting or not seemed to me dubious. 'Why warn X but prosecute Y?' I asked him. 'The decision isn't mine. The Board has its policy.' I decided that the policy was to prosecute where the Board was certain of winning. I had to go to court to identify a man in his fifties who had come down in the world. His misdemeanor was going from door to door in the evening and selling brushes, without reporting his meagre earnings. He turned up well groomed, in his best suit, thus creating a bad impression for he looked prosperous. He pleaded guilty so I did not have to identify him. He was given six months and, when he came out, had to pay back, by weekly instalments, the money he owed the Board.

Some of my colleagues suspected me of being up to no good because I lived in the neighbourhood and, as they said, backed up the unemployed. I enquired, innocently, about the office branch of the appropriate union and was at once dubbed a Communist. The National Unemployed Workers' Movement was a thorn in the flesh of the Board. It was mainly Communist-led but had socialist members. In general the N.U.W.M. men had an aggressive attitude towards the Board's investigators who were hardly to blame for the policy of the Government.

I remember that a single man or woman had sixteen shillings a week, six to cover rent, the rest for all other expenses. A man or woman over fifty—or it may have been fifty-five—had an extra shilling for comforts. One of the most worrying things was the Wage Stop Clause. An unemployed man might not receive more than he had previously earned. The extra nourishment allowed for an ailing child was half a crown a week, to be spent on milk, eggs and a quarter of a pound of butter. One mother admitted that she gave all her other five children a taste of 'real' butter. Margarine at that time was horrible. Before the child got his grant we had to keep a record of his weight for six weeks, to make sure it kept going down.

Pay day for most of my men was Friday. Saturday was not a bad day for them. In the evening both man and wife went to a pub. On Sunday they had the one really good meal of the week, with 'afters', usually stewed fruit and custard. The rent, usually about ten shillings, was to be seen on Monday morning on the mantelshelf, ready for the rent collector. There was little left to carry on through the week. The children seemed to exist on a piece of bread with a scrape of jam, or, with luck, a penn'orth of chips. By Thursday they were in a bad way. I often heard a child say, cheerfully, 'We don't have no dinner on a Fursday.' Even the supply of bread had run out. So had the fuel. No fire on a Fursday.

The poorest, one might say the worst managers, bought coal from a coal shed, fourteen pounds for fourpence, seven pounds for tuppence. The best coal was then two shillings and fourpence a hundredweight so it was cheaper to buy by the bag but not often possible.

The Jewish women did better on very little money. They made good soups and tasty scraps fried in oil. There was more variety in their catering. On the other hand I sympathised with the non-Jewish women who recklessly spent twopence on pickles. The whole family needed a fillip. One block of flats was occupied by men living alone, four of them sharing a sink and a tap on the landing. The bachelors were pitiable. They spent their money on a cup of tea and a roll at a caff while the elderly widowers made a savoury meal out of a bone or two and a pound of 'block ornaments'—the trimmings of the butcher's joints. This was to be bought at fourpence a pound and, with some pot herbs, made a fine stew, usually cooked in an iron saucepan over the fire.

Children, if they were seriously underweight, had 'doctor's milk' at school but when they caught up with the average, were taken off the list and slow deterioration set in. Practically all families bought sweetened condensed milk marked 'unfit for babies'. Tea was always stewing in the pot because not to offer a caller a cuppa was considered beyond the pale.

Wives of unemployed men got free dried milk for babies at the clinic and were given bundles of yellowed, used woollens supplied by well-wishers. Weakly babies sometimes had special food supplied. I think the clinics and the health visitors saved many an infant life, but there were many cases of rickets needing cod liver oil. The panel doctors were pretty good but they had to deal with people suffering from chronic under–nourishment. The insurance stamp at that time covered the man only. The children came under the school medical service and the Care Committees, and such voluntary bodies as Invalid Children's Aid did wonderful work, but the wives of unemployed men had to report to the Public Assistance doctor, the parish doctor as they called him. They hated it so much that they did not go. If they could afford it they paid a shilling to have a tooth pulled. A private doctor charged from two and sixpence to three and sixpence a home visit. Some of these East End doctors were dedicated men who did a marvellous job, often referring cases to hospital.

A man who had been long unemployed could run out of medical benefit so that he had no alternative to the parish doctor. Usually he did not go unless obliged. Many of the undernourished unemployed had ulcers or incipient ulcers, as you could see by their drawn faces. Sometimes their wives gave them chips to relieve the monotony of bland foods. They suffered, of course, and as likely as not sent to the chemist for a bottle of something.

On one surprise visit I heard the wife tell one of the children to say her husband was out, but then she changed her mind and asked me in. 'Matter of fact he's not so good today.' 'Is he in bed?' 'Sort of. I'll go and see.' After some talk in the bedroom she asked me to go in. The man looked ghastly but declared he was fit for work. He was propped up on several pillows, with the blankets pulled up to his chin. 'Good job you didn't call this morning,' he said, with a wry grin. 'You'd a found me knotted up, yelling blue murder.' 'Have you seen a doctor?' 'Not me. I managed by meself. Just passed a stone. Show the lady, Liz.' The stone was in a small jam jar. Two of the children ran in to have a look at it. It was not very big but it looked horrible. 'We turned the kids out into the street,' he said. 'The wife gave me a hand. Wonderful what you can do if you're put to it.' He wiped the perspiration from his forehead. He said he'd be up and about the next day, able to sign on at the Exchange. I let him sign his declaration in bed. His hand was a bit shaky but he managed.

Another elderly man was in much worse shape but still signing on. I had seen him doubled up in the street but no doubt he was able to straighten up at the Exchange. 'I'm O.K.' he said. 'Nothing but a bit of indigestion.' His wife left the room. I could see she was crying. 'She upsets herself,' he said. 'She's like that. She don't need to.' This man had been a general labourer but he was thin and shrunken; his eyes had gone back into cavernous hollows. 'They got it in for me at the Labour,' he grumbled. 'They never send me after a job. I dunno why.' He had done no work for several years but previously had had a good record. 'This country's in a rotten state,' he said. 'If I was a bit younger I'd be off to Canada or New Zealand.' I went out. The wife dried her eyes and saw me to the door. I said her husband needed good food but I couldn't see how he was to get it when he was unable to work. 'It's not that, Miss,' she said, in a low voice. 'It's his fistula. Can't you see he's on the way out?' 'Surely not. He can't be as bad as that.' 'Look,' she said, buttonholing me. 'I know what a shocking state he's in. It scares me stiff, waking in the morning and finding him green as a corpse on the pillow. Supposing he goes off sudden. I'll be blamed, won't I?' 'Why don't you get the doctor to call?' 'He's out of medical benefit. He won't have the parish doctor so what can I do? I'm scared, honest. There's his sister Maggie'll be down on me like a ton of bricks if he goes off sudden. What'll I do?' It was easy because his doctor was my doctor, a remarkably kindly, humane man. He waived formalities. He dropped in next day for a chat and the ambulance was round in a few hours. The man who wanted to go to New Zealand lived about a week.

There was usually a good neighbourhood spirit in the small streets and in the old blocks of flats. In a case of death, everybody contributed towards the wreaths. There was always an enterprising woman to organise such affairs. Funerals were spectacles enjoyed by all, but the feeling of awe went deep. Babies were insured from birth at a penny a week. This was more important than saving. The insurance policies were handed over to young people when they left home or married for though they might have a thin time in this world they intended to go out with full honours. I once heard a woman say to a tearful old granny whose luck was out, 'There's a lovely funeral round the corner, Ducks. Go along and cheer yourself up.'

The one I remember best was in Bethnal Green. Six-storey stone blocks of flats were built round a courtyard and in the middle was another block, shutting out a good deal of light. When the hundreds of children were playing in the yard, the noise was excruciating, but that day there was a hushed silence. All the windows were occupied by spectators talking in low tones. The big gates were, for once, thrown open. A handsome motor hearse stood in the yard, the top piled with wreaths, crosses and the *Gates of Heaven* done in white lilies. The undertaker, in silk hat and tails, supervised the piling on of flowers which were brought out from various stairways by four mutes, equally impressive in toppers. As each wreath was lifted up and shown to the onlookers, sighs of admiration and pleasure went up. The hearse was driven slowly out into the street, to head a procession of Daimlers for family and friends. The mourners were in deep black. The undertaker opened each car door and bowed them in and they sat solemnly, each woman with a handkerchief to her eyes. When all was ready the undertaker motioned with his silver–topped cane and the hearse moved off slowly, to circle the neighbouring streets where the dead man had been known. The undertaker walked proudly alongside. He knew he was the star of the occasion. His hat was in his hand. He frowned at any man who did not instantly whip off his hat as the cortege approached. The four mutes walked decorously beside the cars, hat in hand.

It was a point of honour to spend all the insurance money on the funeral and the funeral feast. I was once invited to the funeral of a man I had known and liked. We assembled round the handsome coffin that stood on trestles in the small living room, covered with wreaths. We returned to the room after the funeral to find two long tables spread with plates of cold ham, pickles, cucumber and such things. Beer circulated, followed by the usual cups of tea. The man's workmates, though they had been fond of him, managed to crack a few jokes as they feasted. The undertaker came in for congratulations. His bill was settled on the landing and he tossed off a glass of brandy before he left. 'It was a lovely funeral,' the guests said on departing. 'You done him proud. You've nothing to reproach yourself for.'

Most women spared a shilling a week to the clothing club. This had to cover children's clothing as well as household replacements. The tallyman was a good friend, even if he charged more than the cheap shops. Mothers found bargains at jumble sales and on market stalls. One woman told me that if she were rich she would buy a new pair of corsets. She had worn one pair for 16 years. The general feeling was that one had to be a bit near the mark, respectably dressed, especially on Sunday and at Easter, the great time for new clothes. Children usually wore rubber shoes in summer, wellingtons in bad weather—very bad for the feet. Night clothes and dressing gowns were almost unknown. One little girl on a school journey was surprised to be given 'another dress' to go to bed in. Another had a 'real' bath for the first time in her life. Children were bathed in a tin tub, the whole family using the same water. On the whole they were well turned out and clean except in the school holidays, when they were horribly unkempt.

We investigators trudged round the district alloted us carrying our papers in a black government bag. While the man was signing his declaration that he had done no work, the woman usually slapped a cup of stewed tea on the table for the visitor. I fixed a squeaker in the bottom of my bag so that when little children became too noisy they were startled into silence by a series of squeaks.

The U.A.B. could give a grant of up to £2 towards replacements if the condition of clothing and bedding, pots and pans, was sufficiently serious. I had to inspect everything and make a careful list of the pawn tickets, but many applications under the pots and pans clause were turned down. If it was granted, I had to supervise the spending of the grant. I was familiar with pawn shops as we often had to get sheets and blankets out of pawn. During my investigations I saw flimsy sugar bags used for sheets and piles of old clothes used as blankets.

I was once given the task of setting up a home for a man, wife and four children after their home had been completely destroyed by fire. On Friday afternoon I was called into the office and told I was to supervise the spending of £5, the largest sum ever granted to a single case. The extraordinary thing was that we succeeded. On Saturday morning I met him at the Employment Exchange, a lean, dark, very serious young man. We drew the money and, as it was a bleak morning, I took him to the nearest Lyons cafe for coffee, roll and butter. Even though I told him I was not dipping into the grant, he was shocked at such extravagance, but we had to plan what we were to buy. In fact he and his wife had already made out a list of bare necessities. 'Clean beds we must have,' he said. 'Last night my little ones lay on the floor. It's not good. My wife cried all night.' His eyes were red-rimmed too. He talked of the rigid economy they both practised to make a good future for the children. 'She shaves me every day with a cut-throat razor,' he said. 'She won't let me waste money on safety razor blades.' So I was not surprised that he proved to be a great man at a bargain. We went to the famous street market, Mile End Waste. We examined second hand beds first and rejected any that might be verminous though the little horrors were adept at hiding themselves in daylight. 'Swab it with paraffin,' a stallholder advised but we shuddered and passed on. He managed to find 3 good clean beds with brass knobs and clean mattresses. I had only to pay for the goods and take the receipts, but he had to carry the things to a friendly carter in a side street, who chalked the name on them and returned to his tea and chips.

I suppose we covered the full length of Mile End Waste half a dozen times. We were becoming well known as he described the fire and the plight of his little ones at every stall. We were pressed to buy pots and vases but he had no use for fancy stuff and we concentrated on tables and chairs. Our list included lino and we were lucky to get a roll of new lino with lozenges of green and brown. 'Poor quality,' the man said, fingering the shiny surface. 'Whadyer expect for half a dollar?' 'Two bob.' 'Take it. I'll starve.' This man had never made use of pawnshops so there were no pledges to redeem. We bought new army blankets and new, very hard pillows. He secured a bargain of salvaged cotton lengths his wife would make into sheets. We fished out a handsome teapot without a lid and then went rummaging at other junk stalls for a lid to fit. The tin kettle was new. It cost sixpence. He found some very nice mugs, all different, for the children and an extraordinary assortment of cheerful plates, picked out here and there and bargained for. He wanted to buy cups without saucers but I could not bear the thought so we hunted out saucers that more or less matched. We went to a junk shop and bought an assortment of cutlery, including a wafer thin poultry knife he said was just what his wife needed. The shop also provided us with pots and pans and a rolling pin. By now I was getting very tired. He had only to lay out the balance of the grant, fifteen shillings, on whatever amenities it would run to. I left him fingering second-hand curtains. 'My nice home, all gone,' he was saying. 'We carried out the little ones. Not a hair of their head was singed. Please God in time I will make of our poor home a palace. The muslin—how much?' It was 2 o'clock when I left him, with a sheaf of receipts, confident that he would not waste a penny.

There were some lucky families chosen for Sir John Boyd Orr's experiment in adding extra nourishment to the diet. This was, of course, done with the permission of the Board, who did not deduct from the family's allowance. I called at one house where there were half a dozen boys and girls and was interested to see them cutting into a huge piece of cheese. 'It ain't 'alf good,' a boy said. 'Mum, where's me milk? You never give me none.' 'Little liar,' said his mother, pulling his ear. 'They're eating like nobody's business. Cheeky with it. Where's me cane?' But the children ran out laughing with their mouths full of cheese.

The effects of long unemployment were terrible. Men on the scrap heap could become cynical, aggressive or hopeless. The hard thing was to persuade them they were not 'done for'. A lot depended on the attitude of the family. The man had lost his position as chief wage earner and young people resented having their earnings taken into account by the Board. Many left home. One man of sixty, with a family of adolescents, drew just five shillings. Unexpectedly he was left an annuity of three pounds a week by a Canadian whose life he had saved, but he would rather have had a job. A very charming and refined elderly Jew, once a hand-made cigarette maker, was supported, except for five shillings, by an only son who longed to get married. I watched the man's health deteriorate and was not surprised to hear he had a bad attack of shingles, but the far–sighted son had kept him in a Friendly Society and while ill he. had thirty–five shillings a week. Mutual rejoicing. In another case the man, elderly again, was very depressed because his wife and wage–earning daughter treated him with contempt. I met the wife and suggested she should try to cheer him up but she tossed her head and retorted, 'Let him get a job and we'll see.' The next week he hanged himself. At the inquest she said he had never been depressed, nor had he threatened suicide. This was an extreme case of a family situation not uncommon.

Casual work centred around the docks and the breweries. Unskilled labourers turned up twice a day for call–on. I often saw a crowd of men hurrying towards a brewery for one o'clock. The foreman liked them to turn up regularly. He knew most of the regulars by name. One man had a half day's work now and then but one afternoon when I called he was in despair. 'I had a rotten cold on me. I blew me nose hard, see. Blow me if he didn't call me name and I never heard. I'd gone deaf all of a sudden like you can. Foreman won't call me out again, not likely. He give me a bad mark, see.' I was told that the scrimmage at the dock gates was appalling. In one very nice united family the man was rewarded for having worked by being given a small piece of meat for his tea and half an ounce of tobacco. A man who started a heavy job after years of unemployment crawled home, done in, but after a week or two of good food he was marching home upright.

We had few women on our books. Most of them were approaching pensionable age and, if they had been in tailoring, had poor eyesight. Although tailoring was seasonal—two seasons a year—girls usually managed to keep in benefit. They bought smart, fashionable clothes by weekly payments and they bought one stocking a week, price sixpence. Men who had managed to keep going for years on seasonal work, generally tailoring, hated to come down to the dole and show their bank book as well as their rent book. They felt deeply disgraced. The nearer people had lived to the poverty line, the more cheerful they were about their unemployed state. Some working men and their wives had a healthy contempt for the manners and morals of the middle–classes. They preferred a public house sing–song, winkles and jellied eels at a street stall and, when in funds, a music hall or a trip to Southend. In September hundreds of families went by lorry, with their cooking pots and blankets, to the hop fields of Kent where for countless years they had stripped hop vines by day, crowded into local pubs in the evening and slept happily on straw in huts. It was a pleasure to see thin, underfed children come back with colour in their cheeks, and apples bulging their pockets. Before the machines took over, the hop fields provided the only real holiday many East Enders ever knew. The mums had a busy life with hop picking and cooking, but it set them up for the winter.

I remember old Granny Forth, already a great–grandmother, a veteran picker, sitting on a lorry waving the old brown teapot from which she was never parted. I had last seen her doing *Knees up Mother Brown* outside her favourite pub. She was of Irish extraction. She put out what she called the Pope's flag when the Union Jacks went up. She was acquainted with all the ghosts the Irish brought with them to Wapping—the little man telling his beads at the corner of Farthing Fields; the Lady with the little dog who walked the streets after midnight; and the White Rabbit, an ill luck bringer, that scuttled about near St George's–in–the–East Hospital.

One large family stays in my memory. The eldest boy had never learnt to read. The second was a scholarship boy who struggled to do his homework in the midst of uproar. These children had an extraordinary habit of biting their toe nails. Mum provided a hot meal every day, even if it was only pea soup. The boys went scrounging for specks—apples thrown under the market stalls as no good but providing a useful addition to family meals. Mum kept order with a switch.

Men and women who refused to work or who walked out of a job, perhaps in a fit of temper, had their benefit suspended for six weeks. They could apply to the U.A.B. I called on a man in late middle age who had never been out of work before and did not know the ropes. Nobody at the Exchange had told him to go to the U.A.B. and for five weeks he and his two schoolboy sons had had no income. He had been worked out of a good job as a tent maker by a rival at his firm, who had worked him up to a state of asking for his cards. His wife had died shortly before. There was a photograph of a beautiful girl in the room. Unfortunately I remarked on it. She had been inveigled into a brothel in Limehouse. This was a cause of deep shame to the man and the boys. 'Had you no brothers or sisters to help you after you lost your job?' I asked him. 'They turned against us on account of the girl.' 'What about the neighbours?' 'We've always kept ourselves to ourselves.' 'I don't think you'll get any money before Friday but if you go to the office you'll probably get some food vouchers.' 'We'll manage.'

One of the pleasantest places to visit was a narrow alley where half the men were out of work. There was a warm friendly atmosphere even though a poor crazed man used to beat on a dustbin lid and pour out obscenities about his neighbours. I was sometimes greeted with, 'It's about time you came round. Somebody always has a bit of luck when you've been. Maybe it'll be our turn.' One elderly couple had some marvellous aspidistras. They always waited for me to remark on them and ask what polish they used on the leaves. When the man was taken on for a short spell, the wife exclaimed, 'Bless you!' though I had nothing to do with getting him work. Another cheerful, skinny man, approaching pensionable age, loved a joke. 'I went to your office last week. Those chaps up there were hopping about like a lot of scalded cats. You'd think they'd rather do an honest day's work.' Only manual work counted in his eyes. A tailoress, a woman who had remarried, applied during a spell of unemployment. The husband, white bearded and serene, was sitting by the fire. As he was almost totally deaf he took no part in the interview. 'I was deceived,' she said, angrily. 'I was told he had money put by but he's got nothing but his pension. He's learned. He could have been a rabbi, but that doesn't put a chicken in the pot.'

I came across one family whose life had become a misery because the man had lost one week's money. It had been arranged that the wife should draw the money and should give him half a crown for himself. It so happened that their name came towards the end of the alphabet so his turn at the Exchange came late on Friday, by which time the children were waiting for mum with shopping bags. By that time there was no food in the house. 'You've shamed him long enough, haven't you?' she said. 'How'd you like to see your old man shamed in front of his mates?' I told her I would do what I could. My report seemed to surprise the officer assessing the case. 'You'd think after what he did his wife would want him punished.'

When Lord Haw-Haw was broadcasting from Germany his talks revealed an intimate knowledge of East End life. They were listened to with interest. I came across one man sitting axe in hand with a pile of firewood beside him. He had just chopped up a table. 'Did you hear Lord Haw-Haw on the radio?' he asked. 'He said the unemployed were chopping up their furniture for firewood. It was as if the bloke had been watching me. It's a beggar.'

Giving things in kind to our people was a tricky business. They could regard it as patronage and resent it. I don't think the little gift of baby's bootees I always gave caused resentment because the cost was trifling. I was usually asked to go up and see the mother who, as soon as she had given birth, took over the management of the household again. Women sometimes said they loved having babies because it was the only time people made a fuss of them. One day when I called on a man with a large family I had to make out a fresh form, starting with the youngest. When I had finished he proudly exclaimed, 'And there's another one upstairs, born yesterday.' Pen poised, with another new form in front of me, I asked the baby's name. 'You got me beat there,' he said. 'Better come up and ask the missus.' One proud father came to the office to report the birth of a little girl, after a whole string of boys. 'We haven't had the bootees yet,' he said. 'What bootees?' 'The ones the lady gives new babies.' So I was reprimanded for setting a precedent and there were some disappointed parents.

One house was awful, furniture broken, bed sagging and the baby's mattress soaking wet. There were two children, according to the case file, a little girl and a baby boy. As I was writing my report I realised that there was no place in that one room where the little girl could sleep. Enquiries were made and it turned out that the child had been taken out of the household years before because the parents were of low mentality and incapable of looking after her. Those parents were smart enough to deceive the Board for several years before they were found out.

On the whole housing was old and poor. As a Northerner, new to London, I was shocked to find families with no back or side boiler, boiling water in a kettle or bucket. Washing day could be a nightmare, though some women made good use of public washhouses. Some of the tiny houses that fell down when London was bombed were bright and cheerful and clean. The kitchen fireplace was the pride of the family, burnished black, with a whitened hearth. Even the back of the fireplace was whitened. But some of the housing was appalling. At the time of the jubilee celebrations of King George V and Queen Mary there was a streamer outside a mouldering block of flats near Mile End Road. LOUSY BUT LOYAL. The oldest council flats consisted of one bedroom, a living room, a tiny scullery, and a lavatory on the back balcony, but whole families had been decently reared there. The newer flats had a bathroom. The water was heated by a gas boiler and pumped into the bath. Some of the old houses in Bethnal Green, a Blackshirt stronghold, had long back gardens full of dahlias and sunflowers. More than once Queen

Mary was photographed in a prize-winning garden. Some of the old property was plagued with bugs, or 'old steam tugs' or 'the red army' as they were called. There was constant warfare against them and in one street, condemned and awaiting demolition, most of the people slept on chairs in the street in high summer. Rats too were a plague and the rodent officer had a busy life.

While I was with the Board, rent strikes spread like a rash through the tenements. They were well organised and were justified as rents were over–high in controlled property. Where a Tenants' Committee functioned, rents were paid to them. Rent collectors were barred. There were pickets at the gates. One block carried the streamer: NO RENT TO THE BLOODSUCKER M. My fear was that our people would be tempted to spend the rent rather than withhold it and that would mean dire trouble later. On the whole they were pretty good and the experience cheered them up. Many tenants had been paying more than the controlled rent for years. At least one owner of East End property charged key money. It was hard on a small shopkeeper holding his shop on a weekly tenancy to have to pay a lump sum once a year or move out. These illegal payments were made at a West End office.

The rent strike started in Brady Street Mansions, where a tenants' committee was formed and rent withheld. No tenant on his own could have kept his rent back without fear of eviction but where whole blocks were involved it was possible. They went for advice to a central committee formed of Communists and socialists who worked out for them the rent they ought to be paying. Block after block of flats joined in. The pickets on the gates made no objections to my going in to see the people I usually visited. We discussed the situation without rancour. 'Supposing we get our rent down a bit, who gets the benefit?' 'Sorry,' I said. 'It's the Board's money, not yours. You'll feel the benefit when you're back at work.' 'Coo! That'll be the day. Whose side are you on, Miss?' 'I'm employed by the Board. I hope you won't do anything rash. Please don't spend the rent money.' I got just as many cups of tea. Some of the men investigators who were refused entry were furious. 'How do you do it?' one of them asked me. 'They don't seem to mind me. I've never been challenged.' 'You must be a Communist. The whole thing's disgraceful. It's all those paid agitators stirring up trouble.' The rent strikes continued until the landlords gave in and the rents came down. Much beer flowed after the victory.

Coloured people were moving in but there was not much prejudice. The men went into the poorest property and rooms were turned into dormitories, hardly an inch to spare between the beds. The tenant was usually a compatriot who made a good thing out of letting. Married couples were usually better housed. I remember a pair of film extras, man and wife, fine well–built types. Through an open door I could see them fighting with chairs but as they were well matched I went quietly away and called again. One very black man was in bed at eleven in the morning but he sprang out fully dressed, boots and all. He had been out looking for a ship at six. Natives of India suffered in their damp rooms in narrow alleys when fog crept up from the river. The man did the cooking and there was always a strong smell of cooking. Poverty had brought Chinese, Malays, Indians, etc to East London, some of them having been connected with East India Company ships. We in the U.A.B. were chiefly connected with Indians who settled in poor property in or near Cable Street and Commercial Road. One narrow alley was entirely occupied by Indians.

Here I am calling at one of those houses, to interview a new applicant. I ring the bell. The door opens a few inches. 'I've called to see Mr Ahmed Ali.' 'He not live here.' 'He's given this as his address.' 'He not here.' 'If I don't see him he'll have no money this week.' 'Wait.' The door closes. A muttered conversation inside the gloomy house. The door opens a few inches. 'Mr Ahmed Ali?' 'You dole man?' 'Yes. May I come in?' Another confab and then, reluctantly, I am admitted into a dark passage. Several suspicious faces peer out of doorways. I ask a few questions and he answers with the help of an older man. Then comes the crucial question. 'May I see your rent book?' 'I not have.' 'Have you a receipt?' 'Not have.' 'You must ask the tenant of the house to give you a receipt and then he must give you a rent book.' The older man finally writes out a receipt on a scrap of paper and I tick off 'receipt seen' on my form. Unexpectedly my client, assured that he can expect to draw an allowance at the Exchange, starts to smile and he calls out cheerfully, 'Goodbye, dole man.'

Sometimes I was asked to act as go–between but it was a hopeless task. One very decent man had been turned out by his wife when she discovered he had been sending money for years to the mother of his illegitimate child. This came to light when he was unemployed and so had to claim for the child. It was the deception, not the lapse, the wife found unforgiveable. The couple met once a week in the street. He handed over the allowance and exchanged his soiled bundle for the linen she washed for him. I was there when another husband was turned out. He went meekly with some spare socks in his pocket and his shaving gear in a jam-jar.

I sometimes had to visit a house where the man had been difficult or aggressive and abusive. I suppose the idea was that such a man would not attack a woman. A labourer of forty came to our area with an appalling record of violence and what is known as threatening behaviour. He regarded me suspiciously until I admired the fine, sturdy baby sitting on the mother's knee and remarked casually that he was very much like his father, as indeed he was. After that all went well. It turned out that the man had a genuine grievance and was the victim of injustice. It was a pity that the workload was so heavy that we seldom had time to listen to the full story. There were some rogues of course. On the other hand there were people like the elderly couple who had not thought of mentioning the grandchild who was living with them. The mother of this child had married five years before and gone off into the blue. The grandparents were astonished to hear that they could claim for the child.

While I was with the Board the old bagel man was taken desperately ill. He had been going to a quack for a remedy for cancer. When at last seen by my own doctor and told that he must go into hospital, his wife called me in to calm him. He was lying under a sort of feather bed with his gnarled old feet sticking out. His white hair was ruffled. His dark eyes were blazing. 'Do me a favour—leave me alone,' he shouted. 'But what's the matter? It's a very good hospital.' 'Without pyjamas I won't go to be a laughing stock.' 'They'll supply you with a nightshirt.' 'I'm not a beggarman. I may be poor but I won't be despised.' The bagel man died in hospital. His wife, who had come to this country from Russia at the time of Jack the Ripper, found the house and the bagel business too much for her so she went to live with her blind son in the sort of poverty she was used to.

Ashton under Lyne

Jack Shaw

The area was distressing. All poor types of streets. Very poor furniture in the houses. Nobody went in for new furniture. If somebody got a set of drawers all the neighbours used to go in and look at them as if it was a wonderful thing. They used to have these brass fire irons round the fire. Some would have steel ones. It used to be quite a thing polishing them up, getting the brass all clean or the steel all burnished up. Then they used to go knocking at the neighbours. 'Hey, come and have a look at my fire irons.' They'd probably spent all afternoon. People then had no ambitions. They were all used to the same thing. Ordinary houses. Furniture handed on. The rooms weren't even decorated, just whitewashed. Like anything else, you'd get them that had a bit more flair, and they used to get dolly blue and all kinds of things and put it in whitewash to colour it. There'd just be an odd house that had a very thin stair carpet. Some had bits of lino on. Some had nothing at all. Just the bare boards. Kitchens was the same. It was all peg rugs. People used to go to the grocers for sugar bags and they used to make all kinds out of them. Peg rugs, aprons for washing with. Kitchens were mostly flags, and of course they used to get down and clean them. In the old days they used to get a hard stone, like a pebble, and rub it on to get all the dirt off. When the donkey stone came out they used to call the women who used it lazybacks. In place of getting this pebble and having to graft and graft, they'd just wet the flags and go round with this soft donkey stone.

There was nothing posh about the houses. Most of them had gas. They had either a mantle or this thing from the wall with a bare flame on. The house was really dressed up on a Friday night. They used to put this donkey stone on the floor, then cover the floor with newspapers 'cos if you stood on it they'd go bloody mad, particularly if it was wet. They'd cover it with paper and put the rug down and it was all posh then. It used to be left like that till weekend. They were so fadistic in them days some of the houses were like little palaces, although it was old stuff. We'd an old white-topped table. We used to play push penny on it. And I'd bring my fretwork in.

Anything like that. But the legs—ooh, bloody hell! Most women then used to wear black woolly stockings. When they was done they used to cut the feet off and put these stockings on the table legs. They used to keep them like that all week, so you wouldn't kick them. Then they'd take the stockings off and polish the legs up for the weekend so when you went in the house you could see your face in them. They used to look at these legs and think they was bloody wonderful. They used to put tablecloths on at weekend. Some had a silky type and some had a thick woolly type. You'd have a coal fire going, and of a night you'd be rolling salt on table, or clear it off and blow football. You'd use them for anything. It wasn't like today. If I started cutting wood up on table now wife'd go bloody mad.

Us lads used to go round in gangs. Just at the back of the pit there's a row of colliery houses where my mates lived. Their fathers worked in the pit. On all spare pieces of ground men and lads were either playing football or pitch and toss. There was a lot of gambling going on, bookies, and pitch and toss schools. Lots of the men used to play peggy for coppers. The peggy was top-shaped and made of wood. You hit the nose end with a stick and as the peggy flew up in the air you struck out with the stick and tried to knock it as far as you could. Then the striker would give his challenge in the number of jumps or skips you could reach the peggy in. Young men could knock it twenty yards or so and they would say 'Ten' or 'Twelve'. If you took the challenge—1d or 2d bet—you took a flying run to the peggy stone and started jumping. If you did it inside the number given you had the money. If not you lost. They used to do canal jumping near Portland Basin. How that started was through gambling. Pitch and toss. If Ashton police came they used to jump over canal to Dukinfield side then they couldn't touch them. But they didn't always land on other side. Then they used to jump the cut for bets.

Blokes used to earn half a crown in the pound as bookies' runners. There was no licensed bookies. The runners used to stand in entries of pubs or else in the ginnel of some place. Some of these blokes would go round the mills and pubs and houses. Anywhere they got bets. There was a wrangle with the police in Manchester. There was a bloke I knew well. I hadn't seen him for a long while and I met his wife in town. She said, 'He's up in court.' I said, 'What for?' She said, 'It was his turn to get caught.' Occasionally the police had to raid the bookies. Now all the police wanted was to catch *somebody*. But they never caught the bookie. It was prearranged.

The bookie owed them only one and that one stopped there so police could catch him. Bookie would pay his fine and give him ten bob. But you couldn't do it with the same one too often. There were that many out of work they were glad to stand there and be a stooge and you'd probably do it once a year.

Around the pits you get pit hills. When the coal came out of pit on a belt system there was people picking it. There was what they called household coal. Then this small stuff what they called boiler coal. And then there was all this slag that was left. They had their own railroad from the pit. They used to bring wagons and dump it any bloody where. It was mostly slag but there was lots of coal in it. When the coal strike was on they were like ants all over it. Next door but one to us was a lad called Lenny Fowles. He had no education, and yet he got to be a leading draughtsman. He was very well respected but he had a lot of ill health. His mother was a widow. Lenny was slightly built but he could play a bit of football. One day I was playing on street when five or six big lads came down. 'Where's Lenny?' 'He lives there,' I said, 'but he's not in.' So they go to his house. 'He's had to go up pit hills and get coal.' 'But we kick off at 11. Go and get all team.' I thought, 'This'll be a giggle,' so I followed them. All bloody football team and three or four supporters got on these pit hills and they filled his bag for him.

Along the canal there's all these mills. They brought coal to the mills in barges. They brought wagons from pit to the shute on the canal and dropped the wagon sides down. They'd have a couple of blokes shovelling the coal. It was dead primitive but it was effective. It went down this shute and underneath were barges. The chaps that was working on barges would only be on two or three days a week, and they'd be related to blokes that wasn't working—brothers and cousins. So on the bridge you'd always see half a dozen or so blokes stood there with caps on and mufflers. This coal would come down the shute into one big heap and the men would be shovelling it. Well accidentally on purpose they'd throw about six shovelfuls into the canal every time they got the chance. When the barge moved on there'd probably be three or four hundredweight of small coal. They used to get a bucket full of holes on a clothes line, throw it across the canal and scoop it up. Fill half hundredweight bags. Then they had prams or pram wheels with boxes on and they used to go round the streets selling. People used to grumble, 'This bloody coal, it's all wet through.' And it was only two bob for half a bag.

My wife's father worked on the railway. You couldn't pinch coal off railway, but he'd got contacts. One of his friends worked on shunting trains that went by White Bridge. 'Put a bucket on side,' he said, 'and every time train goes by I'll throw a lump of coal at it.' They used to have scouts on railway but if anybody had seen him he'd say, 'I were just throwing it at that bucket.' Every time Bill went at night there was about 20 lumps of coal there because he was going up and down all day. They even went to the extent of pulling faces at train drivers. The engine driver would have an excuse then. He knew what it was for.

Insurance companies tried to cash in. If they'd got an insurance book going, they'd make it a part book and they'd have three blokes on it. Let's say the book would be worth £3 a week. They'd get three men and pay them a pound a week and say, 'Now it's up to you. If you get the extra business you'll build the book up.' You was flogging dead horses. You couldn't do it. But they wasn't bothered. They knew that as soon as you started you'd go and see your Aunty Maggie and your Uncle Tom. For the first week or two your incentive were great. You'd think, 'Well I've got a job. It's no more than dole but I'll go and see cousin Frank.' You'd be going round your family and bosses would be laughing up their sleeves because after 3 months you'd say, 'Oh, it's no good.' You'd be handing a book back then and they'd divide that up and advertise it again.

There was a hell of a lot of allotments. And there used to be a lot of knocking off. They used to be up about three or four in the morning going on the Moss pinching lettuce and celery, anything to make a meal. The Moss was more or less peat. That's why they've never built on it. My father had an allotment on the Moss. He paid a pound a year. It was just a matter of growing vegetables for our house. Others had big ones and it would be their full time job. Up at three or four in the morning and horse and cart going to Manchester market. My Uncle Harry did that. It was an all day job. You could hire a handcart for anything. People used to make a living like that. They'd hire a handcart, go on Moss, fill it full of lettuce, watercress, celery. (There'd be a lot of that knocked off). Then they used to come round shouting out, 'Ashton Moss celery!' It was very good. People used to come round selling salt in big blocks. It were only about threepence. We used to break it up with a knife and powder it with a rolling pin. The rag and bone men used to come round. They'd pay a tanner to Ely Waller for the cart. Depending on what you give them they'd either give you a block of salt or some of these stones for cleaning your floor.

Quite a lot of people had so-called ice cream rounds. Mostly Italians, but some local people. There were two brothers, Trainers, and they used to come round at night with a pony and cart shouting, 'Milk, penny a pint!' My dad said, 'It's nothing but bloody water.' My mother said, 'Well, for a penny it's alright. It'll do for rice pudding or anything like that.' There was no good in it. It was just white. But people used to buy it. My dad was working 2 or 3 days a week so we wasn't as hard up as some. But we'd no milk come to our house. I can't remember having fresh milk until I was 15. We used to have condensed milk.

All the older lads were in the Terriers. It was a mode of income because they wasn't working. They got a bounty every year of £5. On top of that they got the uniform. There dozens of them joined for that reason alone. Them that worked in stores would try and knock something off. You could buy a greatcoat for ten bob. A pair of boots for half a crown. It was a common sight winter time to see people with their army pants and greatcoats and boots on. It was a common sight to see the boots, and them grey socks folded up, at the side of the greatcoats in the pawnshops. Women used to pawn their wedding rings and go into Woolworth's and buy brass ones.

Every day there was people coming round canvassing. There were always people with money ready to exploit people who hadn't. Newspapers used to have teams of blokes coming round mithering you. If you'd take the paper for so long they'd give you a life insurance, or else they'd provide you with free glasses. There's a friend of mine who's an optician today. He's not registered but all his life he's been an optician. He started with *News of the World*. He was tall and thin and he just looked the part. His face fit. If you were a bit that way they'd put you on the eyesight testing. If you were on the rough side you'd be an ordinary canvasser. They used to plead with you to get these papers because the only thing they were bothered about was commission. They were working for next to nothing. 'We'll send our expert round to test your eyes.' I said to my friend, 'How can you test people's eyes?' 'Well,' he said, 'there's nowt to it. You've got blank frames and you keep putting different things in till they can see alright. The only thing you have to remember is not to put it back in the wrong slot.' Each slot had a number on and that would be the prescription and he'd sign it with a big flair.

At football matches you used to get people like Jimmy De Looze. He used to be a strong-arm lad. He'd go round doing feats of strength. He used to do all kinds of things. Lift men up and tie chains and bend bars round his neck. These sort of people used to go outside football ground doing all this. Stand on their hands. Then go round with a cap. They'd only get halfpennies in, and buttons. They wouldn't get much more than a penny off anybody.

There were a lot of Co-ops that had halls over the top of the shop. They used to let them off for meetings and educational classes. Some of the wide boys would engage them for dances. Some people were quite good at dancing and took a pride in it. Jack Pickford was a real wide lad. He never worked because there was no work for him to do. But if there had of been it wouldn't have had to be too hard. He was always bothered about his hands, and a lovely collar and tie. But he'd engage hall and he'd flash it all round. He'd no money for advertising, but he'd get as many as he could. It was only about ninepence perhaps, or sixpence. If it was a success he was able to pay band and pay for the hall and have about a pound or thirty bob left. But the margin was that small that anybody in competition, or a bad night and they didn't turn up, he wouldn't even have enough for the hall so you never used to see him after the interval. The band used to go looking for him and all this business. But even they wouldn't be professionals. They'd be playing for about five bob for night. There was quite a lot of these bands. They used to have a kettle drum and there'd probably be a piano and violin. But it was just word of mouth advertising. Occasionally you might see in a chip shop, somebody would be a bit more venturesome and have wrote it out. They used to get an *Evening News* placard and cut it in two and they'd print it on the back. And then some that was a bit more posher still, they'd cut letters out of the newspaper and paste them on and make it look attractive. There used to be more competition-dancing then. Most of these dances used to have a waltz competition or a tango. It was only five bob for the prize but they were out of work and they were desperate. They used to tart theirself up like anything. I remember going to one with Flash Harry and his wife and she came in her clogs. She were done up like Lady Bountiful with a pair of clogs on and she had to borrow a pair of shoes off one of the girls to go in the competition. But as soon as old Flash came in the room they said, 'He's won it.' He were like Victor Sylvester. But they never had a chance. The world just passed them by. During that period they were beat before they started.

They used to have these long-playing piano sessions. Jimmy De Looze had a brother called Cecil. He was a pianist. And there used to be a lad in Hyde—Fox, the marathon pianist. They used to get tents, or go in the Co–op hall. They'd play for two or three days. Cecil De Looze used to play in pictures. They used to be up to all kinds of things just to bring a bob or two in. The pubs used to have their darts team, and dominoes and crib. Driving licences hadn't come out then and you could hire a car for a few bob for half a day. Jack Pickford was always on that lark. He'd go to a pub. 'I believe you're playing at Freemason's Arms tonight. In place of walking or going on bus I'll bring the car and I'll take you all for a tanner a-piece.' He'd come round with this old banger and there'd be about 8 of them trying to get in and he could hardly drive the damn thing. Sometimes he used to break down half way or run out of petrol. You'd always get that type of person who would rise above the others and try to make a bob or two.

One of the things they used to do in some of the clubs and public houses was have a whip round. You'd put in what you could afford. The money was used for that party in that particular room. There were two chaps that were broke and one had threepence and t' other had sixpence which wouldn't go very far. So they went into pub where they knew this thing took place. They sat there for a few minutes, inconspicuous, not letting themselves be seen too much. And then one of them says, 'Well, are we passing the hat round?' So they said, 'Yes.' So he says to his friend, 'Here we are, we're in for the night.' There were people who were in work putting five shillings in or something like that. The hat went round and they put their threepence and sixpence in. Then one of the main people in the room got up and said, 'Now then, what are we going to do with this money? Are we going to buy a wreath, or are we giving it to the widow?'

One chap got his beer for nothing. At that time *The Empire News* used to pay out on twelve results. This chap went into public house and he had just enough to buy one gill of beer. So he bought this gill and he whispered to the landlord, 'I got twelve up. Don't tell t' others.' He drunk his beer and then he went out to toilet at the back. When he'd gone out landlord said, 'Hey, old Charlie's got twelve up on coupon.' So he comes back and one chap says, 'Are you having one, Charlie?' 'No,' he said. 'I've no money. I just had enough for a gill.' 'That's all right,' he said. 'Have one with me.' 'I can't buy you one back.' 'That doesn't matter.' So he has a gill with him. And then another comes up. Of course all through the night he's having a real merry time of it. Then when he was ready for going out one chap says to him, 'Aye, kept it pretty quiet didn't you.' 'What?' 'About that coupon. Twelve up.' He said, 'Oh aye. Seven last week and five this.'

The Black Maria was always being called out to the Labour Exchange. Men would be fighting because they couldn't get any dole money. I knew a man called Bob who was in the police. He said they called it the Hurry Up Wagon. The clerks used to go about and if they saw you hanging about on street corners or in the house you had to go in on Friday and explain why. There was one called Old Blue Nose. He was a real terror. One of the lads had a little firewood round on the quiet. Sometimes somebody would die and there'd be old furniture, so old even that nobody would want it and he used to put it on cart, take it round back and chop it up. Old Blue Nose got wind of this so he was waiting one day. He sees him coming along and he said, 'Hey, where are you going with the firewood?' 'Firewood?' he said. 'I'm flitting.'

As long as people got their food, pinching a bit on Moss, and maybe growing a bit, they got by. Them days there used to be a lot of pigeon pie. Men would go round off-licences and pubs and climb over the back yard and pinch some beer bottles. There were a penny on a bottle. They'd pinch half a dozen and go round and get six-pence and buy a gill. You could sit in all night with a gill. For cigarettes they'd go round streets and pick up dimps and put them in a tin. They used to mix them all up together and make their own. So they were smoking for nothing. They'd nothing else to do afternoons. They'd know some places would be better than others. If they hadn't got enough dimps to make a cigarette they'd mix some dried tealeaves with them. One chap was busy making cigarettes like this. He said, 'I'm just thinking about somebody picking the dimps up that I throw away.'

One way of getting a few bob on the side was pinching scrap metal from old buildings. The best thing was lead. One day two friends of mine, Tip and Woolly, pinched some lead from an old mill in Dukinfield which was in Cheshire. But they took the lead to a place in Ashton in Lancashire. As they were leaving a detective known as Cigar Jim saw them. He took them to the police station. Now Tip (who was the brightest) whispered to Woolly, 'Tell them we pinched it in Ashton or we'll be handed over to Cheshire police.' The Cheshire police were known to be worse than the Lancashire police. So they said they took it from an old mill down by Guide Bridge. The sergeant told a constable who had a motor cycle combination to put one of them in the sidecar and show him where they'd taken it from. Looking round Tip spotted an old unused warehouse. He pointed to it and said, 'We got it from there.' They were fined 10 shillings and that was the end of that.

Another time Tip and Plonk were told money could be earned picking potatoes in a place called March which they understood was in Cambridge. The problem was how to get there. Someone told them to go to Guide Bridge railway sidings and get in a railway wagon. These two lads were about twenty at the time and they set off without a clue. They had no food. Just a bottle of cold tea. They got into a wagon on the siding and waited. At last the wagon started moving. Then stopped and shunted again and again. Night came. Early in the morning off they went again. After what seemed like ages it came to a stop and they were so tired and fed up they got out. They spotted a railwayman and asked where they were. 'Hyde,' he replied, which was about three miles from where they set off.

There was one man who'd been a captain in the army and they had to find him something to do. He were called Captain Annerty and they made him chief of Fire Brigade. He was the only paid one and I don't suppose he'd get much. All they had was this cart but they had no horse. My friend Frank's dad was second in command but he worked in mill. Theirs was the only house with a phone in. It wasn't a private one. They used to turn a handle and it rung in their house. When a fire happened Frank's mum would come to school for Frank. He'd leave school and run for his dad and then he'd go to t'other mills to get three or four more. And that was Fire Brigade. When they got there one of them used to have to go for th' ice cream cart. The horse pulling Oliver's ice cream cart were the fire horse an' all. If he were out selling ice cream there were a coal horse they could call on. Captain Annerty, if he was sober, he'd yell, 'Come on!' and they'd get horse in shafts and set off. More often than not fire was out be time they got there.

When I left school I went butchering. I used to knock a bit of meat off on quiet. I'd go in the back and cut a lump off and put it under my apron. Then I'd give it to Joe Harrison's mother or to one of my other mates. She used to think it were wonderful. The idea in my dad's mind was that I was going to learn a trade. But there was a lot of butchers and he picked the wrong one. He was just an old family butcher. He was probably only making enough to keep his self. He give me five shillings a week. Then I got seven and six. When I got about eighteen I come to ten shilling a week and he couldn't pay me any more. He said, 'I'll give you a reference and that's about all I can do. I just hope you can get a job.' So that's when I had my first sample·of the dole.

I used to go to the Labour Exchange twice a week. Tuesday to sign on and Friday for my money. I can remember the first Friday coming out. It were liking something out of a play—a queue of blokes down each side of the road with trays and they'd got razor blades on and french letters, all kinds of things. Anything to make a bit of money. Beer money for some, but some had been struck off dole and they were doing this sort of thing to keep alive. Some people couldn't pay the rent and they just went to the workhouse. But there would be that type even then that had a bit of go in them. They'd build a little stock up and go round knocking on people's doors. They'd have nothing, only cuff links and collar studs, boot laces and candles. You wouldn't have give a pound for all that was there. I suppose the idea was to flog as many as they could and go and get some more and make a bob or two each time.

Some of the men were that hard up they used to go round streets singing. And there used to be some morbid songs. Sometimes there'd be somebody in bed ill. They'd say, 'Go and give him two-pence to go in next street.' There was one used to sing:

Precious jewels, precious jewels
To make up His Kingdom
Are little children, little children,
Bright gems for His crown:
Like the stars of the morning
His bright crown adorning,
They shine in their beauty
Bright gems for His crown.

He used to sing the first four lines slow, and then he shouted his head off.

After I got laid off by the butcher I went on the dole for a bit and then they asked me to go on a government training scheme in London. I didn't fancy going because I'd started courting but they gave you an ultimatum that you were refusing a job. So I went. I wanted to learn coach trimming. The blokes there said you'd be lucky if you got a job. And if you did you'd find it difficult to make a living if it was one they found for you. Towards the end of my six months they said, 'There's no vacancies for coach trimmers but you'll be offered something. A barman or bus conducting.' All unskilled jobs. When it come my time it was a cellerman in a pub in Park Lane, living in, fifteen bob a week. I said, 'No, I don't fancy it.'

The reason I put in for coach trimming was because my brother was a coach trimmer. Now our Bill had done a whole picture house for £20 and thought he was a millionaire. And when he'd done, he did the manager's three piece suite with material that should have been on the seats and got free tickets to go to the pictures for six months. Well I didn't fancy going into this pub and as I was courting and had been away six months I wanted to get back home. I said, 'If I get back home my brother will find me a job.' They filled it in on an official form: 'Refused job here. Employment found at home.' When I got back and I'd not got a job they played hell with me for coming home. They threatened to stop my dole.

My wife worked in the refreshment rooms at the station. Her father was on the railway. So although she only had a poor wage she was never out of work. They used to start half past seven every morning and they worked till half past ten at night. They had time off but it was pitiful. She'd have what they called mornings off from half nine till half eleven. I wasn't working so we did a bit of courting then. She got five shilling a week. The only thing that made it worthwhile was that they'd have theatrical troupes coming. They used to get little tips. Some of them would be stars and they'd perhaps leave as much as five shilling. But they used to have all kinds of gruesome jobs. She'd go to bed and about two o'clock in morning alarm bell would go. There'd be a train off line and a gang coming on and they had to get up and make them sandwiches. Or some of these cattle trains would be coming and cows wanted milking and she had to go to get somebody from Gregory's farm. They got the milk for free for milking the cows.

My dad was in the mill. He said, 'I worked there forty years and when I left they never said "Good afternoon".' He just come out and that was it. He was on the dole. Then his dole was stopped. The Board of Guardians office was in the centre of Ashton. It was a grim looking place, like a bloody dungeon. You had to go there if you'd no money at all and they made a little grant. Well I'd not been married very long and I came out of work. I went to the Labour and he said, 'You can't have anything for six weeks.' I said, 'How am I going to live for six weeks?' 'Well,' he said, 'you go down Wellyn Wood.' Well that was about three miles away. So I just set off and walked to this place, told them the story, but they only gave me grocery vouchers. Then during this time I got a letter from the Board of Guardians in Ashton. Could I go down and see them. I had to go from Oldham. About 5 miles. Then when I got there they said, 'Your dad's out of work and he's drawing money from here. Can you do anything to help him?' I said, 'I've got no money myself. I've had to walk down from Oldham now. I've got no bus fare.' Then they looked at you as though you was really doing them.

There was no way of entertainment if you hadn't got any money. It was a matter of going for a walk. We used to go for a walk on moors. Or go visiting relatives. You used to see bags of people, whole families, all walking along. They'd think nothing of walking three or four or five miles to the next town. Seeing Auntie. It was just a matter of passing the day on. This Easter Monday I said, 'We'll go and see my brother.' We had no money for the bus and my wife's shoes had holes in. I had two pair so I pulled a pair of soles off my shoes and put them on hers and we walked it to Stalybridge. We took a tin of beans and we had beans and chips. It was real nice. Probably the walk gave us the appetite.

There was another occasion. There was a knock on the door. It was the old woman across the road. She said, 'I've found half a dollar. Come on, I've struck oil.' She found this half crown and her first thought was she wanted to buy my wife a drink.

I remember Ellen Wilkinson. She used to work for Labour Party. She was one of the first—a real fighter. She was only small but she was a ball of energy—she led the Jarrow marchers. She used to come round these slump areas to street corners with an old school bell and there'd be a feller walking round at back of her carrying a chair. That's how she used to do her electioneering. At each street corner she used to be ringing bell on chair and she used to be going at it like Old Harry. The people who were ruling the roost here then were Tories. The biggest one round here was Sir Walter De Freece. When he retired or died another Tory walked in. Nobody knew of him. And I don't think he'd been in six months when he got involved in some kind of swindle, and next election Labour got in.

My friend Bob told me a story about one of his uncles. This chap's dad was that hard up he couldn't live on his own any longer and he'd nowhere to go. Bob's uncle had a house but it was just one up and one down and there was him and his wife and four kids living in it. It come the time when his dad had to go to workhouse and he couldn't walk, and he put him on his back and he carried him like piggy-back. When they got near Scotland Bridge he paused to rest. He said, 'I'll have to put thee down here a bit, Dad.' His dad said, 'Coming along road I were just thinking, this is where I had to put my dad down. I just got to same bridge.' His son said, 'Bugger it. Tha's coming home with us. Tha sleeps downstairs in kitchen.' And he carried him back home to his own house. He was there about 6 months when he died. If he hadn't of turned back his dad would have died in workhouse.

We had a character in Ashton called Soft Walter. He had more money than anybody. 'Penny for Walter.' Folk used to give him something. He used to have a fistful of money and he used to play hell when he got home and his mother took it off him. The neighbours used to say, 'Ooh, they're after Walter's money.' He went in workhouse.

I well remember our Brian being born. He was delivered by a doctor up at Oldham, a Scotsman, he got called up and killed in the war, so we never paid for Brian. The doctors were very good. You'd go to the doctor. He had your name and address. And after, you got a bill, and if you couldn't pay it, which very few people could, each doctor had his own collector. The collectors used to come round each week and you'd pay sixpence. My wife's father and mother used to say they'd never be straight in their lifetime. When the National Health came in all them doctors' bills were written off. The collectors always used to be the same type who were park keepers in them days—they'd be no use today, kids'd throw them in pond—but they were always little wizened fellers.

When Jim Mill's grandfather died the sons went to the doctor and asked what the bill was. The old man had been ill for years and the wife was paying off sixpence a week. The doctor said, 'Well, actually the bill's £40 yet. But I'll tell you what I'll do. Pay me £10 and I'll call it straight.' So the family got together and between them all they paid the £10 off.

At that time there was that Victorian hangover and people were that cowed, they were afraid of authority. There was a government official and he'd been making a tour of schools round here and he'd been saying how depressing and how browbeaten they was. He said the children of the school, every one of them he stopped to talk to, would wince as though they were going to get a clip behind the ear. I used to be like that. That's the way you was brought up. It even stuck to me when I went in the army. When I used to see officers I used to be frightened to death of them.

My father wasn't particularly strict. He'd swear at you and call you 'Bloody empty-headed pumpkin,' and things like that. If you did anything you used to get a real dressing down. And you got little encouragement. It was more knocking you. Once I came home and said some big lads had hit me. He said, 'What're you crying for? Go back and knock bloody hell out of them and if you haven't done by time I catch up with you I'll give you another clout.' They probably thought they were making men of you but if it didn't come out by instinct you was even more frightened.

On Sunday night Stamper Street, which was one of the main streets in Ashton, was the monkey run. That's where you used to go and try to knock on with somebody. But the police used to walk down there and used to knock their sticks on flags moving you on. As soon as you heard that stick you were away. Police and teachers had the authority behind them. They hit you and you expected it. There might be three or four of you at night outside a shop looking in window—you used to make your own games. Looking in a toffee shop window you'd pick a sweet or a colour and t'others had to guess what you were looking at. It was all very innocent but all of a sudden you'd feel something and it would be a policeman with his cape open and he'd bang his cape round your ears and it nearly knocked you on floor. You used to fly like hell.

South Shields

Charles Graham

I was born in 1916 in South Shields, County Durham. Most working class children went to school and played in their bare feet, or in six-penny rope slippers made in Japan. In extreme cases some children would be lucky enough to have what we called 'police boots'. According to the circumstances of the family (widows etc.), children would be allowed to go to the police station and be fitted with boots. Both boots would be punctured at the top with three holes to stop parents pawning the children's boots.

Those who were lucky enough to have boots or shoes used tacks or studs to make them last longer. I went to school one day and lots of the studs were strewn all over the playground, and I was unlucky enough to have one of these go through my foot—I was barefooted. This caused blood poisoning and my foot swelled and I had to go to the clinic. At the same time my mother had slipped from a high kerb and had broken her leg and was in hospital. I had to hop to the clinic which was about quarter of a mile away. I remember the swelling being opened and the poison pushed out. A neighbour, who had been a nurse in the '14–18 war, was good enough to dress it.

The soles of our feet were like leather. Those who survived were tough. I was as strong as a bull. We used to damage our feet, stubbing them and that, but we were always running, playing. We just took it as natural.

Some of us would be bare-footed even in winter. In the snow. But we were hard. We'd go out and start with a snowball and roll it up till it was big enough to carve it out and play inside like an igloo. We had rough old pieces of wood for a sledge and pulled each other round the streets. The old chestnut man used to stand outside the billiard halls in the winter, selling chestnuts and hot spuds.

My mother became widowed when I was seven years of age, and there were seven of us in the family. She had compensation of five shillings per child until they left school and about twelve shillings for herself. We were fairly well off compared to other big families whose father wasn't working and who were dependent on the Assistance Board. My father was in the Merchant Navy and he fell from

'We had a stand-up in the old tin bath. One after the other.'

Back on the surface: miners from Bedwas Colliery stayed down the pit for four days and nights in protest against the corruption of the 'owners' union' – 'the first sit-in ever in this country'.

(*Above and overleaf*) 'So these were the hunger marchers. Just ordinary people, but drafted into an army not through conscription or patriotism, but sheer necessity.'

(*Above*) **No matter how squalid the inside of the house, keeping up appearances was all-important;** (*below*) **Social relaxation: draughts in a workingmen's club.**

'My father would come home in his dirt – all sweaty clothes to be dried out.'

(*Above*) 'Some of the old property was plagued with bugs': fumigating bedding before a family could move into a new council flat; (*below*) The 'hungry thirties': men at a Salvation Army soup kitchen.

(*Above*) A 'Tommy Talker' band: 'they'd go round the streets collecting funds. Then they bought flour and potatoes and issued them to the people on strike'; (*below*) 'For some reason or other we were turned out of our house': an agricultural worker and his wife, evicted from their tied cottage.

a ship's side into the dry dock in Australia. The accident was on the Christmas Eve and he died on the New Year's Eve. I only remember seeing my father about four times. He was always at sea. They'd take a cargo to Africa, say, and load up there with oranges. Then while they were at sea they'd get a cable, dump those oranges at sea, thousands of boxes, and go to another port because there was a better trade. They used to come from Brazil and they used to burn thousands of tons of coffee beans as fuel instead of coal to keep the world prices up. Less and less people were drinking coffee because as people got poorer it became a luxury. My brother was on a tramp steamer and once they had nothing to eat for three days except pancakes. They only had flour. Conditions got worse and worse because people would cut each others' throats to get a job. And the employers knew it.

My mother cried when we heard he had died. All I remember is him coming home with a parrot and a huge sack of peanuts. They used to burn peanuts as well. And use them for packing.

When my father died we were in a flat: a small kitchen, a room that would be the parents' bedroom, and then the small bedroom. There was Sally, Lily, John, Walter, Eleanor and me. Six of us in the same room. In those times I've heard of a brother seducing the sister etc. There were youths of about eighteen years of age in the same room with girls of fifteen, fourteen, thirteen, and so on. Overcrowded, because they couldn't afford the rent of more rooms.

There were a lot of moonlight flits. There was one big stable where they loaned out horses and carts, or long flat barrows. Usually two loads of that would move a family. You'd borrow a barrow for sixpence a day, or 7/6d the week, if you wanted to go round collecting rags, bones, bottles or jam jars, or selling firewood. They did a roaring trade, hiring barrows.

My sister had just one attic room with two children and with only a gas ring. She couldn't cook an economical dinner. Parents would make soup with a bone, some cabbage, a few turnips and so on. But usually we had a slice of bread in the morning. For dinner a penn'orth of each, that's a penn'orth of fish and a penn'orth of chips; and probably a couple of slices of bread at night. That was the staple diet of the average person. It might be changed now and then with a penn'orth of pease pudding and a saveloy from the local German pork butcher's. I was a prisoner of war for two–and–a–half years and I think I got through pretty easy because it was similar in a sense.

We weren't entitled to school dinners. There was people in a much worse plight than we. I remember going into the cafe to buy pie and peas. It was an ordinary cafe and they used to get a ticket to go there and get a twopenny pie and a penn'orth of peas, and that was the school dinner.

My mother was pretty harassed. She did her best with what she had. There wasn't much attention for us kids individually because there were seven of us. When it was possible there was a meal and a fire but many times we had to sit with a candle because we couldn't afford a penny in the light. Most people went to bed very early. Especially in the winter because in the North East it gets bitterly cold. A lot of people who had electricity couldn't afford to pay it so they used to by-pass the meter with electric wires. I remember sitting one night with the light on. I was the only one at home. And these two six–foot chaps came to the door and straight in, pushed me out the way, straight to the meter box. The electricity company were allowed to employ private detectives who could enter your house without a warrant.

My mother remarried. My stepfather was a miner. A skilled face worker. Before they closed the pit he used to have to walk about a mile to the ferry, about four miles to the pit, and when he got down the pit, three miles under the sea. The Rising Sun Colliery. And it was only when he got to the face that he started getting paid. There's one mine there under the sea that flooded. There's 300 bodies still there. When they closed that mine the owner went bankrupt and his brother–in–law sank a shaft somewhere else and they went on getting the coal.

My mother played the piano. We had a piano at first in one rosy period when my stepfather was working.

My stepfather was good, honest, and hard working when he could work. But I saw him going downhill. He became 90% blind in the end. That was through working on the buildings. On certain buildings they use a lot of lime, and he was sifting it, shovelling it through a huge screen, and the dust blowing into his eyes and it does peel your eyes. He wasn't fully aware of the danger from the lime. But even if he had been, he was desperate to get a job. He got the job from a builder who was an old school friend of his. He just worked on the one site until the job was finished and then he was out of work for the rest of his life. He never got bitter about going blind. Like most people who were injured in the mines or anything, they just accepted it because it was like flogging a dead horse if you tried to fight it.

He went without any luxury himself. If food was short he'd go short himself, and my mother too. He never drank and he wouldn't even play pitch and toss. He liked his pipe and he smoked tealeaves. A lot of people did go to the billiard halls and the public libraries but a terrible lot of them just sat in their chair and were afraid to go out. My step-father got to that stage. He'd just sit at home. I've seen chaps with their nails curled right over through lack of use. Men became just like cabbages.

I was about thirteen when my mother married again. We were living in two rooms. Then after a while we moved into this haunted house. I never did see anything. There was two basements with railings outside. There was an old boy who used to sell boot laces, polishes and that kind of thing, and he used to travel all over. He was a clean old chap. And one time he asked my mother if she would let him have a room because he was getting old. One night about three o'clock there's this terrible screaming and breaking of glass. My mother and stepfather went down and he said someone was chasing him down there and he'd smashed the glass trying to beat this chap off. He left that place and he wouldn't go back there.

This place had been unoccupied for a year and before that it was only occupied for a fortnight at a time, but my mother didn't believe in ghosts. Then we let the basement to a young married couple with a child and she went mad. She woke up and there was two blokes chasing her and her husband was trying to control her but he couldn't. She was put in a mental hospital. Another couple who lived upstairs moved out because this woman had woke up and seen a head on the sideboard. My mother moved into that room because it was a nice room and she woke up in the middle of the night and she saw this chap walking across the room and through the wall, and she was absolutely paralysed. When the paralysis had stopped she woke Pop up, sweating like anything, and said what had happened. He said, 'Ah, you've been eating cheese or something. Get to sleep.' About three nights later the same thing happened and she did wake him up but he didn't see anything. But she saw the man walk across the room again and disappear through the wall. Anyway they were decorating a couple of weeks later and they found that there had been a door leading from the next house but it had been boarded over.

My Uncle Willie was a ship's bosun. He'd been round the world a dozen times. Tough as anything. Slept anywhere. My mother always put him up if she possibly could whenever he came ashore. This time he was ashore about three months and she put him in the top room. First night 3 o'clock in the morning he woke my mum. He said, 'I wouldn't sleep in that room for a thousand pounds. I've been round the world. I've been drunk and I know when I'm drunk but I wasn't drunk last night and somebody bent over me then.' And off he went.

My mother had the reception of her second marriage in the basement of this house. There was a couple of grey hens of beer. And they'd got a bit of a brass band down there made up of friends. It was a proper do with cheese and coffee.

My mother left the house because those who promised to share the rent left and those who came in fell behind with the rent. But it was all laid at my mother's door. She couldn't pay the rent or the rates. So she had to get a small place. There were seven of us in three rooms then. My sisters slept in one room, which would be the dining room, in a fold-up wardrobe bed. Then my mother and father in one room and the brothers in the other. That led to a lot of consumption and so on, that type of living.

Every grocer's shop sold 7 and 14 lb. bags of flour, and women baked on a Sunday. Most of the children would be out collecting orange boxes to stoke the fire. It was a great day, Sunday, because there was plenty of bread, and oven bottom cakes, and scones and so on. We used to buy rusty cans of jam cheap in the market. A housewife would go any distance to save a halfpenny. A halfpenny was a candle and that was four or five hours of light. We were lucky in that we had a distant relative of my stepfather who was a butcher and he used to let us have some offcuts of meat on a weekend. Usually sausages was the nearest the average working class got to meat. One of the favourite meals, because of the gas ring, was pan–haggerty. You slice potatoes, put a layer in the flying pan. Put scraps of bacon in the middle then a layer of sliced potatoes again and fill it with water and just boil it away. Or corned beef in the middle. Meat was scarce. I don't ever remember having cheese except for weddings and funerals. And fresh milk was absolutely out of the question. It was mainly condensed milk.

Pawn shops were as common as betting shops are today. In almost every street there was the old woman who offered her services as messenger for those people who were too proud to be seen going into a pawn shop. She was well known to the pawnbroker and could be trusted. She would get say a pound loan, the pawn shop would charge twopence per week until the pledge was redeemed. The messenger would get threepence or sixpence from the housewife. At first the pawn shops would be taking watches, jewellery etc., but as the slump became worse and people were unable to redeem the articles the old man's suit would be in on Tuesday, out on Thursday until it was too worn out to be pawned. The old messenger, however, had her regular customers who could be trusted and was able to take a parcel of rags to pawn for a pound. This parcel would never be opened, the pawn shop charged twopence per week. It was just a way of getting round the law of money lending. The pawn shop was the bank.

Old Mrs King, she was the one in our street. If you were really desperate and you had a watch, she'd know exactly how much to get. She'd get the best price for you, so it was worth her services. The ordinary green person would be fobbed off with ten shillings for a watch that was worth ten pound. Where people were desperate the pawnbroker invariably made sure that if it wasn't redeemed he'd have a huge profit.

I remember her husband, Mr King. He was interested in numbers. Quite clever. He used to get in the billiard hall, played billiards, watched billiards, especially winter when it was really cold and there was no fire at home. And we started noticing things about this chap. He was a very excitable man. One day he came into the billiard hall and he was telling everybody, including me, 'See these hairs?' He said, 'I swallowed two orange pips three weeks ago and they're beginning to take root.' He couldn't get it out of his mind. He was desperate about this tree growing out of his neck. He was a clever bloke before that. They put him away for six or seven weeks to get treatment and every year he got some other obsession like that. Otherwise he was quite harmless. Eventually he got down to studying horses, like a lot of them did. He was so clever mathematically, he'd very seldom lose at horses. He was like these professionals. He would pick out about six or nine horses, the lowest prices imaginable, ten to one on. You could have halfpenny bets then. He'd pick nine horses out. He'd double them, treble them, accumulator, and so on. And he'd probably lay out about fourpence ha'penny on all those horses, and he was really happy at the end of the day if he had ninepence to pick up or sevenpence. Because you could buy ten cigarettes for threepence ha'penny at the cut-price shop. He used to spend every spare minute studying horses. But he always came out with twopence or threepence profit per day which was his cigarette money. He never bought a newspaper, he was shrewd. The newspapers would come out at two o'clock with the one o'clock winner in it. And the newspaper boys would be dashing about the streets, and then they'd dash back and have the two o'clock race winner stamped on them, and so on, until all the races were stamped on or they all were sold. He'd ask the chaps in the billiard hall, 'What won the one o'clock?' And these chaps decided to play a trick on him. They knew what he'd backed. They said *White Plains*. He said, 'Cor!'

and he used to jump right up in the air if he got a winner. Two o'clock. 'What won it?' *Brown John*. 'Cor!' And so on. Six horses. They all come up. He's working it out because he would have won a fortune. Then he went and bought a newspaper. Well that sent him madder than ever, poor blighter. He went right down. He had to go in every year after that. But there was quite a few did go round the bend because of the hopelessness.

When I was at school we lived opposite the railway station and lots of men used to be standing there waiting for trains to come in with posh people coming for their holidays. The rich were really rich. Your old taste buds started when you passed the hotels and restaurants and you could smell the food. But the men used to stand there with these flat barrows waiting. The boys like myself wouldn't be allowed there. 'Geroff!' But we'd get there when the season finished. It wasn't worth the men hanging about but now and again one or two people would come in with their suitcases. I remember one day a huge suitcase as big as myself. I said, 'Carry your bag, madam?' 'Yes.' 'Where to?' And this was one of these big imposing houses on the sea front about a quarter mile away and I could visualise a shilling and I was sweating blood carrying this. We got about half way there and I was switching it from one shoulder to another. 'Do you want a rest, sonny?' 'Yes, just a couple of minutes.' I put it down and my shoulders were really sore. Eventually I arrived there and she said, 'Will you take it upstairs?' And she opens her purse and says, 'Now don't spend it on cigarettes.' A penny! One penny! That's how the rich were. They knew there was so much competition people would do anything for a penny.

There was a rubbish tip where the ordinary rubbish was tipped and there'd be one man and he put dropsies to whoever was in charge and he made a fortune there. Jam jars, bottles and so on. But nobody else but him could get on to that tip. There was hardly ever anything wasted at all. Chaps used to get these barrows and go round collecting rags, bones, bottles; everything was reprocessed.

I sold newspapers. I wasn't old enough to go to the *Gazette* office direct, where I would have got fourpence in the shilling. So I would go to the woman who was a private housewife who was a kind of newsagent and she'd got about a dozen newspaper boys like myself. I got twopence and she got twopence.

When I was a youngster of about ten or twelve one of my favourite haunts was the market place in South Shields. There was the escapologist who would be tied up with chains. There was others making horehound candy. Beautiful smell in the winter. There was a woman with a huge bosom dressed up as a nurse shouting away there with jars of tape worms. She'd get these people and show them one of these tape worms and tell them they must have one and she'd sell these bottles of stuff like hot cakes. The queerest one was four Indians with turbans on, and huge live snakes. They had about ten of these snakes, huge fat ones crawling round one of the Indians, and a big placard up: *Indian snake oil.* They explained exactly how they milked the snake and everything. I used to go there regularly every week. I used to earn a bit helping the stallholders, open boxes, carry this, carry that, put their stall up. The snake oil was for everything. We used to see the regular customers coming back looking and feeling better. It used to cost half a crown a bottle, which was a lot of money then, for a bottle of this pinkish mixture. Because of the times there was a lot of this muscular rheumatism and I could see these old ladies coming back walking better. And the snakes really held the customers while the men did a lot of spieling. I used to visualise them sitting on a stool underneath milking these snakes. I used to help these Indians and one day they told me to get a barrel from under the stall and I had to go to a garage in a back lane just off the market and get five gallon of oil. I took it back to them and they got some pink substance and they poured it in and stirred it and that was it. But it was doing the job.

There was another Indian who was a fortune teller. By law you were not allowed to tell fortunes but his way out was to sell a lucky bean. And the more poverty stricken a person gets the more they go right back to superstition. Any fortune teller will always make enough to live on. Fortune tellers and spiritualists sprang up in all the distressed areas left right and centre. Teacup reading etc. People wanted to find out what was in the future. Is there a likelihood of getting out of this? But his trick was he wrote in invisible ink. He had dozens of pieces of paper and he had a heater, like an oil lamp, on the stall and he'd say, 'You want to buy a bean? And I will give you your fortune.' Then he'd stick this by the heater and chat to her for a minute or two and all that invisible ink would come out and there was her fortune. Marvellous. A miracle. And people really believed that. People wouldn't dare turn a gypsy away without buying something if they had a penny in their purse because they believed in the curse.

In that market place they sold a lot of condemned meat that would be unfit for human consumption. I've been at stalls there with the pork stinking. But they used to sell huge blocks of this for half a crown a time. The crowds would be thronging around. I suppose a lot of people were ill through it.

When you bought a comic you got it for a halfpenny from a second hand book shop. You could read a dozen comics for a halfpenny by inter-swapping them. That was the only books in the average house. Any old books would be burnt to make a fire in the winter. Old boots and socks went on the fire.

I spent many hours on the river Tyne, sharing a very small sculler boat with a friend. We earned a few shillings here and there. As ships came in and moored offshore at the buoys we would take the crew and baggage ashore. There were many ways one could earn a shilling or two on the river. I spent hours on the river with this boat when I was unemployed. I was unemployed a year after I left school and a year before I came south. We used to earn a few bob dredging coal. These big hoppers loading coal on the Tyne dropped coal into the ships but a lot would scatter into the river. We'd lie there and we'd make a kind of fork like a garden fork and it had a net and we'd drop that overboard on a rope and dredge along and you'd have a net full of coal.

All along the coast, especially towards Sunderland, there's seams of coal open to the sea and during a storm it would break this coal and it would be swept ashore and sometimes there's tons of it in the form of pebbles. Lots of people went down there and gathered this coal. I'd take the coal home and some of it my mother would sell to people in the house.

We used to go to the depot where the coal would be loaded on to carts and we'd follow those horses and carts for miles to see where they stopped. Then they'd just loose the back and drop it by the coal hole in the road. We'd ask the woman if we could load the coal in for them for a shilling. Occasionally if you were lucky you'd get half a bag of coal to take home as well.

There was an Arab. He'd buy a big horse and he'd go across to North Shields. Down to the ferry the slope was 1 in 4. It was the same at the other side. He'd go to a colliery in Northumberland and he'd get a huge long cart piled with this rubbish. It wasn't all stone. There was a lot of slate and cheap coal. He'd buy the whole load for about 10/-. Then he'd go down this bank. And that was bad enough, going down the bank, trying to keep the brake on. But to get the horse up the other side he'd whip it and you could see this horse tearing its guts out. We used to hang about the ferry, catching crabs and fish, and the kids used to wait for workers coming from the docks asking them if they'd got any lunch left, and we used to see him. He was fined a couple of times. Once he'd got it to his depot, he used to have a smaller cart and go round the lanes selling the coal at three-halfpence a bucket. But he was a savage bloke with the horses. He'd buy big strong hefty horses and then he'd work them to death. He used to go through two horses a year. The circumstances made him like that. He was desperate to earn a living and that was the only way he could.

The only trouble I got into was falling overboard from my little sculler. To stop the boat from being pinched we tied it to a buoy about ten feet away from the quay. Usually a passing boatman would give you a lift to or from it. But if there wasn't anybody about we had to try to jump in. We'd take turns. Very often as children we'd tie a couple of orange boxes and a couple of planks together and we'd go across the river through this huge shipping lane on that.

We'd jump into the rowboat with the tide going out, and we'd fish until the tide started coming in. This time we wanted to catch the tide and I was late so I jumped in and we went out and there was a ground swell of about forty feet. For the first time in my life I was sea sick. The sleet was coming down as well and we tried to get back and we got to the head of the pier and we stuck in one spot for two hours and couldn't move. We often used to come back about 3 o'clock in the morning and go to my friend's house and have a good old fry–up. If you got out among a shoal of whiting or anything you'd just need to put a piece of silver paper on with three or four hooks and up you'd come with three or four fish because they'd snap at anything. We had plenty of fish.

One chap on the river was known as 'Dead Bodies'. There were quite a lot of suicides during the Depression. A great many of these finished up in the river. This chap 'Dead Bodies' kept his ears to the ground (or water) to hear of anyone jumping in. He knew every tide and current on the river and knew within a couple of yards where the body would come ashore three days or so later on the coast off Tynemouth, even if the victim was from the Newcastle Bridge, ten miles away. He would use a hook on a long pole to tow it to the river police morgue. For this service he would receive 7/6d.

It was very common in those days for children to be dying of diphtheria or rheumatic fever. 'Would you like to see your friend?' And they'd be laid out in a coffin, six, seven, eight or ten years of age. They died of consumption, mostly, because of the overcrowded rooms. The average child saw six or seven of his mates dying before he left school. My brother was seriously ill. I remember him lying on the settee. I was about seven, he was about nine. He was at death's door. I think that was diphtheria. There were seven of us in an upstairs flat, two rooms and a small kitchen. But he recovered.

I can remember vividly the first occasion I was invited in to see a dead friend. We were only about six or seven. 'Would you come and see so–and–so?' And I'd go with a couple of others, and we'd go upstairs . . . and I didn't know anything about it until I got up there. 'Oh, isn't she beautiful?' This was a common thing, like a wake. You didn't go to the funeral. You'd just go and look to see them lying in the coffin. 'Do you want to say goodbye to your friend?' The parents knew that you were playmates and in a sense they wanted to feel that your friend had seen you. 'Your friend's going away now.' At that time, we just took it. That was part of life.

When I left school I remember going round the quay trying to get to sea because this was the dream in that area. But after a year I got a job as a lather boy at a barber's. Five shillings a week. I was there for about eight months. I knew I wasn't going to learn how to cut hair because he didn't want to teach me because he was afraid for his job. This was general. People were afraid of letting you know their little secrets. It was only short back and sides, after all. The old boys used to come in every week for a shave with the cut-throat razor. They'd never been used to any other. My job was just a matter of softening their bristles while he was cutting someone else's hair.

Then I got a job as an errand boy at a grocer's shop. Trade was really competitive. One grocer's shop next door to another. And the desperation of the managers. Usually ex-army officers from the '14–18 war. I used to have to fill these seven or fourteen pound bags of flour and deliver the orders. There was one order I used to deliver on the outskirts of Jarrow. I often wondered why they didn't have their order from the same firm in Jarrow, but they knew our manager and he was so desperate he said, 'It's no bother. I'll get it delivered.' I used to have a sack barrow for delivering and I had to walk about five miles to this place and five miles back. That was an order worth about 30/-. I got twopence tip there so I was quite happy about that.

The manager's two sons were going to grammar school and they used to come in at the weekend. The manager sent them on all the orders where there were tips. I complained because it was so obvious. He said, 'But my boys are doing it for nothing. They're not getting any wages.'

I managed to get work from a lady who owned two hardware shops and a wholesale grocery business when I was seventeen years of age. There were three sons, one an officer in the merchant navy, the next oldest, about twenty one years, travelled for orders and ran the grocery business, and a younger son about ten years old at a public school. They had adopted a young girl of about ten years old. She was very ugly to the point that I am sure my employer thought she would never marry. I was taught by the second son to drive the van, but to make sure I would pass the driving test I was told by my employer to go to the British School of Motoring and she would lend me the fee of 50/- to be paid out of my wages at the rate of 5/- per week. My take home pay was 13/6d before this 5/- stoppage (I would have had 14/- on the dole). My first duty was at six o'clock in the morning when I opened a small tobacco and sweet shop to catch the early morning trade from workers travelling by ferry across the Tyne. I would be relieved at eight a.m., have breakfast and report to the wholesale warehouse at nine a.m., help check and load the goods and start delivering. I very often did not finish work until eight p.m. or nine p.m. (but there was no overtime pay).

Money was so tight that credit was unobtainable, so it was cash on delivery, which means that there was threats and excuses at almost every shop. 'Oh will you wait until I can go and borrow some money off so–and–so up the road?' Or, 'Have you got change of a fiver?' And a fiver was a lot of money for a small tin of biscuits or something like that. Well you're in a real spot there. I'd say, 'Give us your fiver and I'll pop and change it at the bank.' But they haven't got a fiver. Like everyone else they were in desperate circumstances. They needed the goods to sell to make a living.

When I used to be out delivering these wholesale groceries I used to go to a lot of people in Jarrow and it was a terrible desolate place there. Ellen Wilkinson was the M.P. and she pleaded with the government to allow the people in Jarrow to have wallpaper free to paper their homes, just to build their morale up. There was hardly any repairs to the houses because the rents were so low and there were so many moonlight flits. The walls would become damp and the plaster would fall away and that caused a lot of illness among children too. When it came to papering they daren't take the old paper off because all the plaster would come off. So there'd be maybe ten layers of paper. This made a lovely home for lice and bugs, no matter how clean you kept it. The children were riddled with lice in the slum areas. It was a regular occurrence very Saturday night for us, with a small tooth comb and paraffin oil, to kill the nits, on a newspaper. Head inspections at school on Monday morning by the nurse. But they just multiplied. There was colonies of them. Even if you had a house that didn't have lice you were mixing with other children who did.

After a few months of delivering wholesale groceries I asked for a rise, explaining that I was receiving less that I would be getting on the dole. She refused and warned me that if I left the job she would have my dole stopped, so I was forced to soldier on until I found a better paid job.

On one or two Sundays she would ask me to clear and weed her garden. I would work from about ten a.m. until one p.m., have dinner with the family, but the adopted daughter had hers in the kitchen and did all the washing up. Then I would work until about four p.m. and receive 2/6d.

The second son had fallen in love with the young manageress of one of the hardware shops, an eighteen year old honest and reliable girl. My employer accused her of stealing 30/- worth of goods and sacked her. So the son was free again to get down to the serious job of running the business for his mother without ties. But eventually she went into liquidation.

I got a job as a driver for a biscuit factory. I was only 17 then and I had a huge van. And you had to keep going. The first driver said, 'All you've got to do is follow me.' And he was travelling about 60 miles an hour. I'd only been used to a tiny little van. You had to go at 60 miles an hour to get round. There was a regular stoppage by the police. It was a kind of formality. Every now and again we'd be stopped and we'd be fined a pound which was a week's wages. The firm didn't pay it. You paid it. That was part of the job. The orders were packed by the night shift in order of delivery. But very often one would be closed, or they wouldn't have the money, or someone would want to pay for one tin of biscuits with twenty empty ones. It was sweat and blood. I was getting home about half past ten at night.

People used to set up shop in a house, in one room. They'd be open till midnight. You could knock on the door at one o'clock in the morning and buy something, so desperate were they to earn a penny or halfpenny. There was a terrible amount of people on the slate.

I managed to get a job with Wall's ice cream once. With a tricycle. I was getting about 32/- a week. A fortune for me. I got on well and I said to the manager one day, 'How about a job for my friend?' He said, 'I have got a job. Bring him along on Monday.' I dashed to his home really thrilled to think I'd found him a job and his father came to the door. I said, 'Is Jimmy in? I've got good news for him. I've got a job for him. 32 bob a week.' And his face really dropped. He knew he was going to lose a son. Jimmy had two sisters and his mother and father. None of them were working. His father was drawing about 26/- for the family. But if Jimmy was earning 32 bob he wouldn't get anything. So either the son would have to stay at home and keep the family or if he had any visions at all of saving up to get married he'd have to move into digs.

I've been on building sites six o'clock in the morning with about two hundred others where we heard there was a couple of labourers needed. At eight o'clock the foreman come up. 'Go away!' He'd got his two brothers, or his two cousins. And that's the way it was generally.

Once I got a job on a building site in North Shields when I was about eighteen. My stepfather knew the builder. That's why I got the job. My job was feeding the bricklayers. I'd walk to the ferry. Walk about four miles to the building site, and get about half an hour's overtime in the morning to prepare the cement for the bricklayers to get them going straight away. They were building a billiard hall. It was all right on the flat. And then it came to the time when they had to put the scaffold up and they had to have a hod carrier. Well the foreman's brother–in–law got the job as hod carrier. He was a married man with two children. He'd never carried a hod in his life. Nor had I. But I'd practised with it and I'd got the knack. It's just a knack—it's not strength. Anyway this first day the foreman's brother–in–law had to take this hod of bricks up the ladder for the first time. He went up about six steps and he got terrified and he daren't move up and he daren't move down. The foreman and I helped him down. He said, 'I can't do it.' So the foreman said, 'What about you Charlie? Will you do it?' So I took it on. I was in my glory, being fit. I was feeding them all the time and he was down below doing my job. I said to the foreman, 'How about a rise?' I said, 'He's getting elevenpence doing my job and I'm getting sixpence doing his.' 'Ah,' he said, 'he's a married man. You can take it or leave it. There's always plenty of blokes will take your job if you don't want it.'

A lot of the apprentices were used as cheap labour on the buildings. They'd be signed on as apprentices and work for about four years on the site and all they'd be doing was wheeling a barrow and stacking bricks like I was doing. And then when the building was completed the apprentices would be out before they'd even started laying bricks.

Anyway, that lasted about eighteen months. Then I was unemployed and looking for work. Playing about on the river to try to earn a few bob. And then I decided to get out. Some chaps used to take their dole money to the Trow Rocks to try and win the kitty and get out of it. This was the great dream; getting out of the rut.

Well, I hitch-hiked to try to get out of it. A pal and I were making for Birmingham. We got a lift as far as Doncaster. 'Had you heard that there might be work in Birmingham?' 'No.' We were travelling anywhere, just to see. You don't think all the rest's the same as you. You hear vague rumours that there's work somewhere. It was a foggy night when we were dropped by this lorry. A terrible foggy night, thick like. We heard a terrible scream and a crash. We just ran and we could see that these two lorries had crashed. What had happened was that some young chap had been walking in the gutter and the first lorry had run over his feet and he screamed, a terrible scream, and the lorry driver hearing this pulled on his brakes and the other one which was following his lights had crashed into the back. We saw the driver and the driver's mate going up to the front, and there was this chap. The lorry had pulled up right on his head, and it was squashed as flat as a pancake. That really put me off. I said, 'Well, I want to go home.' I could hear that scream. And this was a young chap who'd walked about, doing the same as we were, looking for work.

So we went back and after a couple of weeks tried again, at Birmingham. We got some kind of a job but we couldn't get digs because we hadn't the money. They wanted the money because they couldn't trust strangers. We were living on broken biscuits. We'd get a bag-full for twopence. We'd sleep in the ditch. Eventually my sister loaned me £1 for the fare from South Shields to Charing Cross. I got digs in Hayes End and I worked in Wolff's Rubber Factory. 9d an hour. But later on war broke out and I joined the Army.

During the slump you couldn't join the Army because they were so many. There was such a great demand to get into the forces, to get away from it, although the wages was only 14/- a week, with stoppages out of that. But they were so selective, just like the police. The police could say six foot, and that was your lot, and so much chest, because they had anyone to choose from. I don't suppose 90% of the men in the army with me would have been able to get in two years before the war because of malnutrition. But when war broke out they were all fit.

The first time I saw the Blackshirts was about 1936. I always remember about half a dozen of them coming down King Street, and the middle–aged women and the elderly people crossed the road, and I could smell the fear. I crossed with them. The Blackshirts were strutting six–footers, ex–grammar school unemployed. The attraction was the uniform plus pocket money from Mosley. Old Mussolini sent £30,000. They were selected, just like police were selected. They were coming from their headquarters. I could see the people pause as they approached them. There was no reason for them to cross the road, except they didn't want to pass those men. And I saw the same fear in Germany and Italy when the German or Italian civilians, or the ordinary army, saw the Gestapo, or in the case of Italy, the State Police. I saw and experienced a fear that was deep down. I didn't realise what it was, but it was there. Old Mosley could select because there were so many people desperate, not because they believed in the cause, but they'd get a uniform and stand out above everyone else and seem to have a bit of power. When Mosley visited South Shields, the Palace cinema was practically destroyed. They had a riot. Wherever he went in the North there was always terrible damage because the Blackshirts weren't accepted anywhere at all in the North.

I remember watching the police trying to drag Mosley to his car. He was coming out of the cinema where he had been speaking. Someone had been asking questions and his thugs had got hold of him and bashed him, and his nose was bleeding and this upset everyone. A crowd collected and they wanted to lynch old Mosley because of what happened.

The police were not very polite to any groups of unemployed standing on street corners in those days. The men were used to this. As soon as they saw a policeman they would separate as if they had been plotting to take over the country. The favourite haunt of unemployed were the billiard halls or local libraries where they could get out of the cold, play or watch billiards, play heads or tails for a ha'penny, or in the libraries read the local and national newspapers.

The local copper was an old chap. If someone was doing something wrong he'd just belt them and say, 'Get on!' He knew everyone. The old publican let him have a pint round the back and so on. The local bookmaker would have a half–crown slipped in between a couple of bricks.

Along the riverside lived the Lascars; they never integrated, but they were accepted. Their children went to school with us and we just knew them. They were used as cheap labour. When a ship signed on, the chief mate would tell the Seamen's Union official that he needed so many men. The union official would tell the local hotel–cum–ships' chandlers owner that he needed so many crew. The Indian hotel–owner would pick out the number of Lascars needed, tell them it would cost them a month's pay for signing on. They signed on and received their month's pay in the form of a ticket. On the Mill Dam were ticket changers who charged two shillings in the pound for changing tickets to cash. When the men handed over the month's pay after stoppages to the hotel owner, they would have to borrow a month's pay from him, less two shillings in the pound interest, to buy certain articles such as kit bags, overalls and a 'donkey's breakfast'—a 'donkey's breakfast' is a bit of a mattress filled with straw. The poor blighters sailed a month's pay in the red. A portion of the bribe went to the union official, another portion to the chief mate.

There was a great amount of corruption. When my brother was due to sign on as a cabin boy for the first time, a union official demanded a month's pay for his first payment to join the Seamen's Union. The rest of the crew objected and told him not to sign on, but with their help he stowed away until the ship arrived at Burnt Island in Scotland, where he was signed on and only had to pay the proper dues, which was about two shillings.

There was always trouble when there was ships signing on and they knew there was going to be more Lascars than whites. There was no racialism as such—it was just that they were taking them all from that one group because they were cheaper. The police were afraid of riots. And they weren't too gentle.

Twice I've watched police baton charges. They had mounted police from as far away as Newcastle and Sunderland. I remember watching the mustering of the police and heard the order. There was no way they could escape. There was a hill leading down to the Mill Dam and always when a ship signed on this place was packed. The order was 'Walk!' then 'Trot!' and as they were trotting, pulling out their truncheons, and then 'Charge!' Right in among the lot of them. Hitting anybody. Tom, Dick and Harry. To disperse them. I've seen that twice and it was an awe-inspiring sight. To begin with they'd be fighting each other with half bricks and bottles and then as the police charged the bricks and bottles would be going at the police. To protect themselves in a sense. There was jabbering and shouting and bricks and swearing, and then a kind of a hush as the charge came. Then we saw the people being brought out covered in blood. There'd be about a hundred police charging into this confined space. They were all seasoned men, like commandos. No timid men among them. They were all battle scarred. And as the Depression wore on the police became more seasoned and more ruthless.

Any man would do anything to get a job but there were two places they were terrified of being sent, because once you got that green card and you didn't go for the job, you didn't get any dole. One was Haggie's Ropery, North Shields. 99% of them were women making these thick rope hawsers for the ships. If a man got a ticket to go for that, if they needed a man for something or other, he used to be terrified. These women were practically dehumanised because of the conditions they worked under and lived under. They'd strip him and they'd probably rupture him through their frolicking. Another time when they didn't want a green ticket was when the news boys went on strike—not for a rise but to stop a cut in pay. The unemployment was being cut as well at the time. When the newspaper boys went on strike, and it lasted quite a while, they would send men from the Employment Exchange with a green card, and they'd get bashed up, so they eventually stopped that.

There's some beautiful imposing houses up on the sea front where the middle class lived. But they didn't have any flush-away toilets there. The dustmen used to go round at midnight and clear all the ashes and human excreta, shovel it into horse-drawn carts, take it to a big barge on the Mill Dam and that was taken out to sea and dumped. To get a job like that anyone would give their right arm.

I've seen an ex-grammar school boy, through having a relative on the council, have a job made for him. A tricycle with a little box on, sweeping the streets. But he was really privileged. Only through strings being pulled would he get a job. Even one like that. He thought he was lucky. They used to ration jobs out to the unemployed. And a lot of these were shipwrights, real skilled men. On the beaches in South Shields the sea erodes the sand dunes, and they used to get jobs for two weeks at a stretch on a rota system. They'd plant grass to stop the erosion. A lot of chaps had about six weeks' work in six years.

There were tiers of ships four and five deep for ten miles up the river and even ships' captains couldn't get jobs. At first a ship's officer would sell his valuables. (He was not entitled to dole.) Then his furniture. Then his house. Some would finish up with their families living aboard ship acting as watchmen, their main duty being to keep the fore and aft lights on their idle ships. Most of these ships were to lie idle until mid-1938 when they were sold to Japan for scrap. As a young man I stood with scores of men, old and young, on the Mill Dam, South Shields, watching the Irish potato boats being unloaded by women at the rate of sixpence per hour.

Of course men outside the docks never got a penny waiting. They'd only get paid for the time they're unloading. Outside the various docks there would be rough old cafes where you could pop in and buy a thick slice of bread and dripping for a halfpenny. And lots of these chaps would be hanging about existing on two slices like that.

A lot of young chaps used to pop across the ferry to North Shields and buy two or three boxes of herrings. People couldn't afford cod and so on and they had to sell everything cheap on the quay. And they'd go round the back lanes shouting, 'Plenty a penny, kippered herrin's.' People would come out thinking they'd said twenty a penny but they were actually ten a penny or eight a penny. Quite a lot of young chaps used to make a living like that, hiring one of these barrows for sixpence.

My sister managed a fish and chip shop. Her wage was 7/6d a week. She used to go to the North Shields quay. She'd have to be up about half past 4, quarter to 5. She'd walk to the ferry because it was too early for trams, then she'd walk from the ferry to the fish quay ready for the auction of fish. These Scottish fisher girls used to be on there gutting the fish that was bought by the big customers. All their fingers used to be bandaged up, and all the morning and all the afternoon in the freezing cold north-east wind they'd be gutting these fish for about fourpence an hour. She'd stand on that quay and buy the fish. Then she'd go back home and have her breakfast. The shop opened for a couple of hours at dinner time, and then in the evening up till midnight. She thought she was in clover because at least she had her fish and chips. If we went in we might get a few extra chips but it was so curtailed that there wasn't much room for dishing out a free meal.

A family would move into a room with no fire grate. They'd have a gas ring and their cupboards would be orange boxes and they'd decorate them with a piece of curtain. All their possessions would go into two or three orange boxes.

My brother–in–law was a real hard–working chap. He was a general labourer and the builders in the town knew him as a good reliable worker. If there was work he would have it. He got married to my sister when he was about 22. Fortunately they didn't have any children at the time but such were the conditions then that once you got married your parents moved into a smaller place where it was cheaper, and therefore if something went wrong you couldn't move back, as a couple or even one. Well, he was working at the time. One of the very fortunate ones. While he was working he broke his little finger. He was off for weeks and weeks. It was a bit dodgy on the knuckle. He was offered a penny a week compensation. He accepted it in case the employer wouldn't employ him any more. Then he got his 26 week on the dole and after that he couldn't get a job. He applied to the Board of Guardians. He dreaded that. They all seemed to be big fat chaps. Smoking cigars. They said, 'There's a ticket for you, and there's a ticket for your wife,' and they were for separate workhouses. He just disappeared for several days living rough and he got work somewhere miles away. He came back happy as a lord. It was a very common thing. They were trying to stop the working classes from having children. They asked him, 'Why did you get married in these circumstances?' although he was working at the time.

When my sister got married they got a lovely present from some of her husband's mates. You used to get small eggs from Poland, twenty for a shilling, and they came in these long egg boxes. These chaps spent hours planing and sandpapering, and made a beautiful set of drawers from them as a wedding present.

Another brother–in–law had a job in the merchant navy. His ship was sailing round the world two years at a stretch. He was coming ashore with £50 or £60 in his pocket because he'd been away so long. He'd buy a couple of new suits. Within a week his ship's revictualled and he's away out. He was so close to us and yet he wasn't aware of the slump. All he's got recollections of is everybody happy to see him, bringing out his presents from abroad, and them all wanting to make a fuss of him, giving him a cup of tea, and bring out whatever best they've got. It wasn't a slump for some. It was great. On the railways, in the post office, you were the elite, anywhere you had continuous employment.

My brother used to get double pay during the Spanish Civil War for running the blockade to get the Government supplies in. He was in port there and the bombs were coming from Mussolini and Hitler and there were oil tankers all round him burning all night. He was twenty one and his hair went white with terror. He told us how they ate the rats and the cats there. There was a lot who joined the International Brigade and went to Spain.

Another of my sisters married a man who was one of the elite in the docks. He was an iron-ore handler. He used huge shovels and filled these big buckets which they had to pull out. The iron ore would weigh about six stone on each shovelful. It was savagery. You had to be tough. They were fortunate because if he wasn't working one of his brothers might be working in the docks and they helped each other. But she hadn't a clue about cooking. None of my sisters had a clue except cooking fish and chips.

There were regular gangs employed to unload iron ore etc. To get into one of these gangs was impossible unless a relative had died. However, there was casual labour and men would wait outside the dock gates hoping a ship would be due in. The ganger would choose from the desperate men waiting for a job. If the person's name was Smith who was trying to obtain a day's work, he had more chance than a man whose name was Carruthers—the ganger found it easier to write Smith than Carruthers. The ganger would arrange to pay the men at a public house opposite the docks a couple of hours after knocking off work. If there was no treat or bribe from a paid worker, that worker would never get another job at that dock.

It was the good old days for the foremen, the gangers and so on. They were like kings. And no doubt their natures changed completely. If the chaps didn't do what the foreman said, it was out. They could entice a woman, break the home up, and Bob's your uncle. They could afford it. It was rampant. A woman desperate to feed two or three kids would do anything. Not all of them, but it did happen.

There was the old Italian who started off selling icecream. He made it himself. He'd push it round until he got rich enough to employ a woman to push it round while he served. He paid her half a crown a week. Eventually he had lots of barrows and he employed boys. Just after I left school I worked for a little while pushing this icecream barrow. He started off with a little tiny shed for making his icecream in and finished up with two icecream parlours. All because you could get the cheap labour.

There was a lot of homosexuality in the depressed areas because people didn't want to get involved. There was so many forced marriages. A lot of girls' greatest wish was to leave home because the grass is greener on the other field and they didn't see the danger that it would be just as bad or worse. They just wanted to get away.

My stepfather and my mother were walking down the street and they heard a terrible screaming and a woman came tumbling down the stairs and this chap pounced on her and was belting her and she was semi–conscious. My stepfather, who was a big hefty man, got hold of this chap and was giving him a good hiding and my mother was seeing to this woman. She came to, and she jumped up and attacked my father and said, 'What are you doing to my husband?' My stepfather said to my mother, 'I'll never interfere between a husband and wife again.'

Family life was breaking up because of the Depression. People were getting on each others' nerves. Women went off sex because they were afraid of having babies. And the husbands got to a state where they didn't care two hoots. If they did get a few bob they'd get drunk or gamble. Have a good time for a little while. 'Live today for tomorrow you may die.' There was a lot of friction in marriages. A lot of men left home.

A terrible amount of middle aged and elderly chaps became tramps. Because of the poverty and hopelessness of everything the man and his wife would get on each other's nerves. They'd have a row and he'd just disappear and wander the country. Or he'd be afraid of going in the workhouse. A tramp's walking day would reach from one hostel to another. They used to have to do a certain amount of work like chopping sticks up or something like that to earn their meal. If they had any money on them it was confiscated or they had to pay for what they had. So they used to hide their money in the hedges before they went in. Then they went on to the next one the next day. The winter was pretty grim.

One of my pals went to London on a bicycle. Eventually the tyres burst and he had them stuffed with grass. He arrived in London with 7/6d in his pocket. Being a greenhorn he hung his trousers on the bed when he got to the Salvation Army hostel. In the morning he went for his bun and his cup of tea and he reached for his money and he'd been robbed. Typical in those places. And they took his bun and his cup of tea off him. And that really put him against the Salvation Army.

After three or four years of unemployment some men were quite incapable of work, even if it was offered to them. They would do nothing at home or outside to use their hands or minds. They sat in corners of billiard halls etc. for hours on end. On the other hand there were men who travelled from as far afield as Jarrow to Whitburn Colliery tip, a distance of about seven miles each way. They would travel on an old bicycle, tyres stuffed with grass, arrive on the tip at about six a.m., and after stratching about on the tip would leave at about four p.m. to travel home with up to five bags of coal piled on their bike. Getting that home was an operation of real skill and endurance. They would clamber on top when going downhill and sweat blood pushing it uphill.

As Christmas approached volunteers would collect egg boxes etc. and take them to the old tram sheds and turn them into toys, scooters etc. for very poor kids. They didn't get anything for it, just the pleasure of using their hands. Councils offered prizes for the best decorated street to boost the morale of the inhabitants. Hours were spent scrubbing and painting paving stones, making artificial gardens and flowers. Carnival time was a time to remember. All collections going for the upkeep of the local infirmary. There were scores of highly decorated floats and hundreds of individuals in this long interesting parade through the town. South Shields would compete with Roker Park, Sunderland. During Illuminations Week the Marine Park at South Shields and Roker Park, Sunderland, would charge threepence entrance to see a most spectacular display of fireworks. People came from far inland to see one or the other event. Often a million people or more would see these displays in one week.

On top of the Mill Dam there were lots of amusement arcades, one–armed bandits. Lots of people used to hang around there with the music going and that. There was one chap who fasted forty days and forty nights. He lived on water and cigarettes. You could pop in any time of the night. He was like a skeleton. You used to have to pay a penny to get in. There was a man at the fair in South Shields who used to dive into a tank of water. He used to do two dives a night. Then people would hang on till the next dive instead of going home and that kept them spending a bit longer. He'd climb up I think it was about a hundred feet and the tank would be about two yards across and about four feet deep. And he wouldn't just dive. He'd set himself on fire and go over on a bicycle. He had one leg where he'd hit his leg once and lost it. But that's how desperate people were for money.

Practically every town had a theatre. And they'd go round the local girls, sixteen, seventeen years of age. 'Would you like to come into the chorus?' They just had to do a couple of hours' training. Just tap their feet, to make a crowd up. A terrible lot of those girls got star–smitten and they'd go with this troupe and finish up as prostitutes in London. But so desperate were they to get out of the slums they'd do anything.

People played bingo then but it wasn't advertised. There was big marquees where they'd get groceries for a prize. But for every one of those there'd be a thousand where friends would gather in a private house and there'd be about a dozen playing. And for every shilling that went into the kitty there'd be a penny for light and heat. They played for money then, which was illegal.

In the early 1930s Italians imported and controlled the one-armed bandits which were installed in almost every corner shop. The temptation of the kitty which was in full view in the form of about £1 worth of pennies was too much for many poor housewives who had popped in for a penny packet of tea or twopennorth of liver sausage. Very often they would leave the shop without the tea etc., an empty purse and nasty temper which would usually be vented on the children. There was so much distress caused that in about 1936 some legislation was passed. Police raided and confiscated all these machines, took them to the police yard, where they were destroyed with 14 lb. hammers, taken out to sea and dumped.

Usually at weekends in the different halls the local talent would be up. There was some good talent. Singers and magicians etc. Probably cost you a penny to get in. It was very often full. A couple of hundred more might turn up than there was room for. And there were boxing tournaments that came to be known as 'blood kits'. I've been to a few fights, and they'd fight for half a crown, and their brains were gradually bashed and bashed and bashed until they were just like scrambled eggs.

Pitch and toss was like a religion. They had a flat piece of wood and the hanger–on would put the coins on to this board and flick them into the air. He's say, 'I've ten shilling. I'll say tails.' And the chaps who wanted to bet heads would cover that, twopences, pennies and so on, and if it came down tails he'd have the pound. If it came down heads he'd have to pay these out. In the meantime in the crowd they'd be betting each other. That was the only hope they'd got of getting a few bob. They'd dream of buying the wife a dress or some bally thing or other which was ordinarily hopeless. In most back alleys and lanes young and old men would play their few pennies away, especially on Sunday mornings. These antics were comparatively harmless compared to what happened at the Trow Rocks on the beach at South Shields where the temptation to many married men to win the great prize of about £40 was too much for them. Men, including bookmakers, would arrive there from as far afield as Newcastle and Sunderland. On the seaward side of the rocks was an alcove with a sand floor and on the promenade side about 200 yards of open sand, so unless you were watched from the sea you could not be seen. There was usually two look–outs, one–legged or one–armed men, who had a good view all around to warn of the approach of police. Sometimes the police mingled, dressed as holiday makers, and caught them in the act. There were two schools, the bigger school, where they played for a penny or tuppence. When a lucky winner had a good run in this school he could afford to go into the smaller school where the bookmakers etc. were playing for 5/- a time. As this became smaller (men going broke) the stakes would rise to 10/- then £1 until there was only two men who would gamble winner takes all, which as I said before would be about £40. This winner would tip the chap who placed the two bright and well–worn pennies on the small piece of wood in the tosser's hand ready for the toss, and of course he would pay the look–outs.

The billiard hall was the haven. You usually played for pennies and tuppences but the ones who were lucky enough to have a job would gamble on pool. Basically it was like pitch and toss, trying to win double what you started with. They'd gamble on anything. A lot of it I think was, 'Why have dry bread when I might have jam and bread?' If anybody did get any money they'd spend it quickly because the idea was 'Why not have something to remember?'

South Shields is a beautiful place. It's only through lack of work that people leave. They've got beautiful parks there. There's the North Marine and the South Marine Park, and Marine Road is a road where all the courting couples used to meet and walk along. There's a big shopping parade. And many, many years ago the river used to run through there. Then the parks stretch up overlooking the beach. A beautiful place. There's beautiful scenery there. South Shields Pier stretching out to sea. A small bay, and the North Shields Pier, and the river. There's a bandstand where the bands used to play. Beautiful flowers. Then a huge green, finishing up with a big pond and the promenade. And on the top there's 'the top seat'. On that seat one young couple committed suicide during the height of the slump. He cut her throat and then he cut his own. They had a last beautiful view. The cliffs. The sea. Others would just put their heads in the gas oven and so on. But you can hear that couple sitting there. . . 'Well, we'll just have one last good look.'

Bonnybridge and Salford

Betsy Miller

My husband was an iron moulder. When he was in work he would earn three or four pounds a week. More than that sometimes. Depends how much work he had. They'd to wait for jobs coming in. If they'd nothing in they could earn nothing. He'd come home. I'd say, 'You're early home today, Will.' He'd say, 'I had nothing so I just sat in the sand heap.' We lived in Bonnybridge in a little house for years and years and my husband fell ill. I got the doctor. He said, 'He'll have to get away somewhere that's a bit warmer than this. England preferably. Not so cold there.' So we moved into Salford.

My husband was doing bits of work and being at home. If he worked a week he was at home a fortnight. He was a chronic asthmatic, and bronchitis with it. I got the doctor once to him. He said, 'He's the worst case I've ever attended.' Finished up by saying, 'Poor man.' He *was* a poor man. Couldn't get a breath.

The last time he went to work, I said to him when he went to bed that night, 'Don't you get up in the morning, Will. Don't bother going.' 'Oh,' he said, 'I'll go to work alright.' He was alright when he was sitting or lying. It's when he moved he couldn't get a breath. So the next morning he got up. I said, 'Don't go to work, Will. You know you're not able.' He said, 'I'll try.' So he went and the next thing was, in about a couple of hours two men brought him home. And he never got up again.

I went to work every day. Charring. Doing people's dirty washing. I went to their home and some of them brought it to me. I got paid 4/6 a day. Nine in the morning till six at night. You wouldn't get women to do that now. And I don't blame them. Let them do their own dirty washing. I worked every day, sometimes Sunday and all. I was glad to do it, to keep out of debt. It was a struggle. I've seen me that tired I couldn't lift my arms up in the morning. But I never owed anybody a penny. I never bought anything that I couldn't pay for. There were plenty of times when I had no food. So long as I could get food for my husband and Jimmy I didn't bother about myself. I knew I could get whatever I wanted working out. I always worked where I got my food.

There was always washing and charring. The well–off ones, they didn't want. Oh no. The Marks' of Broughton Park, Marks the Diamond merchant, I worked for them for years. Cleaning, and some washing for me when I came home at night. I did all the rooms. I'd say, 'What shall I do today, Madam?' 'Oh, turn out the drawing room and the dining room. And if you've time scrub out the kitchen floor. And do the dishes.' Luxury in every corner. I used to look round and think about what I had got to go home to. I used to think, 'The buggers. They ought to be shot.' There was Mr Lesley we had to call him. And young Mrs Marks, she was an American. She was of a millionaire family. And there was two children. One we'd to call 'Master', and a little one eighteen months old we'd to call 'Miss'. Miss Sylvia. I could've killed the buggers. They had, well, 16 rooms at the very least. There was the cook and the house-maid. But I had all the rough work to do. They both lived in but I went home at night.

Always plenty of visitors. Friends. Parties and dinners. Mrs Marks would say, 'D'ye think ye could come back tonight after ye go home? Come back and do the washing up, Mrs Miller?' Well I'd be glad to do it to get the money. That was one thing; she used to say, 'Now the chauffeur will take you home in the car.' And I'd get a box full of eatables that had never been touched. She would say, 'You take that home with you, Mrs Miller. It'll do for James.' They had the very best of everything. The market people used to be coming to the door. Great hampers of lovely stuff, fowl and fruit galore. Great bunches of black grapes. It used to make my mouth water.

They had a beautiful grand piano. And the Mistress was a marvellous player. She used to sit down and play and I'd set down whatever I was doing and listen to her. The drawing room was beautiful. She would say to me, 'Could you do the drawing room today, Mrs Miller. I have some friends coming and I can't trust the maids to do it properly.' She knew I could clean but she wasn't very handy at giving me extra money. I Hoovered the great big beautiful carpet. You couldn't hear yourself walking on it. And then the furniture. Dust all the dust off first, if there were any, and then polish it. Polish all the surrounds of the floor. Some of them was beautiful polished floors. With loose mats. They all had to be carried into the garden. Put over a line and beat and brushed, and then come in and finish off with a Hoover. Light and clean out the fires, and carry the ashes down. Mrs Marks used to say, 'I like a coal fire, Betsy, don't you?' I'd think, 'Aye, you bugger, but you don't like to clean it out after.'

Mrs Marks said to me one day, 'We're going on our holidays next week, Mrs Miller. Your wages will be paid every week the month we're away.' They were very good like that. I said, 'Thank you very much.' She said, 'Would you like to go and do a bit for Mrs Brekman?' I said, 'Of course.' 'Just tell her,' she said, 'that I recommended you.' So on the Monday morning I went and rung the bell at Brekman's door. The maid came to the door. I said, 'Mrs Brekman?' She said, 'Are you Mrs Miller that works next door?' I said, 'That's right.' 'Oh,' she says, 'you'd better come to the back door.' I says, 'Not likely. No fear. I don't go to any back door. I'll come to the front door and I'm coming in the front door.' Mrs Brekman comes running out. She said, 'Who is it?' I said, 'It's me, Mrs Miller.' She said, 'Oh, come in.' And her eyes were all made up like a film star. She took me into the kitchen and told me what she expected me to do. It was the summer time and the baby, little Diana Brekman, was in the carriage out on the lawn. Of course when I went out to take the mats the little one started to goo–goo and too–too and one thing and another, talking to me in her little way. So I went to her. I said, 'You are a nice little girl, Diana.' Mrs Brekman come tearing out. She says, 'How dare you talk to my little child! A common charwoman.' 'I beg your pardon,' I said. 'I'll tell you something that you've maybe forgotten, Mrs Brekman,' I says. 'You'd have never got Mr Brekman if you hadn't been on your back to him.' And I walked out. She said, 'You haven't done my cleaning.' I says, 'You can do it your bloody self. It's all you're fit for. If you're able to do it.' I says, 'You only ask me to do it because you can't clean. That's all.' She never looked at me after that. That's what you get if you're low enough to go out doing a day's work. It was an honest day's work I wanted to do. My husband wasn't able to work. That's all. I stuck a lot of that kind of thing. There were plenty of incidents like that.

About 6 years I worked for the Marks. Then we moved. We had to move. My husband was ordered out where there was a bit more open space. For his asthma. And I'll never forget what Mrs Marks said. She said, 'And what am I going to do?' She wasn't thinking about me. They were thinking about themselves.

I worked for the Finnegans for a bit when one of my regular people were away. Used to take whatever I could get, rather than go into debt. Ethel Finnegan, she was that fat, and she was the most beautiful dancer. Ballroom dancing they taught. They'd a great big ballroom. And I was to clean the ballroom. They had a big brush with a polisher and you just went up and down the floor, and dusted the window ledges and that, and a man came to clean the windows. I was well paid for that.

Larry was married to one of the Finnegans. He said something filthy to me one day and I nearly knocked him over with the brush. He thought that because I was there as the cleaner he could say anything he liked. But I just took the brush and ran into him. I knocked him spinning. I never spoke to him again and he used to lift his hat to me when I passed him. I didn't tell his wife. She was a drunkard. She was never sober. But they were nice people, the Finnegans. That song *Finnegan's Ball*—'I spent the night at Finnegan's ball'—that was made up of Finnegan's ballroom.

One time I'd been standing out for a loaf. It was pouring down. I got wet to the skin. I went home and through the night I took pneumonia. I nearly died. I got nine bob a week sick pay. My husband said 'How're we going to live?' I said 'I don't know how we're going to live but I can tell you what you can do. You can go down the unemployment place'—his unemployment money had run out—'and you can ask what is the nearest Poor Law office.' I thought, 'We're in a civilised country. Why can't we live like civilised human beings?' He said, 'And what should I say?' I said, 'You know what to say. You're a grown man. We can't live on love, Will.' He said, 'Not very well.' So they sent a woman. She said, 'Well, what's the trouble?' I said, 'The trouble is this, that we've nothing to eat. And nothing to buy anything with that we can eat. So,' I says, 'What're you going to do about it?' 'Oh,' she says, 'what are *you* going to do?' I says, 'I'm not going to do anything. You're going to do the doing. You're going to give me a piece of paper to take to the Poor Law office.' I said, 'I've got two clubs to pay.' She said, 'What are the clubs for?' I said, 'For to bury me because I wouldn't want to be buried at the bottom of the garden. Would you?' The other club was because I had Jimmy to keep and dress. He was always dressed respectably. Proper boots and a proper suit. 'Well,' she said, 'I'll see what I can do for ye.' And she did. A man came to see me the following day. He said, 'What's the trouble, Mrs Miller?' I said, 'Come on in and sit down and I'll tell you what the trouble is.' I said, 'I'm not getting enough to live on. We can't live on a subsistence. We need to exist.' 'Quite,' he said. 'Well, how much are you drawing? Oh,' he said, 'that's not enough.' I said, 'You couldn't live on it.' He said, 'I could not.' He was a decent fellow and I got it all right. I forget how much I got on it. I think it was 28 shillings a week.

I saw a job advertised and it was Butt Brothers and Cooks, envelope makers. So I thought, I'll have a go at this. I'll go and see if I can get an interview. There was dozens after it. But I was first in the queue, so I got it. Part time office work and part time looking after the teas and one thing and another for the staff. That was 27 shillings a week. That was a rise in my wages. We were scraping along. We had enough but nothing extra.

We worked all day Saturday, because that was their early closing day. There was half a mile of corridors. There was one passage and it had fifty windows down each side. That had to be wet cleaned every Saturday. And there was windows all round the offices. There was the general office. And then there were a score of small offices, single offices, for the manager and the directors and clerks and typists. And some of them were bitches. The women was worse than the men. And dirty. Spilling tea. Spilling sugar all over. Bits of cake being tramped into the carpet. All the offices weren't carpeted but the main ones were. No carpet in the general office and 27 men worked in it. There was all they desks. The dusting and polishing was the worst.

I worked in a pawnbrokers. There was one Irish girl used to come, a lovely girl. Molly Kelly was her name. And she'd a beautiful new suit in a parcel. I said, 'Has your father got a new suit?' She said, 'It's not paid for, you know. It's a shilling a week. He can have it every Sunday, and it'll be back here on Monday every week.' I never put stuff in pawn. Never never never. I saw too much of that when I worked at the trade. In with everybody's lice and bugs and all kinds of animals. Everything but elephants.

Will wasn't a good hand at anything practical. He was a singer. A beautiful singer. He wasn't interested in practical things. He'd do jobs about the house and clean up if I was working. When he was able. He slept downstairs. He wasn't able to go upstairs. Hadn't enough breath to walk across the room. He used to try and do a certain amount but he wasn't able. I was out all day. Then I'd have to come home and do my washing. I've seen me washing at ten o'clock at night. Just a little tub and a little stand, and an old fashioned wringer. Hang it through the house in the winter. In the summer I could dry the washing out in the back yard. No hot water. In the first house I was in we had no *cold* water. We had to carry it. Just round the corner of the house was an old fashioned well. I mended and darned. Not a good sewer but I could mend and darn and keep things right. The rent was ten shillings a week. I've never had my own house. You can't, with a sick husband that's not able to work.

The neighbours were all right. Always squabbling and fighting. You know they little streets. You would hear somebody from the other side of the street: 'Oh, yeah. I saw ye coming home drunk last night.' 'Yeah, you've got room to talk.' 'You ought to be ashamed of yourself, and your children starving.' Falling out. Somebody would use somebody else's clothes line to hang their washing out. That would cause a row. Somebody would see a man calling at somebody's door maybe collecting for something. They'd say, 'Yes, we saw a man at your door. We know what's going on there.' All that kind of thing.

Mrs Gilman next door, she was a marvellous neighbour. I lived next door to her for 18 years and I never had a wrong word with her. She was a little fat jolly woman. Her husband was a brass moulder. At times he was in work. At times he was laid off. She was the same as me. She had to go and get it off the Public Assistance. The Means Test. We used to help one another out. If I went short of sugar I used to say, 'Can ye lend me a cup of sugar, Mrs Gilman?' 'Aye, could you lend me a bit of tea?' She was a really decent sort. She'd only one son. And I had the one son. And they were fast friends.

On the other side there was Arthur Martin, and Harriet. She was a prostitute. Her husband knew but he couldn't do anything about it. He was the decentest little fellow you ever met. I said, 'Where's Harriet?' 'She's out,' he said. 'Oh, what would you do with her, Mrs Miller?' I said, 'What would *you* do with her, Arthur?' He said 'I've tried, I've followed her. She's got away. Anybody she'll pick up. Anybody on the street. Fifteen to eighty. Anybody'll do.' I said over the wall to her one morning, 'Hello Harriet.' She says 'Good morning.' I said, 'How'd you go last night?' 'Oh,' she says, 'he were a nice feller. He gave me an orange.' I said, 'Was that all ye got?' She says, 'He gave me fourpence. It was all he had.'

They had the loveliest girl, Laura. And a boy, Edwin. Edwin was 13 year old and he over–grew his strength and he was as fat as fat. He was about 5 foot 10. He died. When he was dying he said, 'Dad, go and bring Mrs Miller and tell her to come and hold my hand.' I went. When he turned round to me the glaze was coming over his eyes in death. 'Just hold my hand,' he said, 'and don't let that bugger come near me' — his mother. It was the last words he said.

That was a real tragedy. I broke my heart about that boy. If only he'd been properly fed and properly attended. They told her what to do at the hospital. They gave her strict instructions how he was to be fed. She was too busy out. Well, my husband used to say, 'She can't help it. It's a disease with her.' It was a pity for her. She had no time for the children. Neither Laura nor Edwin. Well, they say it takes all kinds to make the world up. And it does. Some good, some bad, and some indifferent. Some that cares and some that doesn't.

There were a couple lived across the street that had a little girl. She died. The mother was a drunkard, the father was a strict teetotaller. I'd say, 'You're the man. I'd half kill her. I'd make her that she wouldn't be able to go to the pub.' She used to take the money for the children's food, and drink it. I was stopped by a drunk one day, and he says, 'Hello.' I said, 'Hello.' He said, 'Are you going anywhere tonight?' I just lifted the back of my hand and I said, 'No. I'm not going anywhere tonight, not with you or any-body.' I let him have it. You got all that.

When Jimmy left school he was near 15. He got a little office job. He had it just for a few months. He would have had to work years before he matured into it, but eventually he would have got a good position. It was something in the advertising line. He was lucky to get a job. He did very well at school. Used to get first in everything. He says, 'I'm not going to go to a job like that. I'm going to be a wri-ter.' I says, 'What the devil are you going to write?' He says, 'I'm going to be a song writer.' He was always singing. From he opened his eyes in the morning till he closed them at night. He started to learn the piano. I bought a lovely piano. Well, got it on the hire. I'd paid an awful lot on it. He said, 'Aw, I don't think I want to bother about the piano. I think I want to sing.' 'Well,' I said, 'You'll need the piano if you want to sing.' He was in his late teens. It was girls then.

I remember once, they were queueing up for everything. I got the word one day that they were selling bread. You'd to queue up for a loaf. So I was just in time to get a loaf, and a woman says, 'I need that more than you. I've 5 children and they're all starving.' I said, 'Oh, go on. You have it. I didn't know.' We had none. We had just to get what we could. It was a terrible time. I have reason to remember it. A man lying sick. Not able to work. Poverty and ill-ness. All the way through. And yet I managed to get Jimmy to school every day. And have time to sit down and talk to him about things that mattered.

Jimmy used to say, 'Ask my dad to take you out tonight.' And he'd have five or six in and they'd be talking politics. Sixteen year olds. I'd say to Will, 'You go and have a drink.' He'd have a drink and come out and we'd walk around. Around Salford. There were young ones that lived in the same street I lived in that would have shot anyone as quick as looked at them through the political position. We used to sell *The Daily Worker*. People used to come to the house for it. I went to the Communist Party meetings every week. I heard Harry Pollitt. He was a fine man. And Tom Mann. 'Fight, fight, fight, tooth and nail. Fight!' That's what Harry Pollitt used to say. 'Fight, fight, all the way through. Till you get what you want. You'll never get it without a fight.'

I remember once there was a raffle. It was a Communist Party gala day. 'Go on, take a ticket, Mrs Miller.' I said, 'I'll have two of they.' Threepence each. And I won a pair of blankets. Lovely blankets they were. Some better–off person had bought them and put them into the raffle.

My brothers were iron moulders like my husband. They emigrated to Australia from Scotland. They're all in Australia. Everybody belonging to me. Jimmy was about 15 when they went away. He doesn't remember them. They went away because they couldn't get work. My eldest brother John, he went first. And when he had been out there about 12 months he sent for my next brother, Tom, and Tom went away. And he had only been out a couple of years when they sent the passage money for the whole nine of the family. So that was 11 of them that was away, and my father and mother. Only my sister and I was left here. Maggie and her husband both died.

Of course there were plenty of people worse off than myself. Women that couldn't manage. Women that didn't know how to make a cheap meal. There was one butcher, a big Scotch butcher, in the Shambles in Manchester. I'd say, 'Have you any pieces today?' He'd say, 'Aye. How many d'ye want?' I'd say, 'Twopence worth.' For twopence I'd get a parcel, all fresh meat cut off the ends. Come home and make a marvellous stew with it. Well, some of them that thought they were high and mighty was too grand to do that. They'd rather sit down and take a bit of margarine and let people think they were well off. But I didn't mind. It fed me and fed my husband and fed Jimmy.

And Millers, Millers the fish shop. They were no friends of ours but it was Miller. And I used to say, 'Well, you're a relation of mine. What have you got on the slab this morning that you can spare?' I'd get a great lump of fish. 'How much is that?' 'Oh, give me fourpence.' Just for the sake of something going in the till. I said, 'Now here, Mrs Gilman next door to me's ill. Could you spare a bit for threepence for her?'

I remember a brass band coming up. And there were a family across the road, Hubert and Lizzie Oxhole, and they came out and they were both drunk and they started to sing. She'd been taking her clothes off and she was standing in nothing but her knickers dancing in the middle of the street. She'd been going away to have a lie down. Never turned a hair, just danced. The two of them.

There'd be street musicians. Maybe four or five fellows. One with a violin. One with a concertina. One with a cornet. And one of they little shoulder pianos. A whole band. And a singer. And some of them were marvellous. All out of work. And they would collect. One would come to the door. They would play for maybe twenty minutes, and sing, and then one would come round with a cap. And you'd see the halfpennies going in. I always gave them something because I was living among a family of singers.

When my husband was able he went and sang. I said to the doctor, 'It surprises me how he's able to sing. With his asthma. He's hardly able to talk.' He said, 'It's the excitement, Mrs Miller. Whenever he gets excited the asthma disappears.' And whenever he stopped, bad as ever. Well it killed him in the end. He was a young man, practically. When my husband died that was the worst of all. I thought I'd never get over that. He wasn't able to work but he was a marvellous fellow. He really was.

Barnsley

Clifford Steele
I lived in a place called Cudworth near Barnsley in the middle of the South Yorkshire coalfields. The collieries are virtually all around. My father worked at Grimethorpe Colliery which was a rather big one employing three thousand men or so. And that was the crux of the living really. If we had a full week's work we were in clover. The atmosphere of the home was brought to life. It oozed out of the whole household that he'd come home with a good packet. We were able to buy things. You could sense my parents were happy. There wasn't the friction. And then when trade was bad generally it got to a stage where collieries had to agree to work three days and shut down three days.

The 1926 strike was really a catastrophe. It brought everybody, working-class, down to their knees. They had to miss the rent. It accumulated arrears. We had to ask shops for credit. We even had to rely on soup being given from the local butcher's for our lunchtime meal. The butcher did it himself. He existed on other people who were working. That kept him going so as a consequence he made that little contribution by stewing bones up and issuing them out to the children. It was the children that were at risk I suppose mainly—nutrition wise.

We used to go sawing trees into logs, putting the logs into a sack, and then pushing it home on a bicycle. It was an interesting job because there were so many of you at it. It was the only means of getting fuel. We went to Lund wood, on the outskirts between Cudworth and Barnsley. That whole wood was sawn down.

The strike brought various forms of fund raising effort. One was a Tommy Talker Band. It was a little instrument—a piece of tin with a hole in the top. You screwed a piece of paper in the hole and you got a similar effect to a paper and comb. Then they evolved an American cornet effort on to these to give the effect of a brass band. They'd go round the streets and people would go to the doors collecting funds. Then they bought flour and potatoes and things and issued them to the people on strike according to the numbers in the family.

Once they started up to work all the debts that accrued had to be paid off. Even if it was only in small instalments. So for some months to come everybody that had suffered in the strike was in an even worse condition. They was having to work, but half the money was having to be paid out in debts that had accumulated over the months.

In the holidays us boys used to go out into the woods for the day. We'd take potatoes and make a fire and bake them for our dinner. On the way home, after a day of swinging from trees and that sort of thing, I've been that hungry I've picked a turnip out of the ground, scraped the skin off with my teeth, and eaten it raw. I've even eaten acorns.

If I went to school with a ball in my pocket, no–one knows what pleasure I got out of that possession of a ball, so I could nod it up on to the tops of the lavatories and coal places as I went up the streets. A margarine box on four wheels and you were really happy. You'd got to use a bit of ingenuity and make your own. One of our pleasures was the twopenny comic. That was swapped around. We really looked forward to Thursdays.

Practically every Saturday night there used to be a fracas outside the pubs. The culmination of the working conditions and all the hazards of living, seemed to be Saturday night when they'd get their ale. Sunday morning they'd see their best friends with a black eye or their nose skinned or something where they'd been fighting each other over some silly argument. Away from the colliery villages, even though they had a big percentage of colliery workers, it didn't seem as bad. I suppose it was just a way of letting off steam.

Tossing two coins used to be a pastime on Sunday afternoons during the summer. They'd call two heads or two tails or whatever. There were a lot that kept pigeons. But the main pastime was having a shilling on the horses. The bookmaker's runner had to stand at the street end and keep out of the way of the bobby and you slipped your money and a note with a shilling each way on so–and–so, and scarper. If he saw the policeman coming he had to scarper as well.

Colliers were a category on their own and they were apt to look on lesser laborious tasks as being a bit cissyish. They were he–men when they went down the pit. I think this is what got lads down the pit. It was said that one railwayman who lived in our street (which mainly consisted of mineworkers) used to come home to half a pound of Cadbury's Dairy Milk chocolate for his dinner. My father enjoyed telling it and I suppose scorned the idea because even at ten o'clock at night he had to have his Yorkshire pudding and two veg and meat. He used to sing hymns about two o'clock in the morning if he got laid on his back after that lot, but nevertheless it had to be. If he went to work five afternoons and came home five nights he had to have five dinners. Imagine how my mother must have felt having to start and cook a dinner at nine o'clock at night. Mind you if I could manoeuvre staying up while that time there was nothing suited me more than having a square of pudding.

My biggest grievance regarding my family life was that I couldn't communicate with my father. Not in the sense that I would have liked. Every lad, at times, looks forward to being able to discuss something with his father and seek his advice. In practical things he could do it, but to discuss anything theoretical was just impossible. You had to accept it. I thought, well, all these other lads have fathers that can read and write. He had qualities, there's no doubt about it. A stabilising influence on us. He'd always his feet on the ground. Never flapped whatever happened. We got comfort in that. It wasn't till I was older I was able to appreciate why my mother read the Sunday newspaper out aloud. It was for his benefit. And of course, when you are dealing with a person like that, through their ignorance they're apt to be somewhat arrogant. He was a good father in the sense that he never squandered his money. He brought his money home—the place where it would do most good. But even between my mother and my father I could see something lacked. His ignorance brought about this arrogance and because of that they couldn't communicate and iron things out.

I passed the eleven–plus but my mother forewarned me that it was no good pursuing the idea of grammar school because they wouldn't be able to afford me to go. They wouldn't be able to afford the clothes, the uniform, and they couldn't afford on top of that for me to be going while I was sixteen. My mother was sympathetic. She wished the position could have allowed me to have gone. You could converse with her that bit more, but she had to accept. The thing that weighed heavily in favour of not pursuing it was the fact that irrespective of education there was unemployment. My father's attitude was, 'What do you want to be going to school for after you're 14? It's only a waste of time.' Since, I've felt that it was an inferiority complex in him that was compelling him to take this attitude. That was the stumbling block. I suppose another point was that, had he been able to communicate and absorb, there possibly wouldn't have been the large family in the first place. That was never discussed. Never. That was taboo. His attitude towards lots of things would be prejudiced by the fact that he wasn't capable of analysing and going deeper into it and reasoning. It had to be a decision on his part and stop at that. You were blocked by that. That wall between.

His attitude was, that there was the rich and the poor, and he accepted that totally. I've never heard him be a red rag in any shape or form. That was a legacy from his upbringing. His parents accepted that there was a lord of the manor in the village. He had to respect that and was brought up accordingly. It had been impressed upon him and was locked in him because he couldn't take it any further. He couldn't discuss it. It was absolutely blocked. It started and finished there. His arrogance again showed in that. It was no good arguing with him against what his parents had taught him.

Next door but one to where we lived was a chap who shouted from the rooftops if he felt any cause to. He kept pigeons. That was his outlet. Educationally he was far ahead of my father. He was the first in the street to get a wireless. He was interested to know how a wireless worked. We got the first invitation to sit with a pair of headphones on and listen to a cat's whisker. That was a great day. Now he, because of his attitude, was victimised and held off work and that stigma from the colliery he worked at extended to all the collieries around and he was black–listed. That was what happened to that sort of chap. I never heard my father criticise the man but what I suppose he did feel was that he was a fool to open his mouth. I could never accuse my father of being bigoted or of unfair criticism to anybody. What he felt inside him I'd never know but he did respect everybody's way of life. It was up to them. But he wasn't influenced in any shape or form. Unless it was an absolute unanimous decision to strike, he'd go and get on with his work and he'd come home without any qualms. 'Ignore everybody else and do what you've got to do.' That was his attitude. But of course what benefits a man such as our neighbour did bring about would be accepted by my father and everybody else. This particular man had his mother living with him and she must have had some sort of pension, however small, but it seemed to keep them above the starvation line. There were people who, however bad things were, seemed to manage to tick over alright.

For me the Depression meant listening to constant arguments over money shortages. The uncertainty of a wage packet caused me to share my mother's worry about an empty purse and I had the

uneviable task of having to ask the shops for credit. I was sent to the
pawnshop once and I hadn't to let my father know. He'd have gone
mad if he'd have thought. But what he didn't realise was how my
mother was having to budget. He wasn't aware of a lot of things that
we had to do, my mother and myself, to keep the cart on the wheels.
He just tipped his money in and thought it did the job. He just
pushed his head in the sand.

I suppose the thing is there were two distinct classes at that time.
If you were born into the class I was born into you accepted it. You
were automatically submissive in your attitude. And yet we didn't
seem to be envious. If a coalowner lived on the outskirts of a village
and the rest of it, we accepted that. He had his big house and his gardens and his gardener but people didn't seem to be envious. It even
went so far as to raise your cap to the schoolteacher if you saw him
out of school hours. Even the policeman walking down the street,
there was a sort of reverence towards him. You felt partly guilty
even if you weren't. Submissiveness was born in you because of
your status. You just accepted these things.

Ultimately there was eight children in our family. Seven boys and
one girl. I had to take the place of a girl really as far as helping at
home because it was just impossible for the mother to cope with
everything. I was near to my mother at every verse end. She hadn't
time to go out shopping herself, to keep the place something like,
and bake, and cater for a man on shifts. My father would come
home in his dirt—all sweaty clothes to be dried out, and catered for,
a bath every night.

That was a chore that had to be done every day. We were lucky
enough to have a proper bath but it was in the kitchen with no water
attached to it. It was just the bath with a wooden board on top. And
it meant using the set pot. That was a brick built stove with a cast
iron container in the middle. A fire had to be lighted under that and
it had to be filled from the tap by bowl. Then the fire heated the
water. And then it had to be transferred from there into the bath
with a lading can—a big enamel pot that held about a quart.

There would be days, perhaps when he hadn't been in such a
dusty place, he'd be satisfied to strip to the waist and wash in the
sink. Then either my mother or I had to wash his back and give it a
right scrub. But when you saw my father's back you just marvelled
that he didn't cringe with every rub of soap and water because it was
literally slashed. They had to work in pants. Bare back. So scratch-
ing about on their hands and knees hacking at coal with a pick, they

never felt it while they were working, but the jagged edges of coal and stone left their mark on you. You were scarred more or less continuously.

In some parts of his life he was asked to work in the Park Gate seam which was really deep. With that came extra heat and dust. He had to carry two quart bottles of water with him. It was a matter of going from home prepared to go straight down the pit when he'd collected his lamp. So it meant walking two miles before he got to the pit head carrying his little bit of snap and two quart bottles of water, and then going down the pit with that and his miner's lamp, and powder when it was his turn to carry it, and then going anything up to a mile underground.

There has been occasions when I've cajoled my mother into letting me stay up while he came home for his supper just purposely to get a little bit of his Yorkshire pudding. And we've waited while midnight some nights wondering what's kept him. Twice he walked in after midnight when he should have been home by ten or half past, and he'd been buried. They'd dug him out and he'd refused the ambulance and walked home. He was only five foot but he was as strong as a little horse. The day after people have told my mother that why he was still alive they didn't know. Once a fall of stone broke his nose and he never went to have it set. There's a blue scar across it today. They were things they accepted I suppose. They daren't say anything about it. If you couldn't present yourself a hundred percent fit you'd lose your job. Even today he has blue marks, with lacerations and dust getting inside, and it never gets out. It's there under the skin.

There were some accidents where a face came in. I forget how many chaps were killed. I think about five where my father worked. There was the big pit, Grimethorpe Colliery, and the smaller pit adjacent to it which was known as Ferrymoor Colliery which wasn't sunk as deep. It just worked the shallower seams. The trouble there was water, where it was dust and firedamp at the larger pit. Apart from the water the conditions were better at the smaller colliery and he did work there for some period. But of course it could be as disheartening plodding about in water as it was in the dust.

The miners were always subject to a day or two days out. If they got four shifts in a week they were lucky. And then there were the odd occasions, perhaps in wintertime when the coal was demanded, that they worked pretty regularly. It was a case of only a few hours' notice. If a man was on day shift starting at six in the morning he had to be hanging about at night waiting to see whether the pit buzzer went. If the pit buzzer went at half past eight it meant there was no work the following day. So it was a case of 'Don't put me snap up, Mother.'

All his spare time was spent on his allotment. He was always productive. He was never still. When I look back I can't imagine how his energy lasted out. To be doing a hazardous and laborious job like he was. I've seen him come home with his wrists swollen twice what they should be. The conditions varied so much. There were days when it was like hacking at flint, and this told its tale in the man's wrist.

It was a type of piecework. The number of tubs of coal they filled they were paid by. Their grievance was that when conditions were bad they had to work twice as hard and they got less pay. If they got a place where the stuff could be shown the pick and would fall down they could shovel that up into the tubs and they were really happy. They got paid then. What they called the butty system was where one man took on the contract and three sets of men covering the three shifts worked in that particular stall, and then the cumulative number of tubs that was filled was supposed to be shared out amongst them all at the weekend. This caused a lot of trouble because some chaps might go on one shift and be really hard put to fill two or three tubs of coal. But once they got over that bad patch their mates could come on the following shift and perhaps have a better day which meant filling more tubs, but naturally they would feel, 'We filled x number of tubs against your few.' This always caused trouble and it did even get to fighting in the pit yard. A lot of the chaps went from there straight to the pubs and the wives were waiting Saturday afternoon for money that never came.

My father never got to the stage of fighting. Of course there were arguments. He wasn't a literate feller but he always had his ready reckoner with him and he could reckon up all right. He'd always kept pigs and livestock and he could assess the weight and what he should be paid. He could only just write his own name but he knew what the weights and measures meant. He'd never ride anywhere. Even if he went to Barnsley which was the nearest town. He'd walk and walk back and that must have been 8 miles at least each way. I suppose he was fortunate in that he had his health, whereas a lot of men went down in mid life with chest troubles, pneumoconiosis and silicosis. He might go to Barnsley on a Saturday when it was market day. He'd just go and look round the market. The allotment that he kept was 2 miles away and before he had his bike he'd walk to that. Days when he couldn't go to work and weekends were spent on his allotment. He always kept a few hens and rabbits. He'd kill a rabbit and we'd have that for a meal. We were lucky in that we had fresh vegetables.

There's no doubt about it, my father was always the industrious type. Saturday afternoons he would go through our footwear and repair all that was necessary. Always with his tatching ends as he called them, his thread and two needles. He'd stitch and put soles on. It sometimes meant cutting a bicycle tyre up to make a sole of. He'd do that rather than allow us to go with a hole in our shoes. Free shoes were issued at school for the most needy, and I remember feeling a little peeved that I didn't qualify.

My mother used to bake a stone and a half of flour on a pancheon. She'd be doing that on her knees in front of the fire twice a week. Washday was a whole day. It started at morning and finished at night. Starching shirts, dolly blueing, creaming her curtains, and all that had to have separate waters. One of my jobs was to wash the pantry floor. It was sometimes 9 o'clock at night before the wash tub was put back for another week.

My main duty was looking after the baby of the family. That was the thing that mattered. To give an hour or two of freedom to my mother. She had to wait for me coming home from school. Sometimes I could get them lads without a brother or a sister to give him a push round in the pram while I went and kicked a ball for 10 minutes or so. It was a bit of a novelty for them to be pushing a pram but of course they got stalled of it after a while. And then when my brothers got a little bit older I found the knack of making a 4–wheeled trolley and popping them in there, and I could combine doing a bit of race track with my box on wheels with my brother inside, as long as he didn't fall out. Of course that happened from time to time. We had to come up the hard way. But mostly I couldn't play after school. There was always a younger brother to look after while my mother washed or baked or ironed or got meals.

I got the benefit of a brand new outfit from the packy man through being the eldest. I had to wear it while ever I could and hand it on. However degrading it was during the week regarding our clothes we always did manage to have a good rig–out for Sundays. We all had to attend church at least twice a day and sometimes three times if we couldn't get out of going to Sunday School. Immediately we got back we had to take our things off and hang them up.

Our family had been lucky. My father and his father had worked together in what they termed a day–hole. A small type of mine owned possibly by one person rather than a company. They walked in to it. The coal was all hand got. No machinery. But they earned some good money. When my father got married he had a hundred pounds in gold sovereigns to put down for his furniture which was a rare thing indeed. All his furniture was brand new from the Co–operative. He put his gold sovereigns down on the counter to pay, which was one of the highlights of his life. So they set off with a bed-room suite and a spare bed and a full suite of furniture for the living room.

When I was a bit older I realised that lads were getting things that mattered and I couldn't get them. When it came to Christmas time we only had a new pair of socks or a shirt, whereas lads would come flashing a brand new torch or a little box camera. It was on them occasions I would tend to show my dissatisfaction. While my mother sympathised my father's attitude was that we were lucky that we got three meals a day. But there were four of us in a bed—two at the head and two at the foot. When I started work we moved to a council house. It got down to two of us sleeping together. I don't think I ever got my own bed. But it was a luxury if there were only two of you.

We could count ourselves lucky we didn't have parents that squandered the little money there was. There was some cases where the children came secondary. But as I got older I was sensitive about babies being born. You got thinking to yourself, 'We're having a job keeping four of us, why should there be five, and then six?' Later I did find out that my mother's sister tried to impress upon her that she could govern these things. Contraceptives were not as talked about as they are today but there still was some means. But my mother was the type of person who thought that sort of thing was wrong. What had to be had to be. This sort of superstitious outlook prevailed amongst a lot of people. We were just coming from one era to another at that time and changes weren't made easily. And so it went on and on. We ultimately finished up with a family of eight children. That was irresponsibility. It took every halfpenny out of their pockets when they should have been having a bit of pleasure as well. They or we never had a holiday.

Things could have been quite a bit different as far as I was concerned. It just didn't allow the things that seemed to matter. There were times when I had to go to school with a patch on my behind, and I've gone when its been a really warm day with my overcoat on to hide the patch. To have a patch on your clothes brought you down just under that level you could tolerate. It was a sensitive point because at that time so much emphasis was put on appearance. You were graded—this was the thing. Even if it was silent.

I don't suppose it was all black. We must have had brighter times on occasions. My pals certainly knew when it was my mother's bake day. Because by gum they used to be queuing asking if I were coming out because of the baking smells coming out of the back door. She used to make macaroons shaped with an egg cup like bobbies' hats. She used to make a flat type of scones with raisins in. Lads would be looking through the crack of the back door to see if they were on the board on top of the bath in the kitchen. That's where she put them all to cool. About 8 loaves and 4 cakes and then this section of macaroons and scones and then rhubarb tart or whatever was going. 'What about one of them, Cliff?' and I'd ask my mother if I could give one to Thomas or Jack. It was usually yes. My mother was as soft as a brush. She'd give her last halfpenny away. If she wasn't watched like, she'd do it, and if things wasn't there my father would blow up. He'd come with a bucket full of peas or beans out of the garden. Well, there'd always be somebody worse off than us. She'd be sending a boiling of peas down to somebody with a large family. My father's argument was, 'Yes, they can bloody well go to the pictures on Saturday night.' 'Well you can't see kids go without food.'

That was the different attitudes. They thought that after a week's work they were entitled to go and have an evening at the pictures. I suppose they were entitled but at the same time there was possibly a family of boys and girls there who were likely to go without something because of it. But it perhaps kept their equilibrium through going. Who knows?

My father was strict to a certain degree. He didn't want us doing anything wrong. He did show his temper and what he was capable of. I don't say he used it, except in the sense of a clip. But when you could see he was really mad you knew it was best to keep out of trouble. I remember walking along with my brother. Somebody had given him half a cigarette, I should think he'd be about 12, and although I hadn't started to smoke he had. I were watching him, engrossed, inhaling and blowing smoke out, and suddenly, out of nowhere, came a resounding thump. We both turned round and my father was there. He'd caught him in the act right and proper. We've had us behinds tanned for various things. Particularly if I happened to sneak off with his bicycle. I hadn't one of my own at that time and, oh dear, did I want a bicycle. I could reach from the crossbar but not sit on the seat. The bicycle leaned against the wall outside so while he were having his dinner I'd try it out up the street. Once or twice I've had a clip for that. The thing was, it was so precious. That was his means of transport. Particularly going up to his allotment. If anything happened it would be a major catastrophe.

But it did make self-sufficiency. I could take a bicycle to pieces and put it together, and even put spokes in wheels, mend peddles that were stripped out of the crank, and things like that. If you could collect a wheel off an old bike from somewhere and a frame from somewhere else and that sort of thing, you could assemble one. I got while lads would come asking me to repair theirs. But at first I used to borrow my father's. As I got older he got more confidence in me. I'd go to the shop without question if I could go on the bicycle. If he wanted something and he didn't want any argument about it he only had to say, 'You can use the bike,' and I was off.

I tried to do what I could. When my brothers were old enough to look after one another I went, after school hours, and looked after a couple of hundred hens. Cleaned them out and fed them and watered them. Bitten to death in summertime with hen fleas. It was for a local insurance man. He had his bungalow on his piece of land and he certainly got cheap labour out of me. I got half a crown a week off him. I kept sixpence and gave the rest to my mum. I went round on Saturday mornings selling his eggs and I got threepence a dozen. But even that was difficult because people could buy Egyptian eggs at thirteen for a shilling. The Globe Tea Company and Meliers used to have boxes outside their shop six foot long and a yard wide and 9 inches deep full of Egyptian eggs.

For a short time I did actually go and grave dig. It was sandstone and shale stone in layers. Corners had to be chopped out with a hammer and wedge. But it seemed a long way to throw a bit of soil, six feet, when you're that small. I've run errands for people and all sorts of things to get a copper or two. And yet, where there was only one, them lads weren't called upon to do all the things that I was.

Saturday evenings I sold the *Green 'un*. It was the sports paper. They came by train to the station and then we had to tram away on the bicycle from the station up into the village. The faster you cycled up like, the first you were on the scene. There was competition. It was quite a feat on Saturday evening, who could get into the village first. Round the streets shouting. And the doors would pop open and you'd sell them a *Green 'un*.

Then I started at fourteen. It didn't appeal to me to go down the pit. I didn't feel, after seeing my father's experience, that I wanted that at all. My father was non–committal. If it was mentioned his retort was, 'I'm not having anything to do with it. You make your own minds up what you want to do. And then there's no come back.' Of course I went after all sorts of jobs and there just wasn't anything to be had. If I'd been able, I've have wanted to go into motor engineering. The thing was, apprentices were taken on until the apprenticeship was completed, and then they were given notice. Lots of jobs and firms were existing on that basis. Young lads doing their apprenticeship and then when they wanted men's money they were fired. That seemed to be the order of the day.

I went to the colliery as the letter lad in the office. Started at six o'clock while two. That job entailed me going round to colliery–owned houses in Grimethorpe, and issuing from time to time notices for men to come and sign on after they'd been laid off. I had to go round personally to see these chaps and in many cases I had to open the letter and read what it said because they couldn't read. And if I read out, 'Will you please attend such a day, such a time, with a view to signing on to recommence work,' I was acclaimed the saviour of the day. Some of the hovels that I went into had only a table and five orange boxes around them. Bare floors. In some cases they'd taken the bannisters down to light a fire. Even the miners were devoid of coal when they weren't working.

One instance stands out in my memory. The lady asked me in, and I stood inside the door. She says, 'He hasn't got up yet. Just stop there a minute, Lad.' She was making oven bottom cakes and she was skimming them across the floor to cool by the draught from underneath the door. With all the poverty we'd suffered I'd never experienced anything like that. We were fastidious to a degree at home, like in hygiene and cleanliness. I thought how the devil can they eat them when they've been on the floor? Then one of the children came in dragging the cakes back with the door and she tapped them back with her foot.

Along with them notices to sign on I had on occasions to take out the electric light bills which was also a colliery project. They generated the power at the colliery and that was distributed to the colliery houses in the village. That was a time when I had to open the door, drop it in, on my bike and away. Or else they weren't all day at getting my bike and taking the back wheel off.

That were a job that went from 14 to 16 and then you were expected to go into the offices or you got a chance to go into the shops: blacksmiths; joiners; electricians; and so on. But at that time they were on three days a week. Someone came along and said to my father there was a vacancy on the railways. They were guaranteed six days a week and I thought I'd be better off there. So I went and had a year or two on the railways. But that meant going away from home. I worked on the railway serving the Yorkshire Main Colliery which is in the Doncaster area. Then I went up to Shepley near Huddersfield. By the time I'd paid board and travel expenses I'd no money in my pocket when I'd finished. I had a guaranteed wage alright, but it was just swallowed up. I went lamp man which was filling, cleaning and keeping the signal lamps in operation. It meant carrying up to three oil–filled lamps up iron rungs to the top of a signal. They had to be changed every seven days. On a frosty winter's day it was quite something getting hold of the iron rungs with your bare hands. Eventually I moved back home because the wages on the railway, although regular, weren't big enough to be paying out board. That and the natural instinct to get back home wherever possible which incurred an expense. I went and asked if I could have a job back at the pit. Well their attitude was, 'You left on your own and if you want to come you'll have to use a shovel.' So I had to take any sort of job that was asked of me. I did that for two or three years. Aerial ropeway and various mundane jobs.

The aerial ropeway is where they load the dirt that comes out of the pit. It's brought out in tubs and tipped on a conveyor and that led it into a hopper, and then from the hopper into the buckets that run on the ropeway. They're loaded and pushed out and automatically clipped on to the haulage rope. There was a thick running rope for the pulley wheels to run on, and a haulage rope continually going round underneath that. There were only seconds intervals between them buckets. I really got some arm muscles on that job.

Eventually I went as the company's weighman. That was weighing the coal as it came out of the pits. The tubs were weighed and credited to the face or unit where they'd come from. The numbers were chalked on underground, and a lad would call them out and we weighed and booked them. Then at the shift end the full tonnage had to be totalled, and the day's tonnage had to be totalled up weekly, and the weekly tonnage was accredited to the men. But the system was that each day two tubs were selected at random, tipped up, the coal segregated from the dirt, and the dirt weighed. The amount of dirt in that particular tub was the percentage of dirt that would be deducted from the men's full tonnage at the weekend. If it happened that they dropped on a dirty tub, the men were penalised by that amount.

I was never out of a job once I started. There were lads that came in and out of jobs all the time. Quite a number, fed up with being out of work, joined the army. A little later on quite a few of my school pals emigrated. Australia seemed to appeal.

We were all pretty docile in accepting our lot. Maybe as kids we argued a bit over duties. When I started work of course I was the big he–man. I had to be catered for. Like my dinner had to be got ready when I came home from work and any shopping had to be done by the next one. I got a bit of prestige then. When I got my new bike I really thought I was it. A white Raleigh racing bike, £5 19 6d. I could pay half a crown a week. Sunday morning was the time for the neighbours to look from behind their curtains.

Leicestershire

Herbert Allen

My father was a farm labourer and he was pretty good at hedge–laying. He didn't work permanently for one employer. We lived in Leicestershire and we always seemed to be moving from one house to another. When I was seven or eight years old we lived at a place called South Croxton. For some reason or the other we were turned out of our house. There was my father, my step–mother, my step–brother (who was eight months older than I was), and two younger kids. It was summer time. Two nights we slept out in a field. We couldn't go off the road into the field until it was dusk in case we should be seen. We slept under the trees. My step–brother and myself had to go to houses with an old tin can to ask them for a can of water to make tea and such. We traipsed about for several days and finished up at a place called Hungarton. We had an old pram with us. I don't think we *had* anything else.

We lived in a bell tent through that summer. The rats used to come in at night time and pinch the food. As the weather deteriorated somebody must have got to know about it because we finished up in the workhouse at Market Harborough, and I can remember how marvellous that was. On our first night my step–brother and myself had to have a bath. I'd never had a proper bath in my life. I was frightened to death. These two ladies gave us a bath and put us to bed. We was in a little room with our dad. (The men were separated from the women.) For tea and breakfast you used to get one round of bread, a good inch thick, and a big knob of margarine on the top, and it was lovely. We were there some time. We had to go to school at Market Harborough. They dressed us in suits—it was the first suits we'd ever had. I don't know where they were stored or what they were stored in, but they had this most peculiar smell—a pleasant smell. We lasted there through the winter.

My father had to leave each day and go and look for work. Eventually he got a job and we was away again. In the workhouse through that winter it was marvellous for us—we was warm, we was dry, we were well–fed for the first time in our lives. And we were secure for the only time in our lives. We moved into a farm labourer's cottage at Great Dalby. The farmer used to pay my step–brother and myself a penny a day to do bird–scaring from eight a.m. till six p.m. Another farmer had several fields that were very stony. He used to pay us a penny a day to carry stones off the fields and dump them round the edges.

By the time I was ten or eleven we'd moved two or three more times and we lived at Burton Overy. All round there is all hunting country. The roads passed through fields and there was a gate at each end of the field. We used to have to go and stand at the gates, every day from school and every weekend, and open the gate for the odd people who came through. There weren't many cars. A few bikes. A few people on horseback. It saved them from stopping and they'd throw out the odd halfpenny or penny to us. We'd have to go up there every day to get enough to buy food. Very often it was a case of: 'Well, you can't have any tea till you've been up to the gates and got some money.' Thursdays used to be the best day. There was a hunt that used to meet on a Thursday, and if you were by the gates about four o'clock just as they was going home from the hunt—especially if they'd had a good day—you got pennies and tuppences thrown at you. You'd get a tanner thrown at you the odd time, and that was marvellous. We had to spend all our holidays there, every spare moment.

On Saturdays it was always 'wooding'. We never bought any coal. I don't remember ever seeing coal in our house. My step–brother and myself used to have to go wooding round the spinneys and the hedges and all that. We'd have a pram and a home–made truck and we had to make three journeys. You'd got to walk four or five miles to the woods and pile the old pram right up, put bits of wood up the sides so you got a real good height. If ever we was hanging around the house it was always: 'If you've got nothing to do you can go and do some wooding.'

We used to collect blackberries, mushrooms, violets, watercress, and sell them at Leicester market. We'd go collecting before we went to school with a great big old clothes basket. Leicester was a good county for mushrooms. We'd sell violets for tuppence a bunch. You can live in the country. When the nice fresh leaves are first coming out on the hawthorn you can eat that to your heart's content (we used to call it bread and cheese); and later on in the autumn when it all turns to the little red berries, you eat those. You ate little pig nuts out of the ground. I don't know what plant it is, it's got a white top and the root is like a little nut. They're ever such stringy, horrible things really. You can eat sour grass—it's a green leaf that grows among the grass—ever such a bitter taste, but you can chew that. And even these rushes that grow in the river, the bottom below the water mark is all nice white stuff. I don't know what you call it, but you can eat that. And of course, turnips, swedes, cow cabbage. When you're hungry you'll eat the lot. You could always build a little fire with wood (as we used to when we was at the gates—when it was cold we always used to make a little fire there). We used to get all sorts of eggs: water hens; pigeons; wild duck. The hens were all loose in the fields and they'd lay their eggs anywhere, under the hedge and that, so you'd have hens' eggs without too much trouble. Where the sheep are there'd be the locust beans. They're ever so nice and sweet, they are. The farmer comes along in the morning and shoves the beans in the trough, and you know what time he comes, and as soon as he's moved away you share it with the sheep. And the salt they put out for cattle. There's any manner of stuff. You could get rabbit. You could live for a goodish while without hardly buying food.

My step–mother used to go to the market with the blackberries and mushrooms but we would take a few bunches of violets. You'd walk. You walked everywhere. You cut across the fields. Distances didn't mater. I was eleven before I went on a bus or anything. That was when the bus started taking us to Oadby school. I did travel in a car once. When we was at Burton Overy my step–brother and myself was in the church choir—my parents didn't go to church but all us kids had to go—and the parson took all the choir lads to the pantomime at Leicester. He piled all eight of us in his car.

I remember another adventure. That was at Burton Overy as well. I don't know what the occasion was. It was in the summer time. My step–mother and my father took my step–brother and myself to Leicester. We had a haircut at the barber's and an ice cream. We must have been really well–off at that particular time.

The biggest event that you looked forward to was the two parties at Christmas, one for the church and the other at the school. They were a really good party: jelly and cakes and a cracker, and Father Christmas would come and give you something. They were the events of your life. At Christmas you used to hang your stocking up and you used to have an apple and an orange in it and hopefully a new penny (you didn't always get the new penny) and a few nuts, and whatever you got for Christmas. One year I had a tanner bus from Woolworth's full of biscuits.

When we were turned eleven we went to Oadby school, and there the teachers used to buy my step-brother and myself a halfpenny bowl of soup at dinner time. We was very ashamed because, although there was a lot of poverty, we were some of the poorest of the poor. There were six of us children, and obviously the more children that came along the more we got hard up. We were more or less half starved. For your tea there was always a round and a half of bread and margarine—no more—and a cup of tea. You might get sugar and milk in it; you might not. I remember my father going to work many and many a time on dry bread and tea (no sugar or milk), and he'd got to do a hard day's work on that. And of course he'd walk to work, perhaps ten miles.

I had no proper shoes to go to school in. I had wellingtons with the tops cut off. I can remember being taken to Leicester market for second-hand clothes and having to try these trousers or whatever on at the back of the stall. My step-mother knitted a pair of short trousers for my step-brother to go to school in. Now and again people would take pity on us and send a bit of bread or a bit of cake round home.

Close by, there were people with plenty of money. There was the big halls and the manses and the manors. We used to go carol singing on Christmas Eve. We'd go miles and miles and miles, and we used to go to a village called Carlton Curlieu and there's a big hall there. We'd go to the tradesmens' entrance of course. You'd be fetched inside. 'The Master wants you to come in.' You'd be taken into this . . . I suppose it was a drawing room or something. It was a big room with a big fire and that. We'd sing a couple of carols to the master and mistress, and it was always a tanner. Then we'd be taken down to the servants' quarters, and that would be a mince pie and a drop of lemonade and a penny or twopence. We didn't keep the money—that had to be handed over. That was good money to buy food or whatever. All around Leicester there was a lot of big houses. It's the place for the hunting fraternity.

Our house at Burton Overy was two up and two down. A living room and a scullery. A toilet about half a mile down the garden. No gas or electricity or anything. You had a paraffin lamp in the living room and candles everywhere else. And when you went to bed: 'Don't drop the candle fat on the floor!' No floor covering of any description. The scullery would be brick floor, the rest wooden floors—bare boards. We had the usual few hard chairs and table. No table cloth or anything like that. You scrubbed the table. It used to be always drilled into us: 'It doesn't matter how poor you are, you can always be clean. If you can't afford boot polish you can spit on your shoes and get them clean.'

We had a stand–up in the old tin bath in front of the fire, so we did get a bit of benefit from the wooding. Saturday nights was always bath. One after the other. The first lot would get some clean water—the last one, it wouldn't be so clean. You couldn't keep heating the water up. But you hardly knew what it was in the winter to be warm, so you just got out of the bath and off up to bed and that was it. Teeth cleaning was an unheard–of thing.

My parents had one bedroom and we were all in the other. There was only the one bed. Some at the top of the bed and some at the bottom. The iron bedstead. The old straw palliasse. The main point was to try to get in the middle. It didn't matter about being all crowded in together. We were never warm. No such thing as pyjamas or vests or underwear. You went to bed in your shirt.

You made the utmost use of your garden. Spuds, cabbages, kidney beans, because you got a big return on those. If you set about seven pounds of spuds you'd get an enormous lot back. You'd get a threepenny packet of cabbage and there was probably a hundred and fifty seeds in that. Even if they didn't all grow, the majority of them did. You'd get, probably, fifty or sixty cabbages. Lettuce are the same. My step–mother didn't pickle anything because she couldn't afford the pickling vinegar and spices or whatever they used to use. You just lived basically from week to week. Sometimes she'd make a little bit of jam, but you needed sugar and usually you hadn't got any sugar. You wanted a penny for a two ounce packet of tea. You wanted tuppence for half pound of margarine.

I think our dad's wage was about thirty bob a week for hedging. He wouldn't ever get any more than that.

He used to go ferreting for rabbits; pigeon shooting when he could borrow a gun. That used to supplement our diet quite a bit. He never owned a gun. Christmas 1934, we'd got no Christmas dinner to come. My step–brother and myself had to go with our dad and try and get a rabbit for Christmas dinner. It was a bright moonlight night. We daren't go out till the people had come home from the pubs and that—we didn't want to be spotted by anybody—so it was gone midnight before we even went out. We stopped a couple of hours round this here hole trying to get a rabbit, and we never did get one neither. *And* we lost the ferret down the hole.

My father wasn't a lazy man, he was a hard worker, but I never remember any period when we wasn't desperately poor. We never had any new clothes—only when we went in the workhouse. For hedge–cutting, with all the thorns and everything else, you must have some good gloves, and very often he hadn't got any, or they'd be sewn up and patched up and bodged up one way or another. You do it in January, February, March time when it's very cold, and I can hear my step–mother saying: 'Somehow or other we've got to get you some gloves.' You had to provide your own axe and billhook to do it. Us kids weren't allowed to touch them in case we blunted the edge—he'd got to earn a living with them. Dad was a good worker. A hard worker. As a hedge–layer he was sought after. The rest of the year he'd try to get some hay–making or a bit of general farm work here and there. Farmers were poor and they only kept on the barest minimum of labour.

There was a period when he was an under–gamekeeper. That was a pretty good job. He lost it through no fault of his own. He was working for a Lord and Lady Somebody. I remember one night my step–mother telling him Lady So–and–so had been killed in a hunting accident. I don't know why, but that was the end of his job.

I had very fond feelings for my father. I can only remember a couple of times when my dad was at home (he was poorly—there was no holidays from work), and I remember how nice it was. It was a lovely feeling when you came home and you knew dad was going to be there. Why, I don't know, because it didn't make any difference really. There was no extra treat or anything. Perhaps we didn't get so many good hidings when Dad was at home.

I used to love to go over the fields wherever he was working. He might perhaps be thinning a spinney out, or might be hedge-laying. If I went, there was always a little bit of his dinner—it was only bread and margarine, but there was always a little bite. It was only cold tea out of the bottle, perhaps with not any sugar or milk in it, but there was always a drop. We might make a fire and have a little brew up. I used to love to go and see our dad. I used to get up with him, about a quarter to six, every morning of my life.

The old gent used to drink quite a lot, and they couldn't afford it. My step–mother was very strict and very hard, but she had a hell of a struggle on. If our dad had got the money he would drink it—straight in the pub Saturday dinner time as soon as he'd got paid. There used to be the most enormous rows. There was a lot of friction. Of course, poverty does cause friction. There was some terrific rows. It got to fighting and that. I used to be frightened to death.

With my step–mother it was a case of keeping out of the way, because I don't suppose there was a day of my life went by without a good hiding. Dad didn't *have* to hit us. He just *told* us. What he said *was*. That was it. But at the same time there wasn't that way that there was with my step–mother. With her it was all smack, smack, smack, smack. She did have a nasty temper. Of course she had a hard time with my father and a shortage of money. How did you bring a family of kids up with hardly any money?

We weren't no angels neither. We were bad enough at bringing trouble in the house. We got in a fair bit of trouble through causing damage in hedges where we went wooding. (But we'd got to have some wood.) The farmers knew us. They'd send the police down the house, and when we saw the police we used to scarper. There was another place we lived, out at Blaston. There was a farmer there that used to keep the milk in churns in the barn until the cart came the following morning to pick it up, and we used to nick a drop and have a drink of the milk. Of course, the cops came along over that. There was a bit of scrumping and all that. There was a big hall at Blaston, and there used to be grape vines and quite a big orchard, and we got in there and tried to help ourselves and things like that. Everybody used to do the same. There was another trick we used to get up to. There was a little shop at Blaston run by an old lady—a very old lady she was, she could hardly see—and this here shop was dark inside. We used to get a farthing, wrap it in silver paper, rub it on our hair till it got ever so smooth, and go to the shop and pass it off as a tanner. You could get these great big biscuits—ever such damn great things they were—and you'd get four for a penny. We used to do that quite regularly.

I was fourteen on the fifth of December, so at Christmas I left school and got a job in a boot and shoe factory in Leicester. Three weeks later I ran away from home. I was fed up. My step–brother was eight months older than I was. His mother used to favour him and my father used to favour me, and there was constant rows. Rows, rows, rows, really rows—nastiness, fighting. We used to bike to work—we both worked in the same place. Anyway this particular morning I got a puncture and I asked my step–brother to lend me his pump and he wouldn't. He said it would make him late and he'd probably get the sack (as he would do if he was late), and off he went. I suppose I got a bit awkward so I decided I wasn't going. I'd got an Aunty in Leicester. I went to my Aunty and asked her if she could lend my dad five bob. After a bit of questioning she let me have this five bob and I hopped on a train and ended up at a place called Ramsey in Huntingdonshire.

I went round and round and round. Only for a couple of days, but I covered a fair bit of ground. A bloke named Cade gave me my first job. Two bob a day I started on. It was all horses then. Sugar beet, or corn, has got to be hoed all the time to stop the weeds from growing, and the horses have got to be kept straight. The chap at the back has got to be guiding this machine with all these blades on (because if you cut two or three plants up the old farmer's soon in a bit of a tizzy). The chap couldn't keep his eye on the horse all the time so he wanted a lad leading the horse. And then of course you soon learned to single the beet. You go along the row with a hoe and then you go along on your hands and knees so you finish up with the plants six or eight inches apart. Kids can do that.

I lived in—up a ladder in the attic. Provided you worked (and you was expected to work) he treated me quite fairly. No spoiling you or anything. You worked seven in the morning till four in the afternoon. In the summer you go back again after tea. That's six days a week, and there's always a bit to do on a Sunday morning. If you live in anywhere it's practically a seven day a week job. But there was nothing else to do anyway. I used to do a lot of reading. Only comics and that, there was no library or anything. You only got a newspaper on a Sunday. It was lonely.

There was unemployment, but I was never out of work. A lad could get a job because they only had to pay a lad's wages. They could get two lads for the price of one bloke, and a lad could do most things a man could do. Not the carrying, mind. The sacks of corn used to be eighteen stone (it shows you how hard the men had to work). They had to be carried from the drum up a ladder to the granary. I used to be where the chaff is, or on the stack.

I didn't regret leaving home—there was nothing at home for me—but I used to cry myself to sleep because I was lonely and fed up and all that, and I couldn't see what was in the future. Farms like that are isolated so there was no playmates or anything. There wasn't much time for playing in any case. You was pretty tired as well. I was never very big and strong, and anyway it was a case of: 'I think you'd better get to bed now, my lad. You've got to be up in the morning.' And you mustn't burn the candles and all. Everywhere was the same. The emphasis was always on money because even the farmers were very hard up.

The sugar beet factory was at Peterborough. They sent their men round to have a look at your crop and they advanced you money right through the season till it was harvested. You couldn't afford to pay labourers out of your own pocket until then.

I had two bob a week to spend. The rest was taken for food and board and working clothes—boots and leggings and knee–breeches. But I certainly lived a lot better. I got not only bread and cheese and an onion, or perhaps potatoes and boiled bacon or something, but you'd have a pudding with your dinner every day. That's what kept you there. Nothing else mattered. I didn't really need any spending money. I didn't smoke because you weren't supposed to smoke till you were sixteen. Somebody'd soon tell you: 'Get that fag out! You're not old enough to smoke!' And it would be no good even thinking about going to the pub for a drink because you wouldn't be allowed inside the place. So you didn't need a lot of money really. You'd get a halfpenny worth of sweets. You'd get sixteen toffees for a penny.

I missed my dad. I didn't see him again till during the war, when I got married, after I came back from Dunkirk.

It was a very unfair system, but it was just your misfortune that you were born to be poor.

Rochdale

Jimmy Buckley

I worked with cotton. I lived in Rochdale. It was just industrial, and cotton was the chief occupation. I started when I was twelve years old. Soon as you were old enough you found a job and went to work for the money. I had high ambitions. I was very good at drawing and painting. I used to get top marks for that at school and I wanted to be a sign writer. But my father was a cotton operative, my brother was a cotton operative, my sister was a cotton operative, so as soon as I was twelve my father said, 'You'd better go and see So–and–so,' who was the overlooker at one of the local mills, 'and get your name down.' There was engineering in the foundry but there was a waiting list as long as your arm for apprenticeships in those days. And they only had their names down because their fathers or uncles were foremen or had some influence.

Until I was twenty there was regular work. I worked in the spinning room. They're horrible places. I got 3/6 a week when I started. Then I went little–piecing. I got 15/- then. Then you go from little–piecing to side–piecing. A spinning mule is huge and there would be 12 pairs in a room. They were divided in the middle by the headstock where all the driving powers were and the different bands and straps and wheels. Rollers put the twist in the cotton. The mules move backwards and forwards and thousands of spindles, the whole length, twist that fast they look still. It was awful boring repetition work. You just got used to it. It took 3 days to spin one cop on fine Egyptian. (Where my brother worked it was very very coarse. They doffed every half hour.) The material was so fine they had to have covers on the drivers to stop the draught because it blew the ends down. If anyone let faults go through they were warned and if there was consistent snarls they were sacked.

There was one incident when I was side–piecing. The mill, which had been privately owned, had been bought by a cotton corporation from Bolton. This corporation just sacked the bosses wholesale, from the carder to the manager, and brought their own people in and they weren't sympathetic towards us. Proctor, the man I worked for, was a very clever, experienced spinner. It sounds funny for me to say it but you had to be clever to be a spinner because it was a very complicated job. Proctor was the shop steward and he spoke out. So Proctor and the man who worked on the next pair of mules were victimised. They were the last of the spinners who would send out work with snarls in and yet they were accused of it. When the overlooker complained of bad work Proctor was annoyed. He said, 'You can't spin a bloody top, owt about cotton.' They were threatened with dismissal and we came out in sympathy. We said we would sit down. We stopped the mules in strike against it. That's the only strike I've been involved in. We sat there all day. No–one came. Where before the manager would have come and talked to us, in this instance they didn't. The man who came at a quarter to five was arrogant and unconcerned about these two men. He just came through and said, 'If you're not at work in the morning I'm going to close this mill.' Proctor asked us not to carry on with the strike because it would mean all the mill closed down and everyone thrown out of work, all the girls in the card room, and all the spinners. So they just finished and we, reluctantly, went back to work. After that it gradually went worse and worse until we never knew when we were working. Every time the overlooker passed, your heart missed a beat. If he waved his hands in front of him it meant, 'Bare spindle—stop indefinitely.'

When you're side–piecing, you have two mules, and the side–piecer looks after one half and the spinner is in the other. There is a boy who is the little–piecer who does the clearing, cleaning, sweeping, the brewing up and all that. All day your thoughts are miles away and you're doing the work automatically. The temperature is 95 to 100 degrees. There's humidifiers, long steam pipes across the room with very finely perforated holes and they're sending out steam. You can't spin unless you have a certain atmosphere. It has to be very hot and very damp. It hits you like a slap when you go in at the door. The floor is wood. It's so oily you have to work in bare feet. You've just a pair of white corduroy overalls. They have to be corduroy to stop the oil soaking through, because you could develop spinner's cancer from the poisonous mineral oil getting on your body. People have been known to die from that. There's so much oil.

There was so many kinds of ropes and bands, and the spinners had to know how to put all these on. In rope when it's new there's a kind of elasticity. All that had to be pulled out before it was used or it would stretch before you'd had it on the pulleys ten minutes and you'd have to take it off again and take a piece out. We used to fasten it to a wheel end and all the spinners would pull the stretch out of it. There'd be about six foot of stretch when you pulled at it. They all got a rag in each hand and, like a tug of war, they pulled at the rope for about five minutes. About twelve men. Then it was ready for putting on. When a man had pieced a band you couldn't see the piecing. We used to have a pot of marmalade handy and when we stopped the mule at lunch time you used to put a spoonful of marmalade in the centre of your hand and stroke it on the piecing. The piecing just mingled with the band and all you could see was the shiny part where the marmalade had been. That band would run for 12 months sometimes before it would break.

I won 5/- with a joke about that. There was a paper called *Cotton Factory Times*. They used to pay 5/- for a joke if they printed it. I made one up. A spinner asked his little–piecer to go out at dinner time and get him some marmalade. The little boy went and was gone some time and then came back. 'Have you got the marmalade?' asked the spinner. 'No,' said the boy, 'they didn't have any so I got you two ounces of ham instead.' I won 5/- with another joke. A spinner had forgot his lunch. So at dinner time he asked the little–piecer to run home and fetch it for him. The lad went out and after a bit he returned. 'Have you got my dinner?' asked the spinner. 'No,' said the boy, 'your wife didn't have anything for you.' 'Well what did she say?' asked the spinner. 'She didn't say nowt,' said the lad, 'she just gave me an orange.' 'And where's the orange?' said the spinner. 'I ate it,' said the lad. 'You silly chump,' said the spinner, 'that was my dinner.'

The noise was shocking. It was really horrible when you were stood near a headstock. It would have sent an average person crazy. The noise just felt to be boring into your head. We didn't talk with speech. You talked with actions. You can imagine hundreds of grinding wheels, and spindles revolving, and cog wheels going, and straps belting round. If you shouted at the top of your voice you couldn't hear so you had to learn to talk with your fingers. If I wanted to go to the toilet I'd put my fingers under my braces. If I wanted to know what time it was I'd go like pulling a watch out— they were pocket watches mainly in those days. With it being so hot and clammy you were sweating all the time. You drank pints and pints of water. If you wanted to go for water you made a sign of drinking. We used to have breakdowns. Something would go wrong with the headstock and the mule would default and break all the ends across the whole length. The spinner had to wind all those loose ends back on and you used to go round and signal at every wheel end so that the little–piecers would come and help.

There was only one thing we used to shout and that was 'Fire'. We used to go all through the mill and shout 'FIRE' as loud as we could and point to where the fire was. I don't know why there weren't more fires because everything was saturated with oil. There are about thirty to forty oil points in one headstock. Before we started every morning we had to climb up the headstock and oil all the spindles. We had to go along the bottoms of the spindles in the morning and all along the tops in the afternoon. They're horrible things in a spinning room, fires. I've been involved in five. They start so suddenly and in a few seconds the whole place is ablaze.

As long as the mules were running the spinners were earning money. They were paid on their hanks. They ran the mules to the last second, even pushed them up for the last draw. We used to start getting dressed about twenty past five. We put our trousers on, our socks and clogs, and then went to have a look round to see if everything was alright. This particular day I was practically ready. It was almost half past. We had to wait while the engine slackened. I was stood by the headstock and I happened to look up and I saw a spark in the pulleys of the next pair. Just that spark and in five seconds all the headstock was ablaze. There's a fast pulley and a loose pulley and when the mules stop they throw the strap off the fast one onto the loose. The loose pulley had got too dry and it was red hot and all at once it came out in a blaze. In five minutes the headstock all fell down. It got in our mules. You could see flames running across. We were all trained and used to these things. We'd got extinguishers at the ends and buckets of water. In most cases we fought the fires and put them out before we needed the fire brigade. It caused considerable damage and it took weeks to get a pair running again.

Another time there was a fire. The overlooker was a very short, terribly fat man. He didn't seem to have any neck. We used to be scared of him. He was going down the room where the fire was. They didn't open windows so there'd be no draught and the room was full of smoke. There was a bogie on the landing for the weft carrier—the man who collects all the cops and takes them down the hoist to the cellar to be weighed and damped. Some of the lads got the bogie and they sent it down the room. It caught the overlooker behind the knees and he fell on the bogie and got carried along. He did look funny. Of course it was very like a humiliation for him. No–one would ever tell who did it.

I've seen some sad and serious things as well. There was a nice lad I got very friendly with. He'd only been there a fortnight. He was creeling—that's replacing the bobbins. I was working on my wheel gate on next pair, and I saw four fingers drop on the floor. The wheels caught his hand, poor lad. Of course he never worked there again. It was over twelve months before his hand healed up. Then there was another time. These long driving belts were at least thirty foot long. The driving straps were very heavy, tough, some kind of fibre, and they were fastened with steel rods. You could tell when a strap was breaking. It started wobbling. It was dangerous because if a strap like that broke, like a rope on a ship, it could kill anyone. It went at such speed and it was so heavy. We used to have to run for a 20 foot pole and edge the strap off before it broke. You couldn't stop the main drive. Only the engineer in the engine house could stop that. This time I was side–piecing and my spinner shouted, 'Get out of the way, Jimmy. The strap's breaking!' I ran as fast as I could but before he could get out of the way the strap broke and it spiral-led round him. It spiralled round him and all over the floor and never touched him. It shook me, owt about him, and his face was like putty. As white as a sheet. They had to take him into the first aid room for an hour for shock.

I remember another man I worked for. We had a loose pulley at lunch time before we set on. We used to have to climb on the fallers and stand on the rollers and pull ourselves up on the creel. When he was climbing down, instead of putting his foot on the fallers he put it on a spindle and it went right through his bare foot and come out the other side. There wasn't any laws about compensation then. Even that lad that lost his fingers never got anything. No law about redundancy or anything like that. If you lost your work you were just out of work. You didn't even get paid for your holidays.

There were no amenities. No canteens. We had to take our lunches. We had to sit on the oily floor with our backs up against oily boards to eat our lunch. The toilets had no covers on them and there were no doors. There were no toilet paper. There was an official notice in every toilet: ANY PERSON CAUGHT USING COT-TON WOOL IN THIS TOILET WILL BE INSTANTLY DISMIS-SED. Whoever thought we would use that would have been silly because it was unhygienic. The cotton wool was dirtier than news-paper.

I was born the last. I was the baby of the family. My mother must have been turned 40 when she had me. I was 14 when she died and she was 58. An abscess burst inside her. Today they would have operated and took it away. I heard the doctor say to my father, 'There's nothing more I can do, Mr Buckley.' We knew then we were going to lose her. My brother was fifteen years older than I. My sister was two years older. We were very close my sister and I. We clung together and went everywhere together. My brother was married and had left home. My father was an old man before his time. He was the kind of man that worried. He was going to work at sixty-three and spinning was terribly hard work for a man at that age so we persuaded him to finish. That was about 1927. My sister worked in the card room and I worked in the spinning room. We did the washing every Saturday afternoon. When I was out of work I used to get up early Saturday morning and light the fire under the old kitchen boiler, fill it full of water and boil the clothes, starch them, and poss them for 10 minutes. If there was anything that wanted special attention you had a rubbing board inside the tub. My father used to get our meals ready and keep the dust down, and every Thursday night my sister and I used to get cracking. It was all elbow grease, blackleading and Brasso. The fireplace had a brass tidy and an oven and a little place for hot water. To bake you had to push the coal under the oven and push a side plate down to keep it in. We had a square of carpet and lino. An old fashioned dresser and an organ. And the high mantelpiece. And above the fireplace: CHRIST IS THE HEAD OF THIS HOUSE—THE GUEST AT EVERY MEAL—THE SILENT LISTENER TO EVERY CONVERSATION. We did all our cooking on the fire. We used the kettle to boil our water. We used to fill an old brown and white ginger beer bottle, wrap a blanket round it and take that to bed. Or the oven plate out of the oven. Or even an ordinary red brick with a blanket wrapped round it. Anything to retain the heat. We had gas lights—no electricity. No hot water. No toilet that you could flush. It was a tumbler in the back yard. It had a narrow well about 10 feet deep and the weight of water made this thing at the bottom tumble over. I lived in that house—just an ordinary terrace—from when I was one year old till I was married.

My father was a choirmaster and organist. My sister and I were in the choir. She never had any teenage life. She had to come right from a girl to a woman. She was only sixteen when my mother died. She had the responsibilities and hard work of looking after a home. She had that colitis. You lose the lining of your stomach and she went to nothing. It was shocking to see her. She worked in the card-ing room of a mill where they did very coarse stuff and didn't get laid off till after I did, but eventually all the mills closed down.

All our neighbours were very good. Everybody knew each other and everybody was friendly. Our neighbour had a little girl. She used to come over when she could just totter. I used to sit on the doorstep after I'd been in the hot mill all day and she used to come and play. Another man had a market garden. For years and years flowers came up in that and then it was turned into a rubbish tip. He used to sell greengrocery. There was a man who went out of his mind and was chasing someone up the street with a carving knife with nothing on. They took him away but after a few weeks he was back again. There was a boy who was the queerest child you could ever see. He was thin and tall, and had glasses and protruding teeth and a most vacant look on his face, and a very awkward shambling gait. He became a borough surveyor. I knew my wife from a young girl. She lived in the same street. Her father was a spinner.

Nearly all the men in our street were spinners. They were all out of work. Four men worked at the foundry. There was one other man and he was private chauffeur to Samuel O'Neil who owned the paper tube works. He had four children. His wife was a very dominant strict woman. All her children bar one turned out the wrong way and I put it down to nothing other than her being so forceful and overbearing. Ethel, the oldest, used to go with my sister and I to these socials. They used to be over by ten and we were on our way home before half past and her mother used to be coming up the road meeting her, letting off steam. Well she went wrong. And the boy, who was really clever, turned into a drunkard. The next to youngest girl was forced to get married. It was only the youngest that had any normal life. The mother was a very hard woman. You never saw her smile. She made you frightened to see her. The father was chauffeur and gardener and he kept his job till he retired. He was very smart and all. Peaked cap, a uniform with brass buttons, and polished black leather leggings.

Meanwhile things had worsened and we'd started short time. We worked three days a week and we played three days a week. If we worked Monday, Tuesday and Wednesday we had to sign on the dole Thursday. That was awfully humiliating. The people at the dole weren't sympathetic and good mannered. They treated us like scum. That was their attitude. They were white collar workers and we weren't. We'd be on short time for a few weeks, then we'd go back on regular time, and then the overlooker would come round to the frame end and gesture with his hands and that would mean stop altogether. And we'd just no work to go to. I had a bicycle and I used to go round to all the mills asking if there was anybody off.

Once when we were on short time they got us cleaning windows. I was about twenty foot up on one of these extending ladders. I'd just got to the top when the ladder slipped, the floors were that oily! Underneath the windows we used to have these containers full of O'Neil's paper tubes and I fell straight into these. I wasn't harmed. Not a scratch.

I was about 24 then and like most men do I fell in love. We were on short time, but love stops at nothing. My wife was also a cotton operative but she worked for Dunlop's. They manufactured fabric for tyres. She was a doubler. Doubling's altogether different from spinning. I was 24 when we got engaged and we said we wouldn't get married till I got promoted. You can get to join–spinning. You share a mule with another man and you have no little–piecer and no side–piecer. There's just you and the other man and you share the wage. From that you go to spinning. We saved up. We never went to the pictures. We used to go for a walk and put the money in the bank. My wife was getting more money that I was. She got 2 guineas which was a good wage for a lady. I was getting 26/- a week and I had to pay 1/- union out of that. You had to wait for someone to get sacked or die before you got promotion. I used to be on the overlooker's track. He kept stalling me and stalling me. Eventually I did get join–spinning after I'd been side–piecing for seven years. I was 29 then. I was getting £3.10s when I was join–spinning so with my wife's wage we had £5 a week. You could get five Woodbines for threehalfpence and eight oranges for sixpence.

We got married and we went to Skegness for our honeymoon. We came back at the weekend and Monday morning I went to work as usual and there was a notice on the gate: THIS MILL HAS CLOSED DOWN INDEFINITELY. I was out of work.

I went everywhere to every conceivable thing. I even went, I'm ashamed to say it, on the golf links to offer myself as a caddy. And you couldn't even get that. You went round to mills and old men were doing boy's jobs, little–piecing, for 16/- a week to get stamps on their cards so they could sign on. Then they would draw their dole while their stamps ran out. I worked nine weeks in twelve months and it was most humiliating. My wife kept me. She was still working because Dunlop's were at their peak. It was awful going out every morning looking for work. It was fruitless. I used to go six or seven miles each morning on my bicycle and there'd be nothing. My mill never opened again. Spinning just died out.

I had a friend who worked for a dairy. It was called the Lancashire Hygienic Dairy and it couldn't have been dirtier. It was a filthy place. He was a driver. He said would I like to go and it was a god-send. We went from Rochdale to Cheetham Hill, Manchester at four o'clock every morning to collect the milk. We had a massive can, and mothers used to put jugs on the doorstep with a saucer over. We had gill and pint measures with long handles. We had this big urn strapped onto the front of the trolley. We sold bacon and wrapped cheese and eggs and got a bonus on what we sold. The wage was £2 which was quite decent when you consider dole was only 17/-, as well as the loss of your pride and all that. I did that for eighteen months, and then Lancashire Hygienic folded up and I was out of work again.

Luckily my wife managed to get me on night work at Dunlop's. It was no joke and it was long hours. Eight at night while seven in the morning. First week or two was alright, but when you'd worked nights for a few months you wanted to stop in bed all Saturday and Sunday feeling like a wet rag. I never hardly saw my wife. I used to see her ten minutes at morning and an hour at evening. She used to work Saturday mornings. Then when the war started we both had to work compulsory all day Sunday as well.

Aberdeen

Marion Watt
My father's wage was 18/- a week. There was 10 of us. When he was called up for the army my mother got 16/- a week—and Col. Davidson made us pay for the rent of the house. We was in the gardener's lodge at Balnagask. It was as bad all over Aberdeen. There was a good lot of real well–off people in the fish, on the trawlers, they were all right, and they seemed to flaunt their money about. You used to be that envious, some had so much to spend and others had so little.

We were married in 1923. My husband had been three years idle before that but as I was expecting a baby we had to get married. It seemed that hopeless because every second person was unemployed. He'd a few months' work as an attendant in Dumfries Asylum when he come out of the army, and that was all. He's a Fraserburgh man, his people lived in Torry. We were at the poor end of Abbey Road. There's a better–off end where they own their own houses. We was in a little tenement house where they was let out in separate rooms. Practically everybody round that corner was idle. We had a terrible time, but we wasn't any worse than other people.

I was terrified when we got married, where would we get a house to live in. And I knew we couldna live at home. That was hopeless. And his mother, she took a dislike to me, being expecting. She cast it up all the time. Alec had a chum, he was a water inspector, and he went about the town a lot. He heard about this room that was empty, so we went right away and applied. Grieve the landlord lived round the back. He said, 'Oh yes, he can easy have it,' so we got it for 6/- the week. My father gave me £10, which was a good lot—not much to furnish a house, mind, but we got everything secondhand. We got a beautiful bed for 10/-. Mind, nothing matched, but it didn't matter. We got this great big outsize wooden bed, ash coloured, and it was all engraved at the ends. It was those straw mattresses that ye put on them, but we'd never had anything else so we didn't know the difference. Then we'd a sideboard—well, it was a kitchen cabinet, we got for 15/-, an overmantel and pictures for 15/-, 4 chairs for 10/-, lino 10/-, pails for my water, and curtains and everything out of £10. The old lady had some chairs and she'd a cabinet kind of thing too, and Alec stripped them and painted them. She'd an awful dirty house, it was just filthy, and we'd an awful cleaning to do. Our walls were ochre—pink ochre, yellow ochre. There was gas in the house—no electric. There was a stone floor. It had been an inn at one time. There was still an old lantern hanging from the roof. There was a woman through the house, a Mrs Craig, and she said to me one day, 'Come here and see this.' She opened her cupboard door and there was a hole right through the wall. They'd been selling drink when they shouldn't. Men'd come into a dairy place and come right through into the inn through her press. It was about the first inn there ever was in Torry.

My husband's father was a cooper, at Fiddes's, and he managed to speak to the manager and got him in there for a few months. But it didn't last, of course, it closed down, Fiddes's timber yard and the cooperage. They was making barrels for the herring, but my husband wasn't trained for that. He only laboured, he hadn't served his time. He never had a skilled job. He was desperate that even our girls had to have a training. One worked with a tailor when she left the school and the other was a milliner. He was daft aboot them getting a trade because he missed it himself. He was labouring in the timber yard when it closed down. They stopped making the barrels. There was no outlet. He just tried for anything—anything at all.

They started giving them six weeks at a time on the streets and roads, tarring. Six weeks, then you was paid off and others got their turn. And then one time he was lucky and he got a year and a half on the roads and he thought he was in for good. But right at our own door he got laid off. He was paving Abbey Road and I was waving to him from the window when the foreman came to him and said, 'This is you finished.' They found that he'd been there too long. They'd overlooked him. We thought we was fine, although the wages weren't much, 30/-. Still it was better, and it gave him some self-respect because he was miserable when he was unemployed. He was a proud man and he hated going asking for jobs and them hardly listening to him. He went to the gasworks at 6 o'clock every morning, because they sometimes took on extra hands, and the foreman said one morning, 'I'm fed up seeing your face.' He came home like a sheet—just miserable. That went on, off and on, for 17 years, till 1937.

When he was doing his six weeks on the roads, he was only there a few days when a great snowstorm started. He'd to walk all the way from Abbey Road at the other end of Torry, right to Woodside, which would have been three or four miles. They'd to report every morning but they didn't get a penny for it, and walk all the way back. One morning there wasn't even a foreman there. The biggest half of the men stole a shovel and went out o' the works and went round the West End by Queens Road and all they places and swept the doors. He made 4/-. That was all the money we had that week. I'd two young infants—I needed four pints of milk a day really. We got milk cheap, but you needed money to buy it. I'd the two girlies, and then I'd five boys—all dead–born, and I'm certain it was because of the malnutrition. I was practically living on bread and potatoes. I tried to get something for the girls and my husband. We'd fried potatoes practically every night, along with something maybe for them. Sausages were cheap and I'd an awful good butcher—Bob the Butcher they called him—and he was really good to me. And men in the fish sometimes give us a bit fish, and we managed for that. But mostly I had potatoes and bread and toast. In the winter months I walked over to the New Market. You got a great big rabbit for sixpence and we had that every Sunday, all the months that rabbits were in season.

In the summer time we went away to the Bay o'Nigg and we had a picnic down there with the girls. All our family, my brothers, sisters, every one of them, used to go on a Sunday when it was fine. We used to take potatoes. Another maybe got a pound of corned beef for eightpence. We all took something, and we gathered buckies and boiled them on a small primus stove. We had *some* enjoyment. Once or twice we went to Stonehaven when the children were small. It was only 6d return. I always wanted to see Dunottar Castle. And this day we went. The oldest girl was 3 and Betty was 2. Alec had to carry Betty. But I wanted to see Dunnotar Castle, and he was *flaming*. He says, 'It's too far.' It didn't look far along the cliffs. I persisted. I loved old castles. Well, we walked and we walked for miles along the cliffs and when we come there it was closed.

We could never afford a baby sitter to let us out. The Torry picture house was just beside us, in Crombie Road. You got into the front seats for fourpence. We liked the pictures, and if we carried the girls, the whole four of us got in for eightpence. We used to be carrying them still when they were going to school and their legs used to be dangling right down.

The most of the people along the street was unemployed, looking for jobs. When the snow came on they used to queue the whole night to try to get a job in the snow. They got 10d an hour and Alec'd work as long as they would let him. They never got home through the day and they got 6d for a pie and a cup of tea. There was dozens of men queued up all night and the foreman came out and said, 'You, and you, and you.' Frozen with cold they'd stand—and yet they'd say the unemployed was lazy.

Then Lady Cowdray at Dunecht House started a scheme. She had hundreds of acres of estates and she wanted these great stone walls built round every bit. The men had to live in bothies on the estate and they'd to keep their wives and families in Aberdeen besides that—and she was paying 10d an hour. She got some single ones, but the married men couldn't do it—and then they were called lazy because they didn't take the work. They'd to have 2 pairs of good dungarees and 2 pairs of boots. How could they afford it?

There was so many unemployed in the town. The Broo was only giving 21/- for the four of us. The Board of Health said it wasn't enough to keep you alive and that the Councils would have to help the unemployed themselves. They started a scheme to build the golf course at Hazlehead and you would get seven and six more on your dole for working three days a week. So of course they all did that. The Hazlehead golf course was built with sweat and tears. They were soaking up to their oxters with the peaty boggy ground. His feet was frozen. He used to come home exhausted. My brother gave him an old bike. We used it for years.

He got a job in Gibb's granite yard in King Street. He took awful bouts of malaria fever because he'd been in Egypt in the war. He used to shake all over. This day he took ill at his work and he came home. Next morning he got his books sent to him and when he went to sign on at the Unemployment Exchange they said he wasn't entitled to any money because he'd left his job without cause. Well, you can never beat authority. They put him to the Parish, and the Parish gave him a chit for 14/- to get food, but no money. We'd no money for rent or anything like that. Oh they were hard. He got that for 3 weeks and then he'd to go before a Board. They discovered he hadn't left this job without cause so they gave him the back money, but we'd to pay back what we got from the Parish. But that was the finish of the granite yard. There was always someone ready to take your place. They used to undercut one another—take it for a few shillings less. They'd have cut one another's throats for a job. But my husband wouldn't do that—he was determined he would never take a job at less than anybody else.

My father took a job as a jobbing gardener when Col. Davidson died, but he wasn't doing very much. He gave Alec a few weeks when he was busy one time and paid him better than anybody else. He gave him £2 a week. Then in 1937 Alec got into the gasworks, after trying for years and years. And he was only there a few weeks. He'd ulcers of the stomach for years and he got word to go into hospital. You got 18/- insurance money when you were ill, and they hardly paid it till you was back to your work again. After a fortnight I hardly had any money. I went to the hospital and Sister come to me as I was leaving and she says, 'You must bring a big tin of cocoa for Mr Watt tonight when you come in. The doctor's ordered cocoa.' You had to bring in all your extras and cocoa was an extra. They never got an egg unless you took it in. I hadn't a penny to buy a smattering of cocoa, so Alec says to me, 'Go to the Parish when you're going home.' I went in fear and trembling to the Parish. The clerk at the desk would hardly listen to me. He said, 'Go to the insurance offices and kick up a row there about your money,' and slammed down the hatch in my face. I sat down in a chair in the corner and cried. I didn't know what to do. And this man come along and he says, 'What's wrong?' He took me into the office and gave me tea. He rang up the Britannic offices and gave them a right telling off about leaving people starving. And he gave me 35/- right into my hand. He says, 'When your husband comes out of hospital, come in and we'll give you extras for him.' Well, they sent me 2 pints of milk every day, and they made his money up to 35/- a week the time he was off ill. That was the only kindness we ever had from anybody.

He was sent out to the convalescent home at Cults. I'd no money for buses and I'd to walk and I was seven months pregnant. I walked twice a week from old Torry, about eight miles, and I walked back. On the Wednesdays, the girls were at school and I walked by myself, but on the Saturday the 3 of us started off at eleven o'clock to be there by two. My mother stopped in Claremont Street at Mannofield and when we were coming home we went in there and got a cup of tea. She'd a small garden and she gave me vegetables. It's just as well I'd an understanding mother. She'd very little all her life. My father's business failed and he was ill and she was going out to work. He turned ill for years and years. My husband did think about going abroad but you'd still need money for that, and you'd have needed someone out there to give ye a job. He tried to join the army but they wouldn't have him—with the ulcers.

If the girls had to go to anything with their chums, I managed to give them the coppers to go. I tried never to make them the odd man out. When Margaret was eight, they started the milk at school. You'd to pay a penny for the small bottle. You'd to pay for the books too. I paid them up at 3d a week. I was still paying till the next term started. Margaret won the Murray Essay Prize. She was up at the newly built secondary school at Garden City. She was very clever. But we'd to pay for everything and we couldn't do it. We couldn't do it. There was no help. She never took it hard. She would've liked to go to classes for shorthand and typewriting, but we couldn't even afford that.

We were still in one room when the girls were going to school. There was an old old woman, a Shetland woman, in a room in front of mine, and she died one night. I was real good to her. I used to give her soup and I sent any messages she had. I did her washing and I helped her. She was 87. Her son came down from Shetland and him and me was there when she died. The breath wasn't out of her body when I was at the landlord's round the back asking for her room. I said, 'It's a terrible thing I'm doing, but I'm desperate. We've the girls in one room—their bed pushed under our own on castors. Mrs Grieve, can I have Mrs Duffus's room?' She says, 'I was waiting for you.'

It was 6/- for one room, 11/- for the two. We'd no water in the room where we'd been living. We'd two pails; the clean water in the pail with the lid, and the dirty pail. I'd two streets to go to empty it. Out the front door and up the brae. There was toilets and the wash-house there. It was communal—we all used it. They'd say, 'I've left a boiler of water for ye, if ye'd like to go in and wash.' It was those lift–up tubs that you'd to empty yourself, and you'd to fill the boiler from a tap outside the door. I got the water from the wash–house and emptied the dirty water in the toilet. But there was water in the room that the old lady had, so we'd a sink. It made a big difference.

You'd to pay for the doctor, and for years I went with the awful-lest pain in my back because I couldn't afford to go. You'd to pay for the girls too, and you put it off and put it off. My husband was very short–tempered. It was just with me. He thought I could've managed. I wasn't extravagant—I couldn't be. But then men usually blames their wives. But not all the time. Just when he happened to be in a bad mood and anybody upset him, I got it. I used to hear the woman upstair nag, nag, nagging at her man, but I never did that. But I will say she had cause, because he didn't rise in the morning and look for a job, where my man got up early in the morning, every day, and looked for a job. Her man said it was a waste of time, and she used to cast up Alec going out in the morning. 'Look at Mr Watt, away out in the morning, and you lying in your flaming bed.'

Forest of Dean

Donald Kear

I became unemployed a fortnight before my twentieth birthday in 1933. I was a machine attendant at a small local factory and it was the custom of my employer to discharge employees when they became older and more expensive to him and employ younger lads in their place. There was plenty of labour available. Young lads were hanging around the factory gates every day looking for work.

At that time the Forest of Dean was a coal mining area. My father was a miner and his father was a miner—he was killed in the mine in fact, a week after my father was born. There was a rule in the Forest mines at the time that if a lad had not worked in the mines before he was 16 he could not enter the industry when he became older. So entry to the mines was barred to me. I began a period of idleness which, punctuated by all too few casual jobs, lasted for nearly three years.

The first week of unemployment is not at all bad for a single man. There is the novelty of having plenty of time. You don't know that within a month your outlook will have changed. When you first try for a job and there's nothing doing, the foreman puts your name down and you say you'll call again in a day or so and you don't feel bad about it. The second time it strikes you that the foreman is less matey. You caught him on a bad day, you tell yourself. The next time he's plainly abrupt, even mildly hostile. A fortnight later, before you can complete the familiar patter, he says, 'Bugger off! I'll let you know if I want you.'

You begin to regard yourself as one of the unemployed. You are no longer a member of the working class. Society is getting along quite nicely without you. Coal is coming out of the pits; bread is coming out of the bakeries; milk is coming out of the cows; the trains are running; kids are going to school. Society doesn't need you. A man in a job doesn't give a damn about a man who's out of a job. Working class solidarity is a phrase which should have the emphasis on the word *working*. If you yawn they ask if you're tired. They ask you if you've had a hard day. If you've inherited a good stout pair of boots from the days when you were in a job they'll say,

'Them's working boots. What y' wearing working boots for?' If you happen to go to bed early it's, 'Early start in the morning, then?' If you go to bed late it's, 'You're going to be tired tomorrow.' If you eat heartily it's, 'Well, I s'pose you gotta keep your strength up.' If you eat only a little it's, 'You ain't active enough to get hungry.' A man out of work is said to have 'a good job—at the cupboard.' He is reputed to be 'a good steady worker—with a knife and fork.'

I went to sign–on one particular morning and the clerk said, 'Mr J. wants to see you.' So I joined another queue. Listening to whispered conversation told me he wanted to see us to cajole us into going to a training camp, and it seemed he wasn't going to meet any takers. When it was my turn to go in I noticed that Mr J. looked as though he'd reached the end of his very short and knotted tether. He began reciting all the virtues of these camps—the comradeship, the toning–up of muscles, the good plain food, the fresh air, and the fact that it was for six weeks only. Then he dried up. 'What about it?' he asked. 'Well,' I said, 'I wouldn't mind if I thought I'd have a worthwhile job at the end of it.' 'We can't guarantee a job,' he said. 'But I know one fellow who got a job as a barman in Birmingham from one of these camps only last week.' 'I don't see much future in being a barman,' I said. 'What d'ye mean? There *is* a future in being a barman!' 'Work myself up to a brewer?' I said. 'Don't you talk to me like that,' he snapped. 'I don't want that sort of talk and I'm not having it. So bear that in mind!'

Another time I was told to see Mr J. This time it was for potato digging in Jersey. There were about thirty young fellows lined up for an interview. I rather fancied a trip across the Channel though it was dawn to dark work and rough sleeping. Then the applicant who'd just gone in came abruptly out. 'Break it up, chaps,' he said. 'They got more bloody blokes than they got taters.'

When you reached the end of your 26 weeks' unemployment benefit you were handed over to the hatchet boys—the Unemployment Assistance Board and the Means Test man. The total income of all the wage earners in your family was calculated, so that you would have to rely on them—your father, your sons or daughters—to maintain you. Any family unlucky enough to have one of their number unemployed were forced to accept a lower standard of living because they had a passenger to carry. In our family I became the passenger. My benefit was immediately cut to 5/- a week. My father was paid on production at the coal face. When his earnings rose a little the benefit was correspondingly reduced. The Means

Test man went regularly to the office at the mine to find out how much my father was earning so these adjustments could be made.

One day he called at our house just after dinner and dad had just had his meal. There were no pithead baths and my father's pit clothes, shirt, vest and trousers, were on the fender airing before the fire giving off the not unpleasant smell of warmed-up sweat. My mother shifted the dinner things off one side of the table so he could seat himself at it and lay out his papers from the brown leather brief-case which he always carried. He began his usual questioning into our financial circumstances and my father, normally the mildest mannered man I ever knew, suddenly reached his limit. He was a man shortly to start an eight hour stint six hundred feet below ground, lying on his side in a three foot seam, hacking out coal with a mattock, and here was the Means Test man telling him, in effect, the harder he worked the less money he would get. Also adding draught to the flames was the miner's inbred dislike of anyone who got a living without danger and physical exertion. He didn't swear at the Means Test man but in a louder than usual voice he abused him and the Unemployment Assistance Board, and the whole capitalist system. Father was very politically aware. In our village we had had visits from Tom Mann, Ben Tillet and Jimmy Maxton. And all the sincere eloquence he had listened to and applauded over the years seemed to come violently re–alive and it poured from him. The Means Test man retreated, packing his case as he walked to the door, leaving his pen, hurriedly retrieving it and, finding his own way out, slammed the door shut. I'll never forget the silence which followed. Father breathing heavily, mother sitting looking nowhere, and me wishing I was dead for bringing such trouble into our house. Father ended the silence. 'I'm not going to work this afternoon,' he said. 'There's nothing in it.'

Nowadays everyone is trying to give up smoking. In those days the problem was how to carry on with it. With so much time to con-sume and the constant nagging feeling of hopelessness and insec-urity you craved a smoke continually. You could buy five Wood-bines for twopence. But this is no bargain when you haven't got two-pence. You'd go for maybe a week without a single drag and then when you were given a cigarette you inhaled so deeply you half expected to see it coming out through the laceholes of your boots. For years afterwards the old habit of one good drag and pinch it out and pocket it persisted, hoarding dog ends until they disintegrated into dry dust. It may appear a childish sort of thing to have a feeling of pride about, but I'm proud to recall that I smoked my own dog ends when I had them but never once did I pick up a dog end from the road. Though I once picked up three broken cigarettes on a woodland path. Also a discarded tobacco wrapper often yielded the makings of a cigarette. It is possible to make a smokable cigarette from tea if much care is taken to roll it tightly, but the quality of the smoke is discouraging.

It was during my dole days that I became a compulsive reader. I read anything and everything which came my way, from Jack London and Anatole France to medical dictionaries and odd volumes of electrical engineering encyclopedias. There were weekly talks on the wireless specially addressed to the unemployed by a man called John Hilton. I came to have a great respect and liking for him. His was the only sympathetic voice the unemployed ever heard. He recommended reading as a pastime for us. 'Long way ahead in the future,' he said, 'someone will want to know where you got your know–how, your handiness with words, and you'll tell 'em you were unemployed in the '30s and you did a lot of reading.'

Via a distant relative of the proprietor of a local garage I got six weeks' work while they were short-handed during the holiday period. I enjoyed those six weeks. I sold petrol at the pumps, served in the shop, entered payments in the ledger—they sold bikes on hire purchase—swept the forecourt, vacuum cleaned the showroom, washed the windows, hosed down the toilets, cleaned cars, ran errands, helped in the garage. It pleased me to know they were pleased with me. They would, they said, have liked to have kept me on. They would be sure to let me know if at any time they needed me. And then the ride home with the gloom of knowing that I would be attending the Labour Exchange again in the morning.

I had another job about five months later. Electrician's labourer, cutting channels in plaster and concrete for electrical conduit, and at odd times, in a dilapidated shed at the back of my employer's cycle and radio shop, repairing and repainting old bikes, mending punctures and fitting tyres, and attending to the charging of radio accumulators. But business was bad and when the electrical wiring contract was completed I had to go.

It was shortly after this job ended that I really got the blues. I was getting nowhere. I'd heard talk of men down in South Wales who'd never worked, who'd left school, gone on the dole, courted on the dole, married on the dole, fathered a family on the dole and who, as prospects promised, would grow old and die on the dole. I became suspicious of every word and look from my parents. I imagined slights where no slights were intended. I spent all the time I could away from home. I walked miles through the woods alone without interest or aim. I rode my old bike with no thought of destination. I was drawing no benefit from the Labour Exchange. I was completely without money. I was conscious of wronging my folk each time I drew my chair up to the table to eat. I began to think of suicide.

But instead of committing suicide I applied for entry to a Government Training Centre to take a six month course. I was sent to a city 35 miles away to attend a Selection Board. It was all very quick. Your name was called and you went into a room in which there was a big table with five or six men sitting along one side. There were no chairs on your side. They checked your name to make sure they'd got the right bloke. They asked you to read aloud from a Ministry of Labour leaflet—eyesight and intelligence test cunningly combined. Then they wanted to see your hands. Apparently they could tell a potential bricky or hairdresser by the type of hands he possessed. I was booked in for a six month course in fitting. My hands were fitter's hands. Each trainee was paid 22/- per week. 17/- of this went to the landlady for bed, breakfast and evening meal. The Centre provided a dinner every day except Sunday. 5/- a week did not allow much social life. We were not encouraged to stay in lodgings in the evening. Sitting in the kitchen with the landlady and her husband had no appeal for any of the parties concerned. When it was dry we walked down to the city centre and watched the traffic and passersby. On a wet evening we went to the arches—a wide railway bridge which formed a tunnel over the road providing a meeting place for Centre lads. I remember black windy nights with the rain shimmering in a mist round the white globes of the street lights. The smell of wet clothes and the feeling of damp soles and damp trouser legs. The hoping that the three fags would last the evening and leave one for the next morning.

'Is there any room for one more at your digs? Want a move, do I? Christ, *do* I? Four kids. Colds all the time. All sitting round the fire. Sniffing and snotting like a bloody harmonica band.'

'It's clean enough, but she's a mean bastard. We never have the same grub that she and the old man have. I wouldn't mind so much, but it don't half show up when it's all laid out on the same table.'

'She's alright in the dark if you don't let yourself remember what she looks like in the daylight. Her old man's no good to her. She says he'll bat away for threequarters of an hour and then only bring up a bit of phlegm off his chest.'

'Sunday morning, see? Half seven. I wake up and I say to Fred that I could do with a cup of tea. We toss. Fred loses. He goes down to make the tea. When he gets there he finds the landlady's hidden the tea, or there isn't any, or she forgot to fill the caddy. But he finds some cocoa. So he makes 2 cups of cocoa. And he brings it upstairs on a tray and tips the lot into the bed. God, I said, she'll think we've had a bloody miscarriage.'

'I've only got a tanner and I've got no fags and it's late. I come to a fag machine, put my tanner in, pull the drawer and it jams out half-way. I can't get the packet out. There's nobody about and it's darkish. So I cut part of the top of the packet away with my penknife and I've poked out two fags when I see a copper coming. I've done nothing wrong but I move away. That copper would have had me for nicking fags. He wouldn't have had the machine for nicking my tanner.'

'My uncle said to write to him when I got settled in. So I did. And, with others bits of news as well, I mentioned the number of second-hand clothes shops there were round here and how I was consider-ing trying to save up a couple of bob to buy a pair of shoes for even-ings. In the hope that he'd send me half a quid. I'd forgot we take the same size. He sent me this bloody old pair of *his* shoes and this one pinches my big toe like buggery.'

'The Means Test man said, "Does your mother in law eat at the same table?" And my old lady bawled, "No. She has some in the corner with the bloody cat." '

There was a friendship between my Lancashire lodging mates of almost a family quality. Although they came from different towns in Lancashire and had never met before they came to the Centre, they were like brothers. We had just got into bed one night, the light was out, only Bill's fag glowed in the darkness. 'Where's thee bin t'neet?' Bill asked. 'Down the park agin,' Jim replied. 'On thee sen?' 'Yeh.' A pause. 'Thee's wanta stop going down there on thee sen,' Bill advised. 'Sommat's going to 'appen down there one neet and they'll blame it on gormless booger like thee.'

It was the first time I had ever stayed from home. Living in a city was entirely strange to me. When the novelty of being at the Centre, being in lodgings, had lost its shine of newness, then came homesickness. I found a small dried oak leaf in the turn–ups of my trousers during my second week. It seemed strangely valuable to me and I kept it in my suitcase. Sometimes I got a panicky sort of urge to run and run until I reached long grass and trees and bracken and clean fresh air. On the other side of the city I discovered a huge goods railway siding. I would walk to this siding, nearly three-quarters of an hour's journey, and rest my eyes on the coal trucks bearing the names of Forest of Dean collieries, Cannop, Parkend, Princess Royal, Norchard, and feel nearer to the Forest and less unhappy.

The atmosphere at the Centre was the exact opposite of what it should have been. Instead of giving an impression that here was a chance of a new life with a trade in your hands, you felt this was a place of punishment for a collection of idle layabouts on the criminal fringe. From the Chief Instructor down to the timekeeper at the gates, the main job of them all appeared to be to bully, to frighten, to squeeze the trainees to an even lower sense of degradation than long periods of unemployment and means testing had already given them. Rarely did you hear a kind word or a word of praise. Ordinary civility, too, was a rarity; politeness never. Some lads had their personal calendars in the lavatories with a stroke for every day completed. Discipline was rigid. A trainee arriving two minutes late was fined 6d. If you were caught smoking in the lavatories the fine was 6d. The main function of the Chief Inspector appeared to be to charge into the lavatories at irregular intervals, book and pencil at the ready, and demand, 'Name and number.' I hated the Centre. I was looking for a way to leave. There were only two. The first was to complete the six months course—the second was to get a job.

One evening after tea the landlady's husband was talking to me about jobs he'd had. One was putting up telephone poles in the open countryside. 'Nothing quite like a job in a Post Office outside gang,' he said. 'Just you and your mates and your van, complete with stove and kettle and china mugs, way out among the fields and hedgerows, and the sun shining and a sky full of larks.' So I wrote a letter to the Sectional Engineer of the local depot explaining where I was and why I was there and how much I wanted a job as labourer in a Post Office outside gang. In less than a week I had a reply asking me to attend his office for an interview. Then the long wait. As day followed day with no letter my hopes began to fade. It was expecting too much that in a city with so much unemployment I should get a Post Office job. And then on the mantlepiece, propped behind the clock, a Post Office letter. 'We can offer you employment . . . '

Lancaster

John McNamara

When you was out of work you drew the dole. And, irrespective of how many years you'd worked, you only drew this benefit for so many weeks and then you was automatically cut off. Your next thing to try and raise some money was Means Test. If you were lucky you'd get a piece of paper which would entitle you to get groceries to the tune of whatever they allocated you. But you wasn't always lucky. When you were trying to get this piece of paper, the chappie would come round from the office, wherever it was manipulated from, and come into your home. You might have a gramophone or something like that. He'd say, 'That's a luxury, that. You could do without it. Is furniture paid for? Is this?' And they went thoroughly and embarrassingly right into the whole business. It was so sickening that a lot of people wouldn't suffer it. They'd rather be hungry.

There was me Mam, and meself, and an older brother. He was a half brother actually. He was out of work. My mother didn't go to work. She was too old. I was working. But the top money was £2 and you could be twenty–odd and still not getting it. I wasn't getting much more than my 17/9 what I started work at. Happen getting a pound and coppers. My brother applied for this Means Test and didn't get it. I was supposed to keep the three of us off that pound and something. The rent had to be paid. The coal, the light, the food.

My brother was in and out of work. He did mostly navvying. Happen they'd be running a water pipeline somewhere in the district. He'd get a job there. But when it come to an end he went on the dole. He might get another job before his dole terminated. Or he might not. When his dole ran out I'd have to support him again. There was always a job for a youngster because he was on low money. So I was fortunate in one way—being young.

Clogs was worn a lot. They had iron hoops on. Lancaster police force had a troop got up as nigger minstrels and they used to give concerts. The money went into what they called a clog fund. If you went to the police in charge of this and they thought you merited a pair for your kid, you could have a pair. There was free dinners for those very poor, but you had to pocket your pride and go and ask for them. You wasn't always successful. And talking of pride, although everybody was more or less in the same category, they'd sharpen their knife on the back step, where I sharpen mine of a Sunday now. They'd sharpen the knife and go through the motions so the neighbours round about could hear. They'd say, 'Mrs. So–and–so's got a joint this week. I heard the old man sharpening the knife.' They hadn't.

I worked in a factory that made floor and wall coverings. I was on inspection, and every piece I passed had my personal mark on it. If something come back from a customer that was wrong, 'You'd better get down road for 3 days.' What they called furlough. Just send you home, penalising you. So there's half your wage gone. They might send you home for a whole week. That was how they punished you for not being observant enough. It wasn't difficult to miss any of these faults because there was only ordinary bulb lighting, and the windows. Winter evenings when the dusk was coming in, the light was treacherous, and when the sun came glancing in at different angles. You was stretching yourself up and down to get the best angle. And the stuff was coming up at you all the time, fast. There could be creases, or they could have missed varnishing. There was lots of faults that could happen during the process before it got to the finished article.

You didn't get increases in your wages automatically. You had to go and ask for them. Happen you'd have to wait about eighteen month or a couple of years before you got a couple of coppers extra on top of your starting wage. And your shop foreman was the be–all and end–all of everything. If he said no it was no. And the one as I had said no in no uncertain manner. 'Get your bloody sel' out or I'll kick your arse!' He ruled the roost. He was the big cheese. But it wasn't his money. If it was of no benefit to him, why should he hold it back? Probably he was on a bonus at the end of the year. I can't think of nothing else. There's no pleasure in keeping money off people if they're entitled to it. It might be many and many a week before you could pluck up enough courage to go and ask again. And even then you might not be successful. 'Get out!' Scared the life out of you. Big ex–rugby player. Even grown men, married men, still not getting the rate for the job.

I had to tell a lie to get my first raise. Your money was given to you Friday night and you always had to say 'Thank you' when you got it. Even though you'd worked for it. Your money was a ten shilling note, and your silver and copper was wrapped up into that like a little parcel. I knew of some lads that used to keep a tanner out or something like that. And that gave me a brainwave. I told the boss next time I went in, 'My mother thinks I'm keeping some money out before I go home, it's that little and I've been here so long.' And that's how I got my first increase. That was another ninepence or tenpence. A long time went on before I got another.

It was no wonder that Lord Ashton was wealthy. 9½ million he left in 1930s. Ryelands House was his place. It was one mass of trees and bushes. He was secluded behind there. There was another estate across the road called Oaklands. He bought that (only for one reason, never occupied it) because it overlooked his place. I worked at both places that belonged to Lord Ashton. St George's works, and Lune Mills down at the end of the quay. There was never any attempt to get a union going. They wouldn't dare because they'd be through that gate—their feet wouldn't touch the floor. And you daren't talk about politics. I could be living next door to you and you didn't know how I voted. You didn't talk about it in case it got back to the factory. He used to employ people to go round pubs listening in to people's conversations. If you was heard to express any views that he didn't agree with you'd get sack. Somebody might say to you, 'Who did you vote for this time?' 'Now don't talk so bloody daft. Don't talk politics to me. Do you want me to lose me job?'

You started at quarter to eight. And that door into them works was closed at quarter to eight. I've been half way across road to the gate, and he's looked out, shut the door and gone in. About turn and come home. He wasn't a villain. It was his job. He daren't do anything else. We never frowned on him for doing it. We knew he was only doing as he was told. He was only a paid servant same as us. But it was a bit of a body blow. To lose one day's pay.

I had an accident. There were two of us lifting this thing and he dropped his end. I split my finger down to the bone. It was a real mess. This were on the top floor of a five storey building. I ran like Hamlet down all the stone steps, across the yard to the ambulance room. He wrapped a lot of bandage round it and said, 'Get yourself to the infirmary with it.' It was winter. There was a lot of ice and I was sliding and slipping all over the place. I was scared stiff of falling with it. It must've been a couple of mile to the infirmary. When I got there they stitched it and dressed it. One stitch must have taken badly so I had poisoning, a lump under the arm and that. If you'd have been off there'd have been no money, not a halfpenny, even though you'd done that accident there. So the only time you didn't go to work was when your legs wouldn't carry you. But I could go to work. My right hand's bandaged but the other's free. I'd to go to infirmary at least two or three mornings a week. Eventually they said, 'It's not knitting together as it should do. We'll stop unbandaging it. We'll let it stew in its own juice.' So they left it for about a week with the same old bandage and from then onward it started knitting together.

In the process of making these materials, the worst part was working in the hanging rooms, carrying the pieces while they were still wet, and being overcome with fumes. It used to make them drunk so they'd be staggering about. They were no good for work then, so their mates used to carry them out and dump them in the fresh air outside the door of the building while they come round. Some of them used to pass out. This is the effect of the varnish that gives the shine to the pieces. The heat and the fumes used to make your nose run and your eyes smart. They'd no protective clothing. You hadn't a mask to wear or anything like that. Come dinner time they'd get their Woodbine out and their can of tea, and that would be their dinner. Didn't want their sandwiches—throw them to the seagulls. I think we'd the best fed seagulls there was round here. Same applied at tea time. They'd be full of fumes—belching. Couldn't face any tea at all. Have to be home three or four hours—sitting on the doorstep in the fresh air. Get to supper time and maybe they'd have a bit of something then, when the fumes had more or less come off their system.

You had to do it because there was always so many people waiting to get your job. There were queues outside the factory every morning, waiting to see if someone had got sack or passed away or anything. And this was the gun that the boss held at your head. There'd be people waiting all the time. All year round. I've seen them huddled down there when it's been snowing and sleeting, coat collar up, hoping that he'd say, 'Just one.' But most of the time he wouldn't want anybody so he'd come out and wave his arms and they'd all trundle off, dejected and cold. No money in their pocket. Fed up. And when you was in work, come Easter, you was out for about a week. No pay. You didn't get paid for holidays. You used to dread it. Then there was short time. You'd work three and sign on three. But you was about a fortnight before you'd get pay off the dole. And the first three days wouldn't count.

We was allowed a half hundredweight of the cheapest floor covering. That was *Lancastrian*. It had a tarred felt–paper base. It was mostly sold abroad in hot countries. The termites won't eat it. It cost 7/6. It would do a floor of a room. But you used to have to be very careful with it because it was only on paper and you was only allowed one lot. On a flag floor, which is very uneven, long before the twelve month was up it was ruined. You was ready for another one.

If you wanted to talk to your mate you waited while your boss was out of earshot. Didn't leave your machine and go and talk. There was one process where you was working in very close proximity to each other. But by God, you start talking? The boss: 'Oy! Too much talking. Let's have a bit more work. Drop it!' There was no ten minute breaks in the morning or afternoon. You daren't take your nose up off your job, never mind tea breaks. If you've had no breakfast and you've taken a slice of jam or something like that, you'd have it down by your machine and wait till boss was out of sight. If he was watching you'd keep your mouth shut. That's how you was, pinching at a slice of bread. You'd sneak it. If he saw you he'd send you home. 'You're not paid to eat food.' Your food and your teacan was left in cookhouse on table. You say, 'Well I'll sit here,' and that's where you'll sit for the rest of your working days. 'Oh, Bobby sits there.' 'Oh, Jimmy sits there.' You put your basket down in the morning when you go into your work and you come out at dinnertime and that's where it is.

On a day off you might say, 'Let's have a walk to Hest Bank.' Or you'd happen walk to Morecambe. You're at the seaside. You'd go scrounging for wood off the tide line when the tide had gone back. Or you'd happen go for a walk in the country. If it was the right time of year you'd go blackberrying. But wherever you wanted to go it was your feet. You hadn't a bike or anything like that. In some cases the whole family went. Mum and dad and kiddies. And happen some neighbours would be going with their kiddies so you'd make a little group. You'd cut a cricket bat out of a piece of wood and shape it so there was a handle to it, and make a ball out of rag. Find three sticks on the tide line and stick them up in the sand for wickets. Nothing that cost anything. You had to improvise everything. You'd take cold tea in a screw–top bottle and make some jam butties up and that would be it. Happen lucky, buy a couple of ounces of corned beef. That would be a luxury. You'd probably walk the road way to Hest Bank—about 5 mile. And you'd happen come back the canal way as a variation. Some people round where I lived used to go down to Morecambe and get winkles and cockles, mussels and crabs. They used to walk to Morecambe with a sack, get whatever they could, and walk back. They'd boil them, and then they'd have a basket on the corner on the pavement. There was always a pink sheet of pins. They'd give you a pin when you bought your penn'orth of winkles. It was something to supplement whatever they were getting. It wasn't a living.

We might pass a day collecting samphire—a sort of seaweed. We'd walk down. Fresh air. Exercise. Away from the streets. And pick samphires or whatever was in season. You'd to be careful not to be cut off by the tide. You'd bring it back, buy a pennorth of vinegar and pickle it. You'd got your pickles just for the price of the vinegar. We was always looking for something that nature provided that we could bring in to supplement the larder. Same as hazelnuts. We'd put them to one side for Christmas. (At Christmas the kiddies didn't have toys. They'd hang up a stocking. They'd get, happen a russet apple and a tangerine if they were lucky, and some hazelnuts and maybe a silver threepenny bit wrapped up.) Mushroom time, you'd get up early Sunday morning, get a few mushrooms and get back in time for breakfast. They helped to fill the plate.

Lancaster market used to be open till nine Saturday night, and whatever beef and pork and sausages they had to sell, they had to get rid of. They couldn't put it away over the weekend because there was no refrigeration, so it would go bad on them in the shop, especially in summer months. So by the time they was ready for finishing, the stuff was right down to rock bottom in price. My mother along with a lot more married ladies knew this. That was the time they used to go to try and get a bit of meat for Sunday. They'd wait till last minute. The butcher would practically throw it at them for next to nothing. The fruiterers never threw fruit away. If they'd gone bad, the bad part was cut out. What they called damaged fruit. There was nothing wrong with it but middle class people and the upper crust, they wouldn't think of buying them. But to us it was a godsend. For twopence you could get a handful of damaged apples or oranges. It was still fruit. The only time you would see a chicken would be Christmas. But it had taken twelve month to get that chicken. Mam would find a penny from somewhere to put in the butcher's shop and by the time the year end come she might have five bob in. Every shop had its Christmas club advertised in the window.

A man would polish up the clothes he worked in for the weekend. Probably put a clean scarf on. Polish his clogs a bit. Then he'd be dressed up. But his clothes still smelled of his occupation. If he had an extra waistcoat or anything, that used to be pawned on a Monday morning and then redeemed again at Friday evening as soon as he come home with his wage. Take enough out and run like hell to pawnshop. You'd want it for weekend to go out in. The pawnshops was thriving. Queues a mile long on a Monday morning pledging. Queues a mile long on a Friday evening redeeming them out again. A watch. Or a wedding ring. Just to buy food. Happen get about five shilling on it.

Getting stuff from the local shop on credit, that was particularly popular. That credit book for food was called a strap. 'Go and get it on strap.' They'd book it down and at weekend, say you owned ten bob, you'd happen give five bob off it. Nearly everybody had a credit book. You'd happen be lucky and pay it all off, but the minute you paid it off Friday night you got another load back on to be paid the following Friday. And through the week, 'Go and get a tin of milk,' 'I'll have a quarter of potatoes,' and so on, and that book was full again.

We used to make our own peg rugs. We used to get sacking and old rags. We cut the rags up into narrow strips. A pile of red here. A pile of blue. Some green. And you worked a pattern out. You poked one end of your rag through with a wooden peg, and then the other end, and left the two tufts sticking up. That used to pass winter time. All the lot of you had a do. Some of you cutting strips. Some pegging them in. Mum, dad, the kids. Near the doorway where you came in straight out of the dirty streets we'd have an old potato sack. You'd wipe your feet on that rather than paddle water into the house. You'd ask the potato man that came round the streets hawking veg to save you a sack. You'd wash it and split it. My mum used to make aprons out of them. She'd get some strong calico material off an old nightdress or something. She'd cut a strip and sew it along the top to tie it with. That would keep front dry, especially on washing day. Used to wash the clothes on the washboard. Either a bar of carbolic or a bar of Lifebuoy solid soap. The dolly legs did the job of what a washing machine agitator does today. They worked that to and fro to swish the clothes round in the tub. And then mangle them.

A woman had a full time job in the home in those days. It was the broom and the shovel to sweep the house. It was the blacklead brush to polish the grate. It was the scrubbing brush and a bucket and a floor cloth and a bar of soap to wash the floors and the tables and the paintwork. And all the paraphernalia to do the weekly washing. Washing day was on a Monday. Baking day was Wednesday. There was a day for everything. You never saw no washing out on a Sunday though. Not on the Sabbath. You may not go to church, but that was respected.

When you come home on a Monday night you'd have something that was left over from Sunday. Fried up. Bubble and squeak. They'd wangle it on a Sunday to try to save something for Monday evening. It was a common thing for a housewife, a mother, to do a hell of a lot of sacrificing. Unknownst to hubby. Unknownst to kiddies. It was nothing for them to say, 'Oh, I've had mine.' And they haven't had a bite. But you didn't find out till it was too late. A good mother went without many a meal. Kids come first. And husband. She was last although she worked harder than anybody. But she always thought it was her place to feed them first.

There was no back way to our house. When the bin men used to come round with the horse and cart they carted the bin through the house. If my mum knew they were coming she'd leave the floor till they'd been. Then she only had to do it once. There was no bathroom. No hot water. You'd to boil every drop. For a wash. For a shave. Cold water tap in the kitchen. There were eight or nine houses all with one common back and two toilets between the lot. The ladies took their turns in keeping it clean. 'It's so–and–so's turn to do it out this week,' and so on. And the coal cellar was in the house. You got plenty of lending and borrowing. If a woman was having a child you'd find somebody dashing in. 'Can I get you anything, Love? I'm going in town.' Or they might come in with a bowl of soup, or a bowl of oatmeal gruel, or happen a nice little milk pudding. And 'Do you want your napkins washing?' If you had a bereavement, they have to be washed and laid out, so one of the neighbours would come in and say, 'It's alright, Mrs Mac, I'll do it for you, Love. Go downstairs and get yourself a cup of tea.' One of our neighbours was Tom Seyers. He worked at the local slaughterhouse. He was a big, massive, red–faced man. They say he could fell a bull with his fist, and he was known to drink blood from the animals as he was slaughtering them. There was an old Irish lady called Annie Trowell. And she had an old clay pipe and part of the stem was broken off. Bowl was nearly up agin her nose. Grand old lady. After we moved out of Bridge Lane we got a Corporation house. The neighbours on the council estate more or less kept themselves to themselves.

Before I got married I was in the Lancaster Harriers. The only hobby I had was the running. But I was talked out of it by the wife's dad. I was courting at the time and he says, 'You're a fool. You're damaging your heart—running like that.' I wasn't glad. I used to like running. Curry's had a branch in Lancaster and you could buy a bike for a shilling a week. A bike were about thirty odd shilling. So I got a bike. I used to ride at night. I only had it for about two year. The crossbar had a flaw in it and the bike collapsed. I took it back but I never got another for it. Before I was married there used to be six or seven of us who mated about on the corner of the street in the evenings, yarning and talking about football and various things. Saturday night was the high night of the week. We'd go to Winter Gardens—dancing. During interval, go and watch the show on stage as well. It was a good six pennyworth.

The first job my wife had after she left school was in a fish and chip shop. Then she went into service for Rev. Baxter. Then he got a living in Derby. Her mother and father needed what few coppers she was earning, so she didn't go. She worked at Sunderland Point at a farm that took visitors in during summer months. The bus only took you as far as Overton. The rest she had to walk, across the marshes. You had to keep your eye on the local paper for the tides otherwise you'd get washed away. So she'd to race across there in winter. On her own. She left there and went in to Lansil's factory. It was nothing to go shares when you was courting. You'd happen go to the pictures once a week. It was strict. Her father said she had to be in by nine. You finished work at half past five, have a bit of tea, wash yourself, comb your hair, and go for a walk.

We got married in December. Her father had died by then, at the age of 43 of a heart disease. We'd saved a few shillings. It didn't cost our parents on either side a penny. We paid our own wedding arrangements: the flowers; the buttonholes; the bouquets; the reception at the hotel; the sandwiches and the tea and what have you. Nothing elaborate. Just a plain meal. My wife bought the material and someone made the dress for her. We bought the ingredients for the cake and someone made it. My first wedding present was my cards on Friday night from Lune Mills. I was out of work that following morning. I'd been working on inlaid linoleum. There was two twelve–hour shifts. Then suddenly, without any warning—chopped in half. I was one of the unfortunate ones.

Voices

Family Life

My father sat brooding over a dying fire. I doubt he moved all day. The final straw came one miserable Christmas when we hit rock bottom. My mother finally cracked and went for my father with the bread knife.

* * *

My mother had an old leather purse, and when I went shopping for food with her, she would squeeze it in her hands until it squeaked like something in pain.

* * *

My father lived in one of his father's houses, and during the strike I remember my grandfather saying, 'Sam, you will pay your rent as long as you can and after that I will take so much a week out of your pay when you start work again.'

* * *

The material shortcomings of our lives were not so heartbreaking to us kids as the psychological anxieties and tensions we would endure when tempers between mam and dad were strained. We were sitting at home one stormy night when mam had just completed redecorating our living room with rolls of tuppeny wallpaper, when in comes my father with two potato sacks full of coal he had carried down the mountain, after hacking it out of the bowels of the hillside. He humps them into the coalhouse soaked to the skin. He asks Mam for a cup of tea. Back comes the apology: 'There's no sugar, Frank.' He must have lost control for a moment which resulted in him taking one of the black soaking coal sacks and slashing it against the newly decorated wall.

* * *

My father was a bad-tempered sod. And of course he used to thump us. He used to say, 'You've got to be cruel to be kind'. He used to have a stick and he used to rap your ankles. The girls were afraid to go out. 'Where have you been?' 'Who have you been with?' I suppose he knew so much of the world, having done it all himself, that he knew what it was all about. He used to thrash my sisters, and he led my eldest sister a dog's life, poor girl. He terrorised us actually.

I was terrified of him. He was typical of a cruel Victorian father. My elder brothers were scared of him until they were well into grown manhood. I've laid in bed and trembled at the rows going on downstairs. Eventually my mother left him and he moved in with his sister. And he was just as bad with her. He didn't speak to her half the time. He was a bad old bugger without a doubt.

* * *

My mam woke Dad up in the night because she'd started labour. She said, 'Frank, you'd better get up and fetch the doctor. I think my time's come.' He just said, 'Aw, put it off till morning.' And went back to sleep. The neighbour who helped with the delivery said to Dad, 'You've got twins. What are you going to call them?' He said, 'Call the strongest after me. Call t'other owt you like.'

* * *

My mother seemed to think my father was not trying to get work and always seemed to be in a bad temper. Then there was a row to end rows and my father said he would not come back to the house.

* * *

My mother was the mainstay of the family. She made the decisions. My father just sat. He was a strange man, like lots of other men in those days. I never got near my father. He never even came to our weddings. He never had a drink of tea in my home. My own children remember him as the man who sat behind the newspaper. He was a very selfish man. Selfish in infantile, childish sort of ways. If there was three scones, he'd want the biggest. If there was two pieces of tart, he'd want the biggest piece of tart. He'd sit at the table with his knife and fork before the meal was even prepared. He'd pick the newspaper up at night and if he hadn't read it it would go in his pocket. Nobody would get that newspaper till he'd read it. There was two newspapers on a Sunday. He would read one, and sit on one. There's no doubt about it that men in that generation were the kingpin of the house. Other people cleaned their shoes. They had a special seat. Nobody dared sit in their seat. My wife's father, nobody dared pass him in case their shadow went on his paper. They were tyrants really in their own way. We were nulled. Afraid. There's more to it than just being afraid. We were humbled. Cowed. We were nulled because of circumstances. Because of life.

* * *

There was one toilet and one washhouse in a yard shared between 4 homes. There were constant quarrels over this. Shouting, cursing, quarrelling, were a part of each day. There was a great deal of violence. Mostly wife beating. The man next door to us had two daughters and a son. He used to belt all his family with a strap. Some people were ready to sieze or grab anything that was to be had irrespective of whether they needed it or not. My father used to say: 'There's one thing the Depression years have done: robbed people of their dignity'.

* * *

It were damned hard money earned, but it were a damn sight harder for a woman to lay it out. I'd got a wonderful manager—the wife. She were one of the best. She had a treadle Singer sewing machine. That was the only thing we ever had on HP, but it were earning its keep as it went along. Somebody would give her an old jacket and she'd cut that down and make the boys a pair of trousers. She hadn't many more months to pay and she were hard up on a Friday night. She'd got about a hundred pounds of blackberries and I biked with them to sell them up at Rushdon to get half a crown so she could pay the sewing machine man.

* * *

I was so used to cutting down dresses for my little girl. One day I told her she'd have to stop off school because she had no shoes to wear. She said, 'Can't you make me a pair out of yours?'

* * *

'Dad's a bit late tonight,' said Mum. 'He's usually home before this time. Never mind you lot, get on with your tea.' Charlie and I didn't waste any time. We'd started eating before Mum stopped speaking. We always had savoury ducks for tea on a Friday. We got them hot from the butcher's round the corner. 'Don't be so selfish,' said Mum. 'Look after Little 'Un and cut up her food for her.' I stopped eating for a moment and reached over to Little 'Un's plate. She smiled as I chopped up the food for her. She started picking up the pieces of meat while I was still cutting. Just then Dad came in. We all looked up and shouted: 'Friday! Friday!' We did this because he always brought us some sweets or chocolate on pay night. 'What did you get for us this time, Daddy?' shouted Charlie. 'This time Daddy,' echoed Little 'Un. Dad didn't answer. He sat down suddenly and looked at Mum. Just stared at her. He hadn't taken his jacket off. He always did that before sitting down at the table. He didn't have an evening paper. Charlie and Little 'Un kept on eating but Mum and I watched Dad. He handed his pay packet to Mum and said, 'That's the last.' 'The last?' 'The bloody last!' 'Oh no, Dad.' Mum looked frightened. Dad looked round at us kids. I felt scared. 'Eat your tea, Boy,' he said gently. 'Get it down you while it's hot.' I nodded and put some food in my mouth. 'You'll be all right, Dad,' Mum said. 'You're a skilled tradesman. You can always get a job.' 'Not a chance. There's blokes as good as me been lining up at the dole for years.' '*I'll* get work somewhere,' said Mum. 'There's piece–work at the shoe factory.' 'They won't take married women. You know that.' 'Yes, but I've worked there before and charge hands know that I'm a good machinist. They'll help me get back.' 'You're dreaming,' Dad said. Mum was crying a little now. 'Bloody hell, don't start,' shouted Dad. 'That's all I need.' She stopped crying, dried her face, and looked at him defiantly. 'All right,' she said, 'take your jacket off and your boots, put your slippers on. Go on, while I get your tea.' She rushed around getting his meal, and slamming it down in front of him, said, 'First things first. Eat— then we'll decide what to do.' Dad looked a bit surprised but he did as she had said. He looked at me and winked, and I suddenly felt hungry again. Mum took the pay packet and started to count out the money. She put all the coins in little heaps and laid the 2 pound notes at the back. 'There'll be them that won't get what's owed,' she said. 'This will go on rent and food. Nothing else.' 'What about coal and the 'lectric?' I asked. 'Only food and rent,' she said. 'You can find wood for the fire in a dozen places and when the light goes out we'll got to bed.' 'Will Dad have to go and sign on at the dole?' I asked. My question made Dad sit up suddenly. 'Not bloody likely,' he shouted. 'No, not me. Bugger 'em! Bugger the bloody lot of 'em! They won't get me begging down at the Labour.' 'Dad, don't swear like that in front of the children.' Mum picked up Little 'Un, who had started to cry. Dad seemed to realise that he'd been shouting and he took Little 'Un from Mum and cuddled her. 'I'll work for myself. I can make anything in wood, you know that. People are still buying things. It's just a question of finding out what they want and then making it for them.' 'But where will you work?' 'I'll rent a shed or something. Maybe an empty shop. Anywhere with a bit of space and some light. There's plenty of places with cheap rents. I'll find what I want, don't you worry.' Mum looked worried though. 'You need money to rent a workshop. And money to buy the wood.' 'I'll find it,' said Dad. He looked sure of himself and I believed him. Charlie stopped eating. 'Did you bring us any chocolate, Daddy?' 'Chocolate, Daddy,' echoed Little 'Un. Dad looked hard at the two younger ones. He smiled and then he started to laugh. So did Mum. And then I started laughing too. Charlie and Little 'Un stared for a moment and then they began laughing just because we were laughing.

* * *

NOTHING OVER SIXPENCE. The people grabbed the merchandise, piece by piece, inspected it, laid it down and picked up something else. It seemed as if they found satisfaction in holding in their hands, if only for a moment, each item which took their fancy. Most of them were smiling, chattering, and shouting to one another as they were swept along. Saturday night out shopping with dad and my brother was always fun even though it meant being crushed and trampled. Dad shouted, 'Move over that way towards the hardware, I need some cleats for my boots.' Dad picked up what he wanted from the shoe repair counter, paid the girl, and we were on our way. 'Go out through the side door,' said dad. 'I want to go to the market.' The cold air outside was a welcome change from the heat and smell of people in Woolies, and my greatcoat (a man's coat several sizes too big) was snug and warm. Although it was about 8 o'clock, men with carts and barrows were still bringing fruit and vegetables to the market stalls. 'Mind yer backs—Mind yer backs!' They pushed and pulled their way through the crowds, trying to get their carts from the road to the stalls. The tram bells rang continually. The drivers up on the front platforms shouted at those foolish enough to walk between the tracks. 'Get off you stupid bugger. Ain't the road enough for yer?' The crowd laughed as the offenders got clear. All the shops along the street across from the market were brightly lit with gas or electric lights but the market was darker. Each stall had its own naphtha flare which lit the counters but little else. The flares always frightened me because they roared and hissed and changed colour all the time. They were sometimes so close to the green canvas covering the stalls that I feared a fire would be started and the whole market would go up in flames. But somehow it never happened and the stall keepers went right on shouting and selling. 'Lovely kippers, lovely Yarmouth crabs. Fresh and tasty!' Many of the stall holders wore fingerless woollen gloves. I wondered if their wives cut the fingers off complete gloves or whether they stopped knitting when they reached the fingers. The noise of the shouting stallholders, the hiss of the naphtha flares and the general din from the shoppers seemed to fit in with the colour of the stalls and the smell from fish, poultry, vegetables, and meat. As we pushed along dad bought cabbages and sprouts at one stall, red beet at another. We stopped at the fish and chip wagon for a penny bag of chips each for my brother and me. The smell of grease and vinegar seemed to fill my nose and made my eyes water. The cockle and mussel stall attracted dad, where he ate three little dishes of cockles before my brother and I had finished our chips. The stall was covered with dishes of shell fish and some of them, particularly the whelks, looked revolting to me. Dad took his watch from his waist–coat pocket and snapped open the silver cover by pressing a button at the side of the winder. 'Nearly 9,' he said. 'Let's get over to Sainsbury's.' He shoved the watch back into his waistcoat, and buttoned up his jacket and coat. We moved across the road from the market to the doors of the grocery store. Assistants were rushing around inside tidying up and trying to get everything in order for Monday morning. Most of the customers were gone but one or two lingered picking up the last of their purchases. 'Now,' said Dad, 'go to that man with the wavy hair at the far end.' I went into the shop and walked towards the assistant. The man looked at me, staring at my greatcoat. 'Half a pound of the cheapest bacon,' I said. 'Right, Son,' he said. He didn't weigh it but from the weight when he passed it over the counter I knew there was about 2 pounds. 'And do you have any cracked eggs?' I asked. He nodded and smiled. I saw that most of the eggs he put in the paper bag were not cracked. As he gave me my change he said, 'I've just charged for the half of bacon. It's the poor that helps the poor.' I thanked him and left as they were turning out the lights and putting up the wooden shutters in front of the windows.

* * *

My father used to spread newspapers on the table. After meals we often heard him say, 'Don't take the table cloth, I haven't read it yet.'

Looking for work and signing on

We used to sign on every 3 days but the queues were so long that signing-on days were reduced to one. Every entrance was guarded by 2 policemen, and every grille around the counters was covered by brown paper. The only contact we had with the clerk was to look through a small slot and say, 'No work'. Then we signed the book he pushed under the grille. A prominent businessman stated that most of the unemployed should be put aboard ship, taken out to sea and the captain given orders to pull the plug out. How the captain was going to get back he didn't say. For nearly five months I remained unemployed, then I received a letter telling me to report to Poor

Law Offices for a Means Test. Three poorly dressed men and two women were seated on a wooden bench in a passage facing the Means Test door. One by one they went in, each one reappearing with a worried and distressed look upon their face. One man turned to me at the door and shouted, 'They're a bright lot of bastards in there. They'll give you nothing.' I was called and entered the room. Facing me was a horseshoe table with nine men sat around it. The clerk placed a chair for me to sit on facing the tribunal. The chairman said, 'You have been unemployed so long it has been decided that your unemployment money will be reduced by two shillings from next week.' The clerk came forward to take my chair away. The interview was at an end. On a Friday in late September I arrived home with my dole to find my mother–in–law helping my wife to pack her suitcases. At the station my wife wished me a fond farewell and whispered, 'We'll be back together again as soon as you get a job.'

* * *

They asked me where I'd applied for work about 4 weeks previously on the Monday. I couldn't remember that far back but I knew I always tried the steelworks on Mondays so I said, 'The steelworks.' So he said, 'That was a Bank Holiday and the steelworks was closed so you couldn't have tried there.' And my benefit was disallowed for dishonesty. They were always tricking people like that. I knew a plumber whose claim was disallowed because he said he'd tried all the places that employed plumbers and they said he wasn't seeking *any* kind of work. Another man said he would accept any work that was offered and he got into trouble because they said he had to seek genuinely insurable employment. And a friend of mine was asked if he was 'Wholly or mainly supported by his parents'. He thought to himself, 'Well, it's not wholly so it must be mainly', and they disallowed his benefit on the grounds that he was mainly supported by his parents.

* * *

I cycled 150 miles from South Wales and went straight to the Employment Office to seek work. The clerk looked at me and he said, 'Another bloody Welshman come for his holidays.'

* * *

One man got work clearing snow for the council. So as not to lose his dole he gave a false name. When the time came for him to step up to the window for his pay he couldn't remember what name he'd given. Men would fight each other for work. With fists, shovels, knives. The losers would sit and cry. The victors' hands would be so soft from years of unemployment that they'd blister and their tool handles would be stained with blood. The man next door to us got a labouring job with the condition that he brought his own hod. He belted his boys till they broke in somewhere and stole one for him.

* * *

I used to wait outside the same bakery every morning with a crowd of other blokes hoping someone would get the sack or would be too ill to crawl into work. One morning there was an accident at the top of my road. My mate who was a roundsman for the bakery was lying in a pool of blood. I didn't know whether to run home to tell his wife or run on and get his job. So I run on.

* * *

My husband didn't work for 4 years. One of my brothers didn't work for 10. Another brother came out of the army and had to sign on. He was asked many questions which he answered in a civil manner until the clerk said, 'Haven't you forgot something?' Syd said, 'What?' 'You should address me as Sir.' My brother reached over the wire that separated them and grabbed the clerk by the collar and tie. He lifted him out of his seat and said, 'I've been sirring things like you for years and I'm not doing it any more. Keep your dole.' The only place he could work was at Clifton pit which was a small village off the beaten track. He walked twelve miles there and twelve miles back. I was sixteen and my mother was getting on in years. She was forty–five when I was born. She was too tired to wait up for Sydney when he was on late shift so that was my job. He had walked to work, put in eight hours' hard graft in a seam twelve inches high, and then had the long walk home. I used to sit prodding his arm while he ate his meal. All the pit muck had to come off in the bath in front of the fire before he could go to bed. First he would wash his head and torso. I cleared the table while he washed his personal parts. Then he would sit on the fender stool and put his feet in the bath. Many a time he's fell asleep like that. But the climax came one night when he just broke down and cried. This was a man who had medals for bravery in India. He was the champion boxer in his regiment and rather than draw dole he was working harder than a cart horse. He was taken out of that pit by the police and sent straight to China because he was on the army reserve.

* * *

My Dad and all the men called him 'Jango'. It was a nickname they had given him in his regiment during the first world war. Now everyone called him Jango, not only the men around our way who had been in the Artillery together but almost everyone who knew him. At school we called his eldest son 'Young Jango' and never thought about it. Jango himself was unemployed—one of those who lined up at the Labour to get his weekly benefit. But I never saw him unemployed. He was always working when I saw him. He seemed to be able to take on almost any job. Dad told me that Jango went out into the country to work on the farms doing casual labour. Ditch digging mostly. Some days he walked as much as twelve miles to work and that meant twelve miles back again after a day of hard labour with only a couple of sandwiches for his mid–day meal. I expect that he would have a swede or turnip from the fields too. In the evenings he sat in the kitchen of his council house with the door open. We could see and hear him there, mending boots while we played around the back garden. He sat hunched on an old chair with no back, a row of small nails sticking out of his mouth from under his bushy moustache. The iron last, on which he held the boots, was clutched between his knees and was wedged into a piece of wooden post which transmitted the force of his blows on the boots down to the concrete floor. He always smiled and spoke to everyone who looked in. 'Hello, my boy. How's your dad?' or something like that. The nails were driven into the leather, not with a hammer, but by the edge of a great flat file. He spat the little nails from his mouth down onto the leather and then pushed them with his huge dirty fingers into the sole. Then down came the great file, never missing, forcing each nail at one clout right into the boot.

You could get vegetables at Jango's back door. He produced potatoes and cabbages from his garden earlier and better than nearly anyone around our way. And they were cheaper than the shop too.

In 1930 when things were not so good and Jango was finding it hard to keep his wife and five kids, he decided to enlist in the navy. Jango had to appear before a local panel of officials. They asked him many questions to test his knowledge. When he thought the examination about finished one of them said, 'Take off your clothes.' 'I didn't know this was a medical exam,' said Jango. 'Get your clothes off quickly,' said the official. I heard Jango tell my dad later, 'I'm sure the bastard wanted to see me stripped just to please himself.' Jango walked out and left the navy to recruit somebody else.

Some days we had rabbit for dinner which Jango sent over in

return for all the washing which Mum had done for the Jango family. This happened whenever Mrs Jango had an addition to the family. I liked rabbit. Mum certainly knew how to cook it. My brother and I would pull out the spade bones from the legs and use them to scoop up the gravy.

When Josh Taylor, who had come back from the war without his legs, wanted to improve his income, Jango and dad made him a little cart. The cart was for carrying sweets and toffee apples which Josh was to sell around the streets. Jango made the axle, the springs, and set the wheels to the frame. Dad did all the carpentry. The cart was connected by a pivot bar to Josh's invalid chair. Each morning Josh's wife filled the little mobile shop with the confectionary she had made the previous evening. Josh would go off in his chair turning the handles which drove the road wheels. Behind came the loaded cart and behind that came any kids who had halfpennies. On Saturday evenings the cart finished its round at the pub and any sweets left were bought by the dads and mums to give to the kids on Sunday morning. Josh always bought a pint for Jango and dad then out of his earnings.

* * *

There was a joke at that time about a man drowning in a canal. A passerby asks where the man works. He leaves him to drown and runs to the workplace. He tells the gaffer that one of his men has drowned and asks if he can have the job. The gaffer says, 'Nay, Lad. The man who pushed him in has got it.'

The Means Test

The Means Test bloke arrived complete with van and men to take the best of the furniture. How I hated him with his smart clothes and the smirk on his face, twirling his stick of chalk in his fingers. I watched as he walked over to two large brass lions standing either side of the hearth, telling my mother they had to go. It didn't matter to him they had belonged to her grandmother long since dead. The poor weren't allowed sentiment. We hadn't much before he got cracking with his chalk. We'd got a damn sight less when he'd finished.

* * *

You were only left with the bare essentials. I bet, today, in some upper class homes, there are thousands of pounds' worth of valuable goods stolen by the Means Test men from the poor in the thirties. And yet if we were caught poaching for a rabbit it meant thirty days inside. It was no excuse that your belly was empty or your kids were dying for the want of nourishment. Mother was given thirty bob to feed herself and five kids. We were left with four chairs, a table, a couple of benches and a couple of beds. I remember thinking, 'Good job we've got no rugs on the floor 'cos they'd have took them as well.'

* * *

Down the road was an old lady everyone called Old Hannah. She used to invite the half–starved kids into her room on cold winter mornings and give them a cup of soup and a piece of bread. She didn't have much furniture but she had a lovely piano. It was always polished. On top stood photos of her husband and children. They were all dead. Old Hannah was told she would have to sell her piano before she could claim money for food. But she wouldn't part with it. She committed suicide instead.

Charity

Over the door was a sign saying *Poor Law Institution*. My mum called it 'The Workhouse', and so did most people round our way. I went inside into the big cold hallway which was dimly lit by a flickering gas lamp. My boots clumped on the bare pine floorboards but no–one seemed to have heard me come in, for nobody appeared through the door in the little glass office. 'What do you want, Boy?' I was surprised by the arrival of a man in the grey poor law uniform. He must have come in behind me from the street. 'I've brought some clean laundry for my granny,' I said. 'You can't go in,' said the man. 'Leave it there. I'll get it sent up.' 'But I thought you wouldn't mind if I went in to see my granny, just for a little while.' 'Children aren't allowed in. It's the rules,' said the officer. He walked off into the office. I lifted myself onto the wooden bench at the side of the hall and laid the parcel beside me. I was determined to get in and wondered how I could manage it. My knees were red with cold. I wished I was old enough to wear long trousers.

There was a sudden draught from the street door. A small procession came in led by a workhouse officer in grey uniform. He was followed by a bewildered–looking woman whose clothes were in rags. Her shoes were tattered plimsoles. She dragged a pram containing two babies in through the door and two more shivering children clung to the handle of the pram. The pram squeaked and squealed across the bare hall on buckled wheels, one of which was without a tyre. The last one to come in was a small slim man of about thirty.

He was trying to look unconcerned; he wore a trilby hat at a jaunty angle and he swaggered as he walked. His hands were thrust into the pockets of a torn overcoat which had once been stylish when high padded shoulders were in. His toes were visible through one of his shoes.

'Sit down,' said the officer. The whole family squeezed onto the seat next to me. I couldn't help staring. The husband tried to pick up one of the children but his wife pulled the child from him and then sat sideways on the seat with her back to him. He shrugged his shoulders and smiled across at the officer who stared back humourlessly. So the husband looked along at me and winked. I felt embarrassed and looked away. The officer spoke to the woman. 'A matron will be here in a minute, Missus, to take you and the children into the women's wing.' The woman nodded. She looked too tired and worn to be able to speak. 'What about me then?' said the husband loudly. 'You'll go to the men's wing, Richardson, when I'm ready to take you there.' 'You're not taking my wife and kids away already?' shouted Richardson. His wife turned and looked at him. For the first time since she'd come into the hall there was some expression on her face. I'd not before seen such contempt on a person's face and the memory of the woman's hatred for her husband stayed in my mind for a long time. But she said nothing. A woman in uniform came for the family. As they trailed through the door the man shouted, 'Sorry, old girl,' but his wife didn't even look round. He seemed infuriated and rushed after her but the two workhouse officers blocked his path. While this was happening I noticed the door to the hospital wing was unwatched so I grabbed my parcel and slipped through.

* * *

We used to play the game of seeing who could make their dripping piece last the longest. Because I was the eldest I had the job of keeping the baby out of the house for as long as possible. We used to sleep 5 to a bed and we only had our coats to keep us warm. We used to get belted for no reason and we were forbidden to play so we wouldn't wear out our footwear so fast. Many a time I heard my mother crying with hunger and I've seen my father cry with humiliation. At school the sight of a child fainting on having no breakfast did very little to melt the heart of some of the teachers who still continued to thrash you on the basis you wasn't trying to concentrate. We just used to get insulted by the teachers who used to yell, 'Get a move on! You're like a mob of unemployed!' Our charity boots were inspected by the headmaster who demanded the uppers should shine like guardsmen's even when there was no soles left.

* * *

I didn't want charity. I would slide under the desk with shame every time my name was called to attend the poor kids' parties and outings. Some of the kids would humiliate me by bringing clothes and shoes more worn than the ones I was wearing.

* * *

The younger men would sometimes listen to the older ones who had fought in the first world war. I remember one in particular who lived quite close to me. He had been through the whole of the war in France and ended up with the knee and calf of one leg shattered by shrapnel, and a bad chest. He had an iron fastened to his boot, a coiled spring that reached up to his knee where it was clamped around his leg. When he moved his leg to walk the spring was set in motion and so lifted his foot up. All these disabled men got by way of pension was a shilling a day. Twice a year he had to appear before a medical board of an army doctor and retired officers who would reduce your pension if they thought you were improving. He eventually died in the workhouse.

Walter was a tram conductor. He went to this bookie's house to place a bet. The house was raided and the bookie and Walter were both charged. The bookie was fined and he paid the fine and his business went on as usual. The court decided not to fine Walter as he would automatically lose his job and they thought that was punishment enough. Walter never worked again till he eventually died from the after-effects of having been gassed in the war.

* * *

One day when the rain was coming down like a stream I waited on the curb near Piccadilly Circus to cross the road and watched three men singing in the gutter. They were so wet that their clothes glistened and shone like silk. They looked desperate and miserable. On impulse I said, 'Would you like a cup of tea?' For seconds no one answered and then one man began to cry and another said, 'Oh, God, yes.' I took them to a working-men's cafe in the market just a stone's throw away and gave them tea and baked beans on toast. At the end of the meal the youngest had to go out to be sick. They had had no food for two days. They were miners and a foundryman from Wales who had exhausted their dole. They had been singing in the streets for weeks and in a good week were able to send 2/6 home.

They slept where they could and ate rotten fruit and vegetables from the gutters in Berwick Street market and scraps from hotel dustbins. Well, in the end I took them home with me. I still had some old clothes of my father's. I was able to send them off next day, washed and fed, with a couple of bob. The neighbours never liked me after this episode and the local clergyman used to cross to the other side of the road when he saw me coming.

* * *

I went in the corner shop and asked if they had any empty boxes. The shopkeeper said, 'Yes. Take the till.'

Medical care

We enjoyed roaming over Kinver Edge, sliding down the hills on dustbin lids, digging in the sand after money the holiday visitors had lost. We'd spend hours searching for pop bottles, taking them to Cooper's shop, getting a penny for each one. We lived right opposite Edge View TB sanatorium. We used to stand on the bank watching the staff take the dead bodies out of the wards. There were no blinds up at the windows. Some days we saw as many as five. People were so undernourished through poverty, through the greed of the upper class, they didn't have the stamina or the will to fight illness. They just gave up.

* * *

My sister was taken ill and the doctor treated her for nettle rash. He told my parents, 'Just dab her with this calamine lotion. It'll soon clear up.' A few weeks after, my brother was taken ill with the same symptoms, only far worse. This same doctor refused to come to see my brother. We got another doctor from Stourbridge. He took one look at my brother and I heard the words 'scarlet fever'. As they put him into the poor peoples' ambulance I noticed his skin was peeling off just as my sister's had done. He was taken to the isolation infirmary. After he'd gone to the 'fever tent' the authorities came and stoved out the house. It was a horrible stench. For a while we were treated as lepers by most people. My brother lay critically ill for some time. I missed him even though we were always arguing. Came the day when dad came back with a pile of comics, drawing paper and coloured pencils. Placing them on the table he said to mum, 'Glad, the kid's going to mek it. Ar stopped on me way home to pick a pot of peas to buy him these'. That night I was allowed to stop up late, mum sitting by the fireside with her knitting, dad at the table drawing puzzles, the kind where you have to find hidden objects in the scenery, me lying on the hearth making a scrap book from brown paper, with paste made from flour and water. It must have been self–raising flour because the pictures wouldn't lie down flat. When dad visited my brother next day he went armed with the puzzles, the scrap book, comics, and a pair of bed socks mum had knitted from unravelled wool.

* * *

When our baby was born we had to borrow a mattress from next door and spread newspapers on it. I used to feed the baby on a bottle of warm water. We put her to bed in a drawer. We made nappies out of newspaper. When I went before the Public Assistance Committee they asked me if the baby was being breast fed and when I said yes they reduced the 2/- allowance for a child.

* * *

Lots of children didn't have any resistance to the diseases going the rounds. In 1933 infant mortality in St Helens was 116 per thousand. The Salvation Army used to hold services for 3 or 4 children at a time in the street and take the bodies away in flimsy wooden boxes.

* * *

I had a friend who lived next door. Her name was Elsie. One day we were playing together, the next day I was told the angels were taking her a long long way away. I took my 2 most treasured possessions to her mother (a box of unopened handkerchiefs my grandfather had bought me, and a doll on a swing which the lodger won for me at the wake). I wanted her to have them to keep her company on her journey.

* * *

The cottage were a damp old house and I'd always got some of the children middling. The doctor told me at the finish, 'If you don't get out of this damn, blasted old house you'll have neither wife nor kids.' We'd got six then. Bronchial pneumonia they used to get. And the missus cracked up one year with tonsillitis. The youngest was ill, only eight weeks old. The missus had to sleep in the same room—one little room downstairs. The doctor had been coming in above a week or two and he kept telling her, 'You can't possibly keep her, Mrs Lawman.' Mum says, 'While there's life there's hope.' And she come up to waken me one night. I suppose I was a bit thick–skinned asleep. I turned over and went to sleep again. I didn't know while she come to call me in the morning: the little 'un had had a change for the better. The old doctor was thunderstruck

when he come in the morning. We had a bill for eight guineas. We
used to have to pay two or three bob a week. My eldest boy had rickets. He was in Manfield Hospital fifteen weeks. The doctor begged
us to let him go in. He had his fifth birthday in there. He had an
operation on both knees. They done a good job on him too, but that
was another five or six bob a week gone.

* * *

There were boards outside all the police stations covered with
notices: MAN FOUND, and a description of the body and cause of
death. Often malnutrition. TB sufferers were kept going on cheap
cough mixture till they pegged out.

Above stairs

At home we thought ourselves to be poor since we seldom had any
new clothes (my father still wore the frock coat he had been married
in in 1903 for my sisters' weddings). We had very dull food, and
drinks only for special occasions. My parents were very austere
about alcohol. They thought it their duty to employ as many servants as possible because of unemployment.

We had two gardeners and our old coachman who cleaned the
car—a T model Ford—and stoked the boiler. These men were paid
30/- a week each and got their cottages, coal and vegetables free.
Our head gardener's daughter was a very clever girl and my grandmother paid for her to go to a teacher training college. The fee of
£50 a year was a quarter of my grandmother's income. We also had
five living–in maids. Being more or less an only child, as my siblings
were so much older, I spent a lot of time with the maids. They were
very cheerful jolly girls, mostly from the colliery district of Derbyshire. It was an understood thing that, on their weekly day off, they
always took a little case with them containing their 'tea'. This, of
course, meant a few pounds of butter, sugar, etc for their families.
Their wages were very small. The cook might get as much as £40 a
year, a 14 year old kitchen maid as little as £12. But their parents
were glad to have them in good service and their uniforms—print
dresses and linen caps and aprons—were provided. The parlour-
maid, who waited at table, had a dark blue or brown serge dress,
and so did the housemaid who helped her if there were more than
six people dining. The meals in the servant's hall, where the cook sat
at the head of the table on a chair and the rest on forms, were probably better than ours. I am certain they kept a more ample table
than we did in the dining room.

We had a joint on Sunday but thereafter it was usually mince or cottage pie. Chicken was thought to be expensive and we seldom had a roasted one except on gala occasions. We did have some game shot on the estate but not very much. Most of it was poached. My father was not a keen shot and, if he had a small shooting party, only a few brace of birds and the odd rabbit found their way to the game larder. The maids did not eat game. They considered it their due to get butchers' meat that had been properly paid for. I think the maids were happy with us. Some stayed a lifetime and stayed our friends always. But domestic service was beginning to be unpopular and the young ones came and went with rapidity. Our household was dull for the more flighty ones. We had no unmarried manservants as my parents felt it might lead to immorality. The village was a mile and a half away, and the drive to the main road, where the buses ran to Derby, was a mile long. The girls did not enjoy walking it on dark nights and those from the colliery towns were afraid of the cows. They longed for bright lights and fun, but they had quite a lot of fun among themselves and their pealing laughter often penetrated through the baize door to our part of the house. We were not supposed to entertain if one of the maids was out as it made too much work for the others. We were taught to be very considerate in this way but we never made a bed or helped with the washing–up except on Christmas Day.

My father liked us all to go to bed early to save fuel and light. He himself retired at 10 and he had a master switch which enabled him to plunge the servants' hall in darkness as a hint that it was time for everyone to go to bed. As a military man he could be frightening and often shouted orders. But the maids had frightening fathers of their own and took it all rather as a joke. They understood him very well and were fond of him. The fire by which we sat in the library was always a wood one. Father cut the logs himself. He hated to see us put a piece of coal on the fire. But the maid's fire was always banked with coal—they were entitled to that coming from the colliery district—and the huge Herald range in the kitchen was said to burn a ton of coal a week. It must have been a terrible job for the kitchenmaid to blacklead it every morning.

* * *

There were a lot of us. We were rich, gay, young, idle. One day we were bored and decided to go for a picnic. We went in a cavalcade of motor cars led by a young man in a Rolls Royce. We had a barbecue in the snow by a frozen lake. After dining the young man thought it would be a jolly wheeze to drive his car on the ice. The ice cracked and the Rolls sank and we all laughed tipsily. Then I noticed a silent wall of pinched–faced unemployed miners watching us. The miners didn't laugh. This young man asked them who they thought they were staring at and told them to be off. They went in silence. Some days later a parcel arrived in Edinburgh at this young man's home. It contained silver cutlery and a note which said, 'These were found by the lake after the snow melted.'

* * *

My father was a regular soldier who retired in 1926 with the rank of Brigadier General. He had inherited our ancestral home five years before and had already sold off about half the land and many valuable manuscripts from the library to pay death duties. My father had his army pension of about £800 p.a. and my mother had a small income of her own. When the 1931 crisis came my father's pension was reduced. Then he started to speculate with his savings from a lifetime of abstemious living. A crooked stockbroker gave him bad advice and he lost the lot, about £6,000, in the Hatry crash. Then farming began to fail and the farming tenants were in trouble. One could see the land was beginning to deteriorate. Rent Day, Lady Day 1932, was dreaded by my parents. Mrs Hardy, the grand old lady whose family farmed the Lodge Farm, sent a lad with her cheque for £114 for the 120 acres she farmed and her house and cottages. The cottagers paid their half year rents of £3.15s. But my father waited in vain for the rent of the big farm of 220 acres where the tenant was already in arrears. The poor chap had failed. He could not pay. The fields were ungrazed, the thistles abounded, the ploughing had not been done. It was a terrible day. We grieved for the man and his family and for ourselves but most of all for the land. When a new tenant was found he had to be allowed the farm rent free for the first year to get the land productive again. My father's solace was to labour himself, cutting thistles and hedges, mending the potholes in the drive. He worked like a navvy. My brothers helped when they were home on leave from the army. In harvest time they helped the farmers with the hay and corn. Poverty in our village must have been rampant but it was largely hidden. People were very proud. There was one labourer's family with more than twenty children. They were a source of great worry to my mother and once she asked the local panel doctor if anything could be done to find them other accommodation than their three bedroomed cottage. He countered by asking how many spare rooms we had.

Another huge family lived in a disused railway carriage. The father was an invalid but there was a new baby every year. One year they got measles and at least one died. On Sundays, on our way to church, we used to take a milk pudding or some delicacy to an old lady in the village. Like many local people she had a goitre—or Derbyshire neck as we called it—which made her look hideous, but her cottage was snug enough. The row she lived in faced the main road and the privies were in the back garden with no other access, so all the 'night soil' had to be carried through the house when the carts came to empty the earth closets. We, of course, had indoor water closets in our big house but father considered it unmanly to use them himself and went off to what was known as 'Buckingham Palace' where there were two adjoining WCs in an outhouse. Male guests were encouraged to follow his example.

In the country

I took a horse–keeper's job at Little Addington. Thirty–five bob a week. You'd got to be in the stable at five o'clock in the morning. You'd got to get your horses watered and fed first. I had ten horses there. You'd got to tidy them up with your dandy brush. At harvest time there'd be a hell of a row if I hadn't got them horses in the shafts by half–past–six when the other men come in the yard. Well, then you'd be working till seven or eight at night. I used to do all the cutting with the horses with a self–binder. It used to chuck the sheaves out ready tied up. You'd got your seeding to do. Wheat seeding in the autumn. Your barley seeding and that in the spring time. Then you'd got your root–ground to get ready where we were going to grow the mangles and turnips and that.

I always reckoned ploughing was the best job on the farm. The old doctor used to say, anybody suffered with the nerves, let them get a job on the farm and take a pair of horses and watch the furrows turned up. He said that'd do them as much good as he could.

We used to get out of the stable at half–past–six in the morning—carry on till half–past–nine. Have half hour's lunch. Some farms would let you take a nose bag for the old horses and some said they didn't want it. Then we used to carry on while two o'clock till we knocked off and then we'd got to go home and untackle our horses and feed them. Then you'd got your straw and fodder and all that to get in. If you hadn't had time to clean your stable out in the morning you had them to muck out. You'd got to sit up at nights when your mares were foaling—April, May and June. You didn't get no overtime. Ten bob a foal if you kept it alive. You'd perhaps sit up a fortnight or three weeks. Always used to have three or four. Then they went out of Shires and in for Percherons. They're a French breed. One year they got our gaffer to take one and I took that out for thirteen weeks. I used to start out from Little Addington eight o'clock time Monday morning and get back Saturday afternoon. Serving the mares. Used to average twenty–five, thirty mile a day. They always said you wasn't supposed to ride the horses, but I had one as I used to ride. I loved horses. You'd got some'at to talk to. You can't talk to a tractor. Some'd go to bed with you. Others'd kick your brains out. We had one mare had a weak foal and I had to stand and hold her nearly forty–eight hours. A good man could save his boss hundreds if he knowed his job. When you were thrashing it were always the horse–keeper's job to take the corn off the drums, weight it up, and carry it away. Wheat 18 stones, beans 19, barley 16 and oats 12. Some farms you got a shilling a day extra for that, but not where I were. They wouldn't let you have a cart if they could help it because that took another man. That were damn hard work, that were, and dusty.

* * *

He wasn't a bad boss. I couldn't say as he treated you bad, but they were like us at that time. They couldn't afford five quid for a stack sheet. We used to have a cover the stacks up with straw at night. You damn well earned all you had. We earned big money and never got it. I first joined the union in 1918. They done a damn good job of work. I've known Christmas Days come on a Sunday and we haven't had a damn minute off for Christmas. About 1919, 1920 we first got half a day on a Saturday—if you could call it half a day. When the union got that in some of the men were worse than the bosses: all the cattle were going to die and be starved to death. We worked sixty–odd hours a week. Then they wheedled it down to about fifty–four. They got us three Bank Holidays. Oh, Gawd blimey, there were a row over that. That were Easter Monday, Whit Monday I think, and Boxing Day. That come in about 1935 or 6. But you'd still got to go and feed your animals. You had to do that for your house. They'd got you like that. I always reckon they were the biggest man–trap ever made, the tied cottage. We didn't get any annual holidays until the last war. Then we got three days. You couldn't get unemployment. So you'd got to keep your mouth shut. I always felt sorry for them blokes down in the fens. A lot of them used to have to stand off dead of winter; they'd got nothing to do. How the hell the poor buggers lived I couldn't tell you.

There was so many tied cottages, and that was the weapon they'd use. You'd got to come to their terms or: 'Get out of my house!' I threw myself out of a job once. The old gentleman died. The farm changed hands. There was a widow woman in a cottage on the farm, and she'd lost her husband. She had three delicate children. The new farmer wanted me to move into this house. He said, 'If you don't come, I shan't want you.' I couldn't see myself going into that house and turning out them three little children, so I didn't go, and I lost my job. But I couldn't safeguard her. That old farmer wouldn't take no rent off her. He went to court and said she hadn't paid the rent. She hadn't got nobody to speak for her, so she got evicted and had to go. There was another man who had a family of nine. He was turned out of his house and put in the workhouse up at Aylsham.

* * *

Our neighbour was an old boy who had all these children. And they had a big bowl, what you wash with, in the scullery. They didn't have plates—they'd all sit round and scoff out of this big bowl. He used to have goats upstairs, and pigs. Those little goats and piglets'd jump on the bed, and jump off the bed onto the floor. You'd see the pigs looking out of the bedroom window at you. They had to keep the animals warm and contented.

Protest

In 1931 they reduced unemployment and means test payments by 10%. It was announced in Parliament in October 1933 that by doing so they had saved over £54 million. You could say they had stolen it from the poor. The BMA worked out that the absolute minimum a person needed to spend on food to keep body and soul together was 5/11 a week. Sir John Boyd Orr found that four and a half million spent less than 4/-. (Another four and a half million spent more than 14/-). In 1934, 66% of applicants to the army were rejected on medical grounds. Employers were quick to realise and exploit the advantages of the situation. Men couldn't refuse a job that paid less than the proper rate, or less than unemployment money, or even commission only, or they would lose their dole. Between 1921 and 1931, 10% of the total population of the North East migrated. And when the men came back to work in the shipyards, to build ships for the Second World War, there were apple trees which had grown from the cores they threw away on their last shift.

* * *

One evening after work I was walking along Murraygate when a procession of unemployed were coming towards me. Suddenly, without any warning, mounted policemen and others on foot charged them with truncheons. The police appeared huge and the unemployed so under–nourished and small. In a few minutes the street was cleared. Later the story was that the mounted policemen were brought from another town and were given whisky or rum before they set out.

* * *

A procession of unemployed had started to wind its way from the Horsefair. The banners read, WORKERS OF THE WORLD UNITE, DOWN WITH THE MEANS TEST, WE WANT WORK NOT DOLE. I felt excited to think that someone had the guts to protest. I stood watching until 2 men carrying a banner which read JOIN THE UNEMPLOYED WORKERS MOVEMENT, shouted, 'Get in the ranks if you're out of work'. And I became one of the demonstrators. Like a big ugly snake the column of marchers stretched for hundreds of yards behind me. Very few policemen were visible along the line of demonstrators. A few minutes later we all knew the reason why. The head of the procession had stopped at the beginning of Old Market Street and the police were ordering the leaders to go round the back streets. This they refused to do. A police inspector then blew his whistle and within seconds hundreds of police came out of the side streets followed by the mounted police. They couldn't have picked a better battleground for their assault. We were in the widest street in the city with five side streets leading into it. With batons drawn the men in blue went to work. Ten minutes later the street was like a battlefield. Dozens of demonstrators and a few policemen were laying unconscious in the road and the mounties were driving their horses into the crowd.

* * *

The day the hunger marchers were expected in Carlisle I said to my neighbour, 'Are you going to see the hunger marchers?' and her reply was, 'What hunger marchers?' Well I went and when the contingent from Maryport marched in they could have been a regiment of soldiers. They were straight as a die and Maryport had done them proud. They each had a new khaki shirt and a new haversack and they were well shod. A repairer had seen to their footwear and, although he was lame, he was going with them to mend and patch what he could on the way. But they had only come 28 miles.

They were converging on Carlisle to spend the night in the Market Hall before starting on their long march to London the following day. They came from all over, but the most pathetic sight was the Scots. They had marched every foot of the way from Glasgow. Ragged, footsore, hungry, heads bent. Our lads had marched in singing Cumberland's own song, *John Peel*. Other contingents had marched in singing *The Red Flag*. But the Scots hadn't the strength to sing. We knew they were coming before we saw them because of a rhythmic sound which as they drew nearer became a chant. 'Are we Red? Yes we're Red!' Repeated over and over. I stood on the pavement with my two wee ones in the pram and cried.

* * *

I went along to the dark, dusty hall feeling nervous and useless. I was frightened by the sight of so many males, mostly lying like wounded soldiers on straw mattresses; shabbiness and the stale smell of poverty was everywhere, in their clothes, the wooden raftered hall, the chipped enamel cups and plates. Most of all, I felt, in their feet, mainly bare, white and anaemic looking, except where red painful blisters festered and dripped pus. A short, young, forceful man came up to me. 'Hold this,' he said, and put a heavy basin into my hands. He looked so out of place, wearing the uniform of the respectable doctor of those days, stiff white collar, black jacket, pin–striped trousers. But there was nothing conventional about his manner. He went from one marcher to another, and I obediantly held the basin while he bathed and tended the battered feet. Awkwardly I held out bandages and safety pins. I felt the most inefficient nurse in the world. So these were the hunger marchers. Just ordinary people like those I had met in the poorer districts of London, but drafted now into an army not through conscription or patriotism, but sheer necessity. 'We come a long way,' some of them told me, 'but we don't want charity. We want work, and food for ourselves and our bairns.'

* * *

The men had been welcomed home from the Great War to a land fit for heroes. But as they said at the time, 'You'd need to be a bloody hero to live in it!'